Hold Fast the Faith

A Devotional Commentary on the
Westminster Confession
of 1647

By
Matthew Everhard

Reformation Press
P.O. Box 2210
Lenoir, North Carolina 28645

1034101

Dedication

There are literally scores of people I need to thank for helping this project to come to a final form. First, I thank my editors Paula Kincaid, and Carmen Fowler for their hours of work on this project. I also want to thank Forrest Norman for his fine work at the Layman and Reformation Press. The Reformed community needs stalwart men and women such as these.

Secondly, I want to thank my colleagues who have assisted in critiquing, reviewing, and guiding this volume: Dr. Jon S. Marko, Elder Mark Van Drunen, Rev. C. Lee Hutchings, Rev. Art Helin, Rev. Dr. Michael Allen, Rev. Dr. Jeffrey Jeremiah, Charlie Deeg, Kristina Pfiffner, and especially my mentor Rev. Dr. Wilfred Bellamy. Their suggestions have been invaluable and have greatly improved this book, although its remaining faults (theological and otherwise) are no doubt fully my own responsibility.

I would like to thank the Session of Faith Evangelical Presbyterian Church for affording me the time to work on this project. My people at Faith Church are my joy in ministry. My prayer is that this book will benefit many churches besides this local church that I hold so dear.

Of course, my wife Kelly is a constant source of love, affection, solace, and joy; her loving support has helped me to become a better man and a stronger Christian. My three precious children inspire me daily. Soriah, Elijah, and Simone: daddy loves you.

Finally, I praise God for saving me through the blood of Christ, whose "doctrines of grace" I have here sought to extol.

-Matthew Everhard

Other Works
by
Matthew Everhard

Christ Our Supreme Joy: Encountering the Glory of Jesus Christ. Kindle Edition. (Brooksville FL: Faith Church Publishing, 2010).

The Children's Catechism: A Parent's Resource for Scripture Memorization. (Brooksville FL: Faith Church Publishing, 2010).

Abortion: The Evangelical Perspective. (N. Richland Hills TX, BIBAL Press, 2007).

Rock Solid: Helping Teens Discover the Truth of Christianity. (Lenoir NC: Reformation Press, 2005).

Table of Contents

Bonus Features

Introductory Essay:

A Copernican Revolution of the Heart

In 1543 the astronomer Nicolaus Copernicus published a startling new book entitled *"De Revolutionibus Orbium Coelestium."* Simply stated, it jolted the minds of all into whose hands it fell. Contrary to the prevailing view in his time that the cosmos had the earth at its center, the telescope-toting scientist made a compelling argument that the Sun was actually the center of the universe! The ramifications of this discovery were, of course, astronomical (no pun intended). Nearly every facet of the people's worldview (including that of the Church) needed renovation. Today we call it the Copernican Revolution.

In a like manner, when we make the spiritual discovery that God is sovereign over all of creation, the maker of all that exists, the sustainer of every atom and molecule, the architect of human history, and the planner of our very own lives as well, a similar revolution takes place in the human heart. Our discovery of the theocentric state of the universe—that God reigns in every sphere of life through the radiance of His Son Jesus Christ—is no accident. This new manner of thinking is nothing less than the drawing, prompting, and confirmation of God's Holy Spirit Himself. This book is designed to foster just such a revolution of the heart.

I graduated from Ashland Theological Seminary with a master's degree in practical theology. My major was a sub-field within theology known as "spiritual formation." I have to confess to the reader in this introduction that I am still not entirely sure exactly what that term means. Even though an accredited and well-acclaimed graduate seminary saw fit to dub me a "master" in this area, I am not certain that *anyone* can truly gain any sort of mastery over this supernatural process.

Since "spiritual formation" is part of the goal of this book, I had better hasten to define exactly what I am up to. For our purposes, let us use this definition:

> Spiritual formation is a believer's life-long process of growing more and more like God's Son Jesus Christ, through the power of the Holy Spirit.

First, let's take a closer look at this definition by breaking it down into its constituent parts, and then we'll explore how the Westminster Confession of Faith is related.

A Believer's Life-Long Process...

We live in a society that is fascinated, yes even *addicted* to quick fixes. As Americans we practically medicate ourselves with real-time technology, television (equipped with digital video recorders to fast-forward through the commercials), fast food, and instant messaging. As soon as we notice an unfulfilled want in our lives we eagerly devise ways to obtain it—right now! By contrast, the process of spiritual formation is just that, a *process*. There are no short cuts to obtain it, no quick routes to get there. You cannot "Google-search" the information you need, and print it off in five minutes. You cannot search a Wikipedia article to quickly get the gist of it. Spiritual formation must be sought after for a lifetime. It is like a journey on foot through various mountains, harrowing valleys, across dangerous bridges and through lonely fields. Yet there is a fixed destination in view.

...Of Growing More and More Like God's Son Jesus Christ

None of us were born as saints that we would naturally or accidentally imitate Christ. In fact Reformed theology teaches us that our sinful natures are totally depraved; there is not one thing inside of us that makes us worthy of God's mercy. Though we were created in the *imago dei* (Latin: image of God), our fall into sin brought misery and ruin. Nevertheless, the journey of spiritual formation has as its destination complete conformation to the likeness of Jesus Christ.[1] The Bible says that Jesus Christ is the "radiance of the glory of God and the exact imprint of his nature" (Hebrews 1:3). Just as Jesus Christ is the perfect reflection of God's glory, so too are we supposed to be imitating and reflecting the character, morality, mentality, holiness, and power of Jesus Christ.

---

1 Romans 8:29, 1 Corinthians 15:49, 2 Corinthians 3:18, 1 John 3:2.

The Apostle Paul, while striving with the immature and theologically messy Galatians, called that particular church, "my little children, for whom I am again in the anguish of childbirth *until Christ is formed in you*" (Galatians 4:19, emphasis added). Perhaps this passage from Galatians is where we get the "formation" part of the term "spiritual formation."

Spiritual formation or transformation is closely related to another important theological term, "sanctification." Sanctification is understood to begin at the moment of conversion and describes the Holy Spirit's continual drawing of the believer into greater and greater intimacy with God the Father. During the whole process, the believer is beginning to take on the holiness of Christ Himself, which was legally imputed to us at justification, thereby throwing off the sin that entangles our lives. Our old nature (or the "flesh" as Paul often calls it) is slowly being defeated by the new Spirit-nature, which has now taken over. This process is completed in death or finalized at the return of Christ, at which point "glorification" is realized. 1 John 3:2 summarizes glorification when it says, "what we will be has not yet been made known. *But we know that when he appears, we shall be like him,* for we shall see him as he is" (NIV, emphasis added).

...Through the Power of the Holy Spirit

This process is one that cannot be undertaken alone. Self-actualization is not spiritually possible. On the contrary, God has given us the Holy Spirit to empower us, to be our Counselor (John 14:15), our teacher (John 14:26), and our sanctifier (John 16:8-11). The same Holy Spirit who originally summoned us into a relationship with God the Father, is also deeply concerned that we continue to grow in our faith. In fact, Jesus said that it is the Holy Spirit's role to "guide us into all the truth" (John 16:13 NASB).

Reformed theologians have taught that the eternal life of a believer unfolds in this grand scope, often called the *ordo salutis* (Latin: the order of salvation):

> **Election:** God's predestination of a definite number of persons, before the foundation of the world, according to the secret council and good pleasure of His will.

> **Effectual calling:** God's inviting and drawing of the elect by His Word and Spirit, persuading and enabling them to embrace Jesus Christ.

Regeneration: the new birth of life in the Spirit; what Jesus called being "born again."

Faith: assenting to the truth of the promise of the Gospel, by receiving and resting in the righteousness of Christ alone.

Justification: the act of God's grace whereby He pardons all of our sins, and accepts us as righteous in His sight.

Adoption: God declaring us His children and treating us as His own family members.

Sanctification: the process of growing in godliness and Christ-likeness, so that we are enabled more and more to die to sin, and to live in righteousness.

Glorification: the final perfecting of our souls in holiness at the time of our death, or at the Lord's return.

Thus, if you are a believer today, you are necessarily on point *seven* of the above list. Points one through six have already happened to you, and point eight is yet to come. Your mission for the remaining days of your life is to draw closer to God, increase your intimacy with Him, enjoy His presence, and be transformed into a living representative of Jesus Christ. It is this process of life-long transformation with which this book is concerned.

How then do we intentionally engage in spiritual formation? This is in large point the great quest of this book. Here we find that the Old Testament saints, the New Testament Church, and many of the post-biblical believers in church history are a great encouragement to us. By searching the Scriptures and examining the lives of those who have gone before us, we learn to incorporate certain "disciplines" into our lives in order to better submit ourselves to the Spirit's leadership and guidance. Prayer, study of Scripture, fasting, solitude, silence, meditation and other life-habits that we discover can all be very beneficial to help us in yielding to the Spirit's guidance.

The Westminster Confession of Faith

One spiritual discipline[2] that the Church has historically appreciated is reflection on its creeds and confessions. Confessions are essentially concise summations of the Church's doctrine. They are statements of our shared faith. For as long as believers have gathered to worship, they have taught *doctrine* in order to pass on the true faith from generation to generation (Jude 3). In fact, the New Testament itself records some proto-creeds that were in use in worship even before the close of the biblical canon. Examples of this type of creed include Philippians 2:6-11, 1 Timothy 3:16, and 2 Timothy 2:11-13. Many biblical scholars believe that these early creeds were memorized in the form of hymns aiding memorization in a pre-literate society. Within the first few centuries after the completion of the New Testament canon, the early church continued to encode its vibrant faith with early formulations of Christian teaching, such as the Apostles' Creed, the Nicene Creed and others.

In fairness, there are some branches of the Christian family tree that reject the notion of keeping creeds and confessions. However the vast majority of believers holding to the historic Christian faith have found great spiritual power in honoring the teachings of past generations. In fact, one major strength of confessional Christianity is the abiding connection that is forged between previous generations and contemporary believers. Clearly, the universal Church of Jesus Christ connects believers not only to others around the world, but also to our forefathers in the faith who have gone before us in generations past. Creeds then, help modern believers to remain humble while avoiding what C.S. Lewis called "chronological snobbery," that is, the belief that one's own generation is somehow superior to all those who have gone before it.

Furthermore, confessions and creeds serve to help assure us that the doctrinal faith that we articulate today has not subtly changed over time by being subject to the warping influence of secular society. Creeds stand as ancient landmarks denoting the "boundaries" of believers' hearts in history. Noting where one deviates from an ancient creed gives a person a clearer understanding of where his or her own theological convictions stand in relation to other believers throughout history. Perhaps this also helps us to discover what direction we are moving. Are we moving closer to Christ? To God's Word? To the heart of God Himself? Or are we moving further away?

---

2 The spiritual disciplines are those activities which call for an active (or sometimes even passive) participation on behalf of the believer in order to draw closer to God and grow in the faith. Just as the physical body must exercise to maintain physical fitness, so also Christ has given us spiritual exercises to keep our souls healthy and well.

The confession that I will be recommending to you in this volume is the standard-bearing creed in the Presbyterian or Reformed branch of Christianity. Influenced heavily by the thinking of Reformation theologian John Calvin (1509-1564), the Westminster Confession (1647) is a confessional exemplar of Reformed theology.[3] The Westminster Confession of Faith is the premiere example of theological intellectualism absorbed in the beauty of the sovereignty of God. The Westminster Confession, and Calvin before it for that matter, were both completely committed to the theological framework that God is sovereign over the entire universe. Therefore, as you study this Confession you will undoubtedly encounter the Living God as ruler of the cosmos, the world, the events of your life, and hopefully your heart.

Historical Context

While the historical context of the writing of the Westminster Confession has been written about at length in other places and cannot be repeated here, a few words about its composition are appropriate. "Composed by an Assembly of Divines convened at Westminster Abbey by the Long Parliament (1643-1648), the Confession was designed to unite the English and Scottish churches in their theology."[4] In the first half of the 17th century, England was in turmoil. Nearly torn apart politically, many believers in Britain looked to the Scriptures and to their Puritan theologians to help articulate hope for their lives. Many hoped that England, Scotland, and Ireland could all be brought together under one confessional standard. More than anything, believers needed their spiritual leaders to help them understand the whole of Scripture in the midst of a rapidly changing and often chaotic political climate.

Fortunately, these theologians and pastors sought to articulate the strong sovereignty of God as revealed in the Scriptures. Commissioned by the English House of Commons in 1643, work began on a new confession. Originally, it was thought that a mere revision of the Church of England's Thirty Nine Articles was all that was necessary. It soon became apparent

---

3 Reformed theology is often called Calvinism for better or for worse. While there is technically a distinction—the former is the larger umbrella under which the latter falls—these terms will be used nearly synonymously in this book. Calvinism, by definition is Reformed. It is a specific branch of Reformation theology. However, not all Reformed theology is expressly "Calvinistic," coming from Calvin or his followers.

4 "Westminster Confession of Faith" in The Dictionary of the Presbyterian and Reformed Tradition in America. Ed. by D.G Hart and Mark A. Noll. (Phillipsburg NJ: P & R Publishing, 1999) p. 276.

that more work needed to be done. They did not entirely reinvent the wheel; the crafters of this document had been inspired by prior works including the Irish Articles of 1615, principally drafted by James Usher, as well as the Genevan Catechism of John Calvin himself. Their final product was nothing less than breath-taking.

After 1,163 sessions meeting in Westminster Abbey, the so-called "Westminster Divines" (comprised of 151 believers including theologians, parliament members, and Scottish advisors[5]) completed a document that would stand as perhaps the most excellent summation of Reformation-inspired doctrine to date. The Confession was approved by the English Parliament and then also approved by the Scottish General Assembly in 1647. While Calvinism itself waxed and waned throughout England's history, the final product of the Westminster Assembly lives on in many denominations today.

The Westminster Confession also includes two "catechisms" (from the Greek word meaning instruction) that were designed to help believers learn to articulate their faith. These two surveys of biblical teaching take the form of question-and-answer sessions, as could be given from a mentor to a student. The Larger Catechism is designed to give thorough definitions of such great theological concepts as sanctification, effectual calling, and sin. Its precision has been of tremendous help to preachers, teachers, and theologians throughout the centuries. The Shorter Catechism is briefer and is suitable for use in Christian instruction for new converts, youth, and even children. These two documents are included as appendices in the back of this volume. These Catechisms are invaluable, and many readers will want to work through them in addition to the main body of the Confession. More will be said about these catechisms in Appendix B.

In America, the Adopting Act of 1729, "an action of the Synod of Philadelphia whereby the Westminster Confession of Faith and Catechisms were adopted as the doctrinal position of the Presbyterian Church in colonial America,"[6] made the Confession a primary theological tool by which candidates for ministry were examined in the colonies of the New World. This act ensured that all ordained pastors and licensed preachers received the Confession "as being, in all the essential and necessary articles,

5 This group was comprised of 121 ministers (Presbyterian, Episcopalian, Independents, and Erastians), 20 commoners or tradesmen, and 10 landowners.

6 "Adopting Act (1729)" in The Dictionary of the Presbyterian and Reformed Tradition in America. Ed. by D.G Hart and Mark A. Noll. (Phillipsburg NJ: P & R Publishing, 1999) p. 13.

good forms of sound words and systems of Christian doctrine; and... as the confession of our faith."[7] Interestingly, the Westminster Confession of Faith was studiously learned by rote, as it was often included in copies of the New England Primer, the booklet by which most school children learned to read.

Today, the Westminster Confession of Faith lives on as *the* primary confessional standard of Reformed denominations such as the Evangelical Presbyterian Church (the EPC[8]), the Presbyterian Church in America (the PCA), the Orthodox Presbyterian Church (the OPC), and several other denominations around the world.

How to Use This Book

This book is intended to be a guide to help you work through the Westminster Confession of Faith on a transformational level, not merely an intellectual level. In other words, my goal in this book is to help you to pray through this Confession in a way that fosters personal transformation and spiritual growth. Weighty matters of the Confession's historical composition will not bog you down. Neither will you find yourself stumbling over the various changes, amendments, and alterations that have been imposed upon the text, as various denominations sought to make it more palatable. In the rare case that these discussions are necessary, notes will be provided for your convenience.

While this book is not intended to be academic, neither is it intended to be "easy." The real work of the heart never is. My hope is that this book will be of primary importance to three groups of people. 1) Impassioned lay persons who are enflamed with a desire to go much deeper into theological truth than is possible in a typical Sunday School class, 2) seminary students from the Reformed tradition that are hoping to discover the power of this Confession, and 3) pastors and elders who would like to show their flocks the richness of our theological heritage in order to fan into flame a greater zeal for the glory of God.

The version of the Westminster Confession that you will be working through is essentially the 1647 version, with only minor updates to the language. For instance, I took the liberty of changing words like "dependeth" to "depends" and changed archaic language like "hath" to "has." My intent is to make the Confession more readable without detracting from its theological content.

---

7 Ibid.

8 The Evangelical Presbyterian Church is my own denomination.

I have also made small (and infrequent) changes to some words, and spellings that have passed out of common usage. For instance the word "sundry" is often updated to "various" and "neighbour" is changed to "neighbor" to reflect an American English. The Westminster Confession was designed to be studied in chapters and blocks of like-themed material. I have kept the original chapter divisions in place. As you read the Westminster, you will also notice that the writers seem to be obsessed with semicolons and colons. Clearly this is the work of a committee! While we often do not encounter prose in this style today, I have left the grammar intact; to do otherwise would have called for a more significant revision than I was ready or willing to be held responsible for making.

Following the content of each chapter of the Confession, I have included my own insights into how spiritual formation can begin to occur using the Confession as our starting point. It is here, following the reading of each chapter, that the reader is encouraged to spend time in meditation, confession of sin, and praise. These meditations and formation exercises are what set this work apart from the many other versions of the Westminster one may find in print. Five principle types of exercises will be included in each chapter, as follows:

Prepare in Prayer

The prayers under the heading "Prepare in Prayer" are just that—short, succinct prayers for the reader to offer to God as you ready your heart and submit your mind for the reading of Scripture and further study.

Reach Back

Sections marked "Reach Back" are small commentaries on the historical or theological content of the Confession. Sometimes the Westminster Assembly wrote things that are either controversial to modern believers, misunderstood, or even viewed as non-essentials today. These sections will help the reader to understand the mindset of the Westminster Divines as they went about their work of articulating the Christian faith. (Often I will simply use the words "the Divines" to indicate the authors of this classic work). Modern believers will be assisted in spanning the gap between the centuries by looking back to the context in which the Confession was written. As we do this, we will often find that the moral standards of the Confession's writers raise needed critique to today's ethical laxity.

Search Inward

Exercises labeled "Search Inward" are designed to lead the reader to look deeper into his or her own soul and reflect on one's own life. *This is often precisely the step that we avoid when we study doctrine!* When reading the Westminster, we will be surprised at how often it suggests something important in regard to our own situation. Far from being a dusty work with little relevance for today, the Westminster often speaks gently to our souls, asking us to search the interior castles of our hearts. For instance its section on marriage (WCF 24) may point us towards a positive goal that we may construct for our own relationship with our spouse. Or perhaps a section on sin (WCF 6) may illuminate an area that we must immediately confess. The Confession's words on the sacraments (WCF 27) may help us to more deeply engage the Spirit of God and encounter the Resurrected Christ as we receive the Lord's Supper. Often what we read in the Confession will prompt us to ask questions of ourselves that are uncomfortable. This is good and healthy. Search Inward sections will often lead us to repent, give thanks, or even to fall onto our faces in the holy presence of the Lord.

Gaze Upward

Sections marked "Gaze Upward" are designed to prompt the reader to burst into spontaneous praise. The Westminster Confession of Faith is an intensely God-centered document. These sections will usually point to passages in the Confession that cause us to give glory to God. The Confession goes out of its way to define the mercies of God, lift up His direction in providence, and magnify His love for the elect. It also highly exalts the God of creation by highlighting His power over the formed universe. Here you will certainly find specific reasons to sing, declare God's greatness, or stand in awed silence before His holiness. The purpose of the Confession is always to help us to discover our chief purpose for living: "to glorify God, and to enjoy Him forever" (Shorter Catechism, A#1). So often we find ourselves encumbered by the sheer weightiness of doctrine, that we fail to allow its power to call us into the assembly of angels, martyrs, and saints to exalt His name in praise.

Step Out

Sections called "Step Out" are designed to move the reader to action. It should never be the case that Christian teaching prompts our minds to move, but not our lives. Christian instruction must always be connected to responsive action. Perhaps at times the reading of the Confession will call us to witness vocally of Christ's redeeming love. Other times, the Confession may call us to make social stands that are unpopular with the world around us. At still other times, the Confession may bid us to take on other forms of spiritual disciplines such as biblical memorization, prayer, or fasting. No reading of the Confession—or Scripture for that matter—should leave us the same as we were before. Each time that we encounter God through the Scriptures, and many times that we encounter Him in the Confession, we are changed and called to receive our life-mission.

One Final Challenge

My challenge to the reader is to "eat" this book in small sections, digesting each chapter of the Westminster in bite-sized portions. As a matter of course, one chapter of the Confession followed by its spiritual formation section will likely be enough for one sitting. Any more, and the mind may be overrun with too many thoughts! In any case, the suggested spiritual formation exercises, if honestly attempted, will lead the believer in such a direction of prayer as will be spiritually edifying to the soul. Please remember that even though the Westminster Confession has literally dozens of quotations of Scripture within, and allusions to many more, it is no substitute for reading Scripture itself. While the Scriptures are the words of God, the Confession is nonetheless the words of men. For this reason, each section will be fortified by special readings of Scripture that are designed to be parallel to the segment of the Confession.

The Confession itself acknowledges its human limitations (WCF 1.10). At the same time, it has served as an inspiration to countless souls, and it is my conviction that it will benefit you too "until Christ is formed in you" (Galatians 4:19).

The Confession Chapter One:

Of the Holy Scripture

1. *Although the light of nature, and the works of creation and providence, do so far manifest the goodness, wisdom, and power of God, as to leave men inexcusable; yet they are not sufficient to give that knowledge of God, and of his will, which is necessary unto salvation; therefore it pleased the Lord, at various times, and in diverse manners, to reveal himself, and to declare that his will unto his Church; and afterwards for the better preserving and propagating of the truth, and for the more sure establishment and comfort of the Church against the corruption of the flesh, and the malice of Satan and of the world, to commit the same wholly unto writing; which makes the holy Scripture to be most necessary; those former ways of God's revealing his will unto his people being now ceased.*

2. *Under the name of Holy Scripture, or the Word of God written, are now contained all the Books of the Old and New Testament, which are these:*

Of the Old Testament:
Genesis, Exodus, Leviticus, Numbers, Deuteronomy, Joshua, Judges, Ruth, I Samuel, II Samuel, I Kings, II Kings, I Chronicles, II Chronicles, Ezra, Nehemiah, Esther, Job, Psalms, Proverbs, Ecclesiastes, The Song of Songs, Isaiah, Jeremiah, Lamentations, Ezekiel, Daniel, Hosea, Joel, Amos, Obadiah, Jonah, Micah, Nahum, Habakkuk, Zephaniah, Haggai, Zechariah, Malachi.

Of the New Testament:
The Gospels According to Matthew, Mark, Luke, and John; The Acts of the Apostles; Paul's Epistles to the Romans, I Corinthians, II Corinthians, Galatians, Ephesians, Philippians, Colossians, I Thessalonians, II Thessalonians, I Timothy, II Timothy, Titus, Philemon; The Epistle to the Hebrews, The

Epistle of James; The First and Second Epistles of Peter; The First, Second, and Third Epistles of John; The Epistle of Jude, and The Revelation.

All which are given by inspiration of God, to be the rule of faith and life.

3. The books commonly called Apocrypha, not being of divine inspiration, are no part of the Canon of Scripture; and therefore are of no authority in the Church of God, nor to be any otherwise approved, or made use of, than other human writings.

4. The authority of the Holy Scripture, for which it ought to be believed and obeyed, depends not upon the testimony of any man or Church, but wholly upon God (who is truth itself), the Author thereof; and therefore it is to be received, because it is the Word of God.

5. We may be moved and induced by the testimony of the Church to an high and reverent esteem of the holy Scripture; and the heavenliness of the matter, the efficacy of the doctrine, the majesty of the style, the consent of all the parts, the scope of the whole (which is to give all glory to God), the full discovery it makes of the only way of man's salvation, the many other incomparable excellencies, and the entire perfection thereof, are arguments whereby it does abundantly evidence itself to be the Word of God; yet, notwithstanding, our full persuasion and assurance of the infallible truth and divine authority thereof, is from the inward work of the Holy Spirit, bearing witness by and with the Word in our hearts.

6. The whole counsel of God, concerning all things necessary for his own glory, man's salvation, faith, and life, is either expressly set down in Scripture, or by good and necessary consequence may be deduced from Scripture: unto which nothing at any time is to be added, whether by new revelations of the Spirit, or traditions of men. Nevertheless we acknowledge the inward illumination of the Spirit of God to be necessary for the saving understanding of such things as are revealed in the Word; and that there are some circumstances concerning the worship of God, and the government of the Church, common to human actions and societies, which are to be ordered by the light of nature and Christian prudence, according to the general rules of the Word, which are always to be observed.

7. All things in Scripture are not alike plain in themselves, nor alike clear unto all; yet those things which are necessary to be known, believed, and observed, for salvation, are so clearly propounded and opened in some place of Scripture or other, that not only the learned, but the unlearned, in a due use of the ordinary means, may attain unto a sufficient understanding of them.

8. The Old Testament in Hebrew (which was the native language of the people of God of old), and the New Testament in Greek (which at the time of the writing of it was most generally known to the nations), being immediately inspired by God, and by his singular care and providence kept pure in all ages, are therefore authentic; so as in all controversies of religion the Church is finally to appeal unto them. But because these original tongues are not known to all the people of God who have right unto, and interest in, the Scriptures, and are commanded, in the fear of God, to read and search them, therefore they are to be translated into the language of every people unto which they come, that the Word of God dwelling plentifully in all, they may worship him in an acceptable manner, and, through patience and comfort of the Scriptures, may have hope.

9. The infallible rule of interpretation of Scripture, is the Scripture itself; and therefore, when there is a question about the true and full sense of any scripture (which is not manifold, but one), it may be searched and known by other places that speak more clearly.

10. The Supreme Judge, by which all controversies of religion are to be determined, and all decrees of councils, opinions of ancient writers, doctrines of men, and private spirits, are to be examined, and in whose sentence we are to rest, can be no other but the Holy Spirit speaking in the Scripture.

Prepare in Prayer
Heavenly Father, as we set out on this journey to understand this great document from Church history, please remind us that nothing written by human hands can surpass the truth of that which You have inspired, the Holy Scriptures. Amen.

Into the Scriptures
Read Psalm 119:1-40 and 2 Timothy 3:16.

Reach Back
The Westminster Confession was written during a time of great controversy. Matters such as the powers of parliament and the role of the king were being debated pointedly. The governmental structure of the Church of England was being contested. Would the Church of England be led by a king, a presbytery, an episcopal hierarchy, or in independence? Political and religious problems were intrinsically tied together. As the Westminster

Divines sought out spiritual truth as a rock of constancy in their lives, many aspects of their national life were in severe turmoil. It is probably impossible for American readers to understand the tensions felt in the 1600's between king and church, the kingdom of man and the Kingdom of God. Political tensions were high. Infighting among believers was ongoing as many Protestants sought to distance themselves from their Catholic counterparts in much of the world, and others fought to bring the Church back closer to Rome! Many of the disputes, even among the Protestants, were of doctrinal matters. For this reason, the Divines sought to understand their political and cultural turmoil in the light of certain unchanging absolutes. Despite the vast array of conflicts within and without of the Church, the Westminster Divines were summoned to bring clarity, unity, and peace to the churches of England and Scotland.

Because of these times of unmitigated commotion and sweeping change, the Westminster Divines wisely opened their theological masterpiece with the changeless Word of God. Here, they posited, is the foundation of all theology. This chapter aptly sets the stage for everything that will follow in these thirty-three chapters; Reformed theology is, if anything, biblical theology. By opening this grand piece of propositional theology in this way, the Divines made it clear, in no uncertain terms, that the Reformation banner of "sola scriptura" would be held high in all that would follow.

In today's parlance, Reformed churches like to speak of the "Three I's" when defining our view of Scripture. Inspired: the Scriptures have God as their ultimate author. The trustworthiness of our holy book is grounded in God's own truthfulness. Scripture teaches what we are to believe concerning God, and what duty He requires of us. Infallible: the revelation of God in the pages of our Bible never fail in their intent to convict and to convert. When the Bible is read and preached, the heart is either softened or hardened; no one stays the same. Inerrant: the very words of Scripture contain no errors whatsoever. The Bible is flawless in everything that it affirms.

Search Inward

Notice the strong language with which the Confession lifts up the Bible as *the* source of divine revelation. "Majestic," "heavenly," "the Word of God," "infallible," "the supreme judge." These are phrases and words designed to show the utmost respect and honor for the written Word. Clearly, the Divines intended to convey their conviction that the Scriptures derive their authority from God, since He is their author, and the revealer of divine counsel. Without any hesitation, we can say that the Divines held a position of inspiration contrary to anyone who would suggest that Scripture was on equal footing with tradition or church councils.

The topic of Scripture's inspiration is placed first in the Confession for one reason: all other doctrines and teachings of the Confession fully depend upon the Scriptures as their ultimate source—as should our lives. Looking into your own heart, do you honor the Scriptures as the very words of God spoken to you? When you study them, do you read for information or for transformation, or both? Do you ever find that a particular passage speaks remarkably clear to your own situation?

Consider again the words of Paul in 2 Timothy 3:16, "All Scripture is breathed out by God and profitable for teaching, for reproof, for correction, and for training in righteousness, that the man of God may be competent, equipped for every good work." And again, the words of the Psalmist, "I seek you with all of my heart; do not let me stray from your commandments" (119:10 NIV). In both passages of Scripture, we see the desire to be renovated, from the heart outward, by encountering the Bible. This renovation often comes at the price of "reproof and correction." This process can be hard, often unbearably painful, as God strips us of our pride and replaces it with a soft heart of humility.

James tells us,

> Be doers of the word and not hearers only, deceiving yourselves. For if anyone is a hearer of the word and not a doer, he is like a man who looks intently at his natural face in a mirror. For he looks at himself and goes away and at once forgets what he was like (1:22-24).

As I was teaching an adult education course called Bible 101, I sought to make this truth applicable to people who were doing a first-time survey though the Bible. And so I devised an acronym to assist students in truly using the Scriptures in a renovating way. The acronym "mirror" is simple. Every time we study a passage of Scripture, we should ask ourselves these questions:

> M: Magnify — What does this text reveal about God that causes me to magnify His glory?

I: Inspire — What does this text show me that inspires me to pray?

R: Reveal — What does this text reveal to me that prompts me to confess my sins?

R: Recognize — Who do I recognize in this passage that needs prayer, salvation, help etc.?

O: Obedience — How does this text demand my obedience to God's revealed will?

R: Respond — What must I do immediately to respond in faith to this passage?

Gaze Upward

Take some time this day to praise God for revealing His heart to you through the Scriptures. Consider that He did not have to reveal anything to us at all, and yet still could have held us accountable. What does it say about our God that He loves His creation so much as to express His will to His creatures through an unchangeable medium such as the Scriptures?

Ask God to make you more like the Psalmist, whose heart delights in obedience and conformity to God's holy decrees. Do you "rejoice in following (God's) statutes" as he writes in Psalm 119:14? Do you find your strength in His promises when you are weary from sorrow, as he pens in Psalm 119:28?

If you find a rebellious domain in your heart, that truly does not delight in obedience to God's revealed will, as recorded in the words of Scripture, confess it to God now and ask Him to sanctify your mind, so that you, like the Psalm writer, can boldly say "turn my heart towards your statutes and not toward selfish gain; turn my eyes away from worthless things; preserve my life according to Your word" (119:37 NIV).

Step Out—Reading Scripture

Notice how the Divines took both time and space to write out the titles of all 66 books of the Scriptures. This is important for two reasons. First of all, this articulates which books are considered sacred writ. We call this list the "canon."[9] Secondly, and more practically, it begs the question, "Have we read them all?" It is true that Habakkuk is just as inspired as Romans. The book of Leviticus is just as authoritative as the Gospel of John. Each book of the canon deserves to be poured over, studied meticulously, and committed to heart.

Now, take a moment to reflect on your devotional habits. Do you read the Scriptures on a regular basis? Weekly? Daily? What changes can you make in your schedule that would be more conducive to a devoted pattern of Scripture consumption? Perhaps you need to cancel a weeknight event, or drop out of an activity that is particularly wearing on your personal energy. If we find that we have created such a full schedule that we cannot follow hard after God, perhaps we need to make adjustments to our priority list in order that we might better make time for our Maker, Redeemer, and Master.

In his introduction to R.C. Sproul's book Knowing Scripture, the respected Anglican theologian J.I. Packer writes,

> If I were the devil...one of my first aims would be to stop folk from digging into the Bible. Knowing that it is the Word of God, teaching men to know and love and serve the God of the Word, I should do all that I could to surround it with the spiritual equivalents of pits, thorn hedges and man traps, to frighten people off.[10]

Packer then moves on to quote Jonathan Edwards in the same vein, "The devil has ever shown a mortal spite and hatred towards that holy book the Bible: he has done all in his power to extinguish that light...He is engaged against the Bible, and hates every word in it."[11]

As we move throughout this study, endeavoring to know God more intimately through His written love letter to us, let us keep in mind the warnings of these two renowned men of God. For the enemy of our souls will do everything in his power to keep us out of this book.

Some of us think of reading the Scriptures as though it were the same as good exercise or dietary supplements: advisable to do as often as possible,

---

9 The Greek "canon" and the Hebrew "qaneh" both mean "measuring rod."

10 J.I. Packer, quoted in R.C. Sproul, Knowing Scripture. (Downer's Grove IL: Intervarsity Press, 1977) p. 12.

11 Ibid.

but maybe not every day. There are too many other distractions that deter us. Others of us treat the Scriptures as though they were food. We need it, but we can survive up to five weeks without it. For others still, the Scriptures are like water, we desperately depend upon it, but still can survive five days or longer without. My prayer is that we would learn to rely on the Scriptures as desperately as we need oxygen. That we would take it in so regularly and naturally, that we hardly even think about doing so. But deprive us of its benefits for five minutes—and death ensues. This is not to say that we must continually have our Bibles open on our laps. Of course that is not possible. But let us pray that the Word of God so thoroughly soaks into our consciousness that we would not be able to suppress the natural respiration of Spirit-dependant living.

The Confession Chapter Two:

Of God, and of the Holy Trinity

1. There is but one only living and true God, who is infinite in being and perfection, a most pure spirit, invisible, without body, parts, or passions, immutable, immense, eternal, incomprehensible, almighty, most wise, most holy, most free, most absolute, working all things according to the counsel of his own immutable and most righteous will, for his own glory, most loving, gracious, merciful, long-suffering, abundant in goodness and truth, forgiving iniquity, transgression, and sin; the rewarder of them that diligently seek him; and withal most just and terrible in his judgments; hating all sin; and who will by no means clear the guilty.

2. God has all life, glory, goodness, blessedness, in and of himself; and is alone in and unto himself all-sufficient, not standing in need of any creatures which he has made, nor deriving any glory from them, but only manifesting his own glory in, by, unto, and upon them; he is the alone foundation of all being, of whom, through whom, and to whom, are all things; and has most sovereign dominion over them, to do by them, for them, or upon them, whatsoever he pleases. In his sight all things are open and manifest; his knowledge is infinite, infallible, and independent upon the creature; so as nothing is to him contingent or uncertain. He is most holy in all his counsels, in all his works, and in all his commands. To him is due from angels and men, and every other creature, whatsoever worship, service, or obedience he is pleased to require of them.

3. In the unity of the Godhead there are three Persons of one substance, power, and eternity: God the Father, God the Son, and God the Holy Ghost. The Father is of none, neither begotten nor proceeding; the Son is eternally begotten of the Father; the Holy Ghost eternally proceeding from the Father and the Son.

Prepare in Prayer

Holy God, as we study Your character and nature today, please remind us that no matter how rigorously we study, Your eternal power and divine nature surpass all human ability to comprehend. In the name of Jesus we pray, amen.

Into the Scriptures

Read Isaiah 44:1-8 and John chapters 14-16.

Reach Back

One of the beauties of reading and praying through the great creeds of the faith is the way that they connect us to Christians of ages gone by. Here, the Confession connects us with our forbearers in the faith by articulating the doctrine of the Trinity. Specifically, this section attempts to emulate the Apostle's Creed and the Nicene Creed (among others) by lifting up the doctrine of the tri-unity of God, as He eternally exists in the persons of the Father, the Son, and the Holy Spirit. This doctrine is truly an ecumenical formulation of God's eternal existence, held by Protestants, Roman Catholics and Eastern Orthodox believers alike. Though we may disagree on many lesser dogmas and doctrines, this section of the Confession is a consistent rallying point at which all orthodox Christians may connect hands and encircle the throne of God in praise and adoration. The Westminster Confession uplifts the three mysterious and majestic truths that the Bible reveals regarding the nature of the Trinity:

> There is but one God.
>
> The Father, the Son, and the Spirit are all fully God.
>
> And yet each person in the Trinity is wonderfully distinct, not to be confused with the other two persons.

Nature does not offer a metaphor rich enough to describe the Trinity. Many have tried to compare the nature of God to things found in the created order. For instance, some have compared the Trinity to water, ice, and steam. All are comprised of $H2O$ sharing one molecular makeup. Yet all analogies fail at *some* point. We need to be very careful that we do not reduce the majesty of God's eternal coexistence by comparisons that diminish His glory. In the above example (that of $H2O$), the analogy does not adequately explain how God is Father, Son, and Holy Spirit *at the same time,* without confusing the persons of the godhead. Theologians have been careful to distinguish between the terms "person" and "substance." God exists as three persons, and yet these three persons have one substance—each of the persons is fully divine.

Search Inward

Note in the biblical readings from John 14-16 how the persons of the Trinity honor and bring glory one to another. The Son is said to bring glory to the Father (John 14:13). The Father loves the Son and the Son abides in His love (15:10). The Spirit is truth and is sent by the Son from the Father (15:26). The Spirit glorifies the Son (16:14). Each person of the Holy Trinity uplifts, glorifies, and loves the other.

Eugene Peterson writes:

> In reality (the Trinity) is our most exuberant intellectual venture in thinking about God. Trinity is a conceptual attempt to provide coherence to God as God is revealed variously as Father, Son, and Holy Spirit in our Scriptures. God is emphatically personal; God is only and exclusively God in relationship. Trinity is not an attempt to explain or define God by means of abstractions (although there is some of that, too), but a witness that God reveals himself as personal and in personal relations.[12]

Now that you have taken a closer look at the relational love of God Himself, look deeply into your own heart to discern if you are beginning to love in a similar manner. While we cannot *comprehend* the Trinitarian nature of God with our minds, we can begin to *imitate* His self-giving love with our lives. Do you seek to lift others up, or to tear them down by your words and actions? Often we feel most at liberty to dissect the actions and motives of those most dear to us—our parents, spouses, children, and church leaders. Ironically, we often reserve better outward behavior for strangers and colleagues than for those most dear to our hearts! By looking at the way the three persons of the Trinity express self-sacrificial love, especially the Son's willingness to submit His own life to the Father's will, how much more ought we to learn to love others from God's perfect example?

---

12 Eugene Peterson. Christ Plays in Ten Thousand Places. (Grand Rapids MI: Eerdmans, 2005) p. 7.

Gaze Upward

I mentioned in the introduction that the Sovereignty of God ought to inspire a "Copernican Revolution of the Soul" in our own lives. We now know (thanks to Copernicus' helio-centric theory of the universe) that the Sun is the center of mass around which the planets orbit. I can't help but wonder what would happen if we were to make just such a celestial change in our prayer lives. What would happen if praise and worship became the central object of our prayers, rather than our lists of requests? As good as those are, I am convinced that prayer requests are *secondary* to our created design to worship and adore Almighty God.

Because God is omniscient (all-knowing) He already has our prayer requests and needs well in hand before we ever bring them to His throne. Do not get me wrong: I am not saying that we should avoid the labor of intercessory prayer. That would be quite mistaken. I am suggesting however that intercession is *subordinate* to the intimacy that is to be formed between a worshipper and God.

Let us receive the challenge that the Confession lays before us today, by refusing to allow our own prayer life to be "people-centered." Let us instead ascribe to God words of praise and exultation, applying the most wonderful language that we can summon, in order to more fully bring glory to our God in prayer. There ought to be times or "seasons" of prayer where we make praising God our exclusive work. For one week or one month, attempt to make your prayers exclusively praise-centered. Don't be concerned with listing out your worries and fears—God will still honor those lists of "help me's" that we send His way. Rather, trust that all of your worries and concerns will be absorbed into your praises and exultations.

Step Out—Contemplative Praise

The simple truth of the Christian life is that praise brings joy. It brings joy to God, and it brings joy to us in Him. John Calvin described it this way, "If God contains the fullness of all good things in Himself like an inexhaustible fountain, nothing beyond him is to be sought by those who strike after the highest good and all the elements of happiness."[13]

---

13 John Calvin, quoted in John Piper, Desiring God: Meditations of a Christian Hedonist. (Sisters OR: Multnomah Publishers, 2003) p. 90.

In today's lesson, our passage from the Confession was especially full of adoration and praise. In fact, sections one and two could easily be converted into heart-felt prayer by simply changing the pronouns from "He" and "His" to "You" and "Your." Meditatively read these sections again slowly, taking time to digest each word to the best of your own comprehension, understanding that many of these concepts are beyond our full ability to grasp. Take time to use the descriptive words in section one and apply them to God's glory in your heart. For instance, you might render section one something like this:

O God! You alone are infinite in being and perfection, a most pure spirit, invisible, without body, parts, or passions. You alone are immutable, immense, eternal, incomprehensible, almighty, most wise, most holy, most free, most absolute, working all things according to the counsel of Your own immutable and most righteous will. Lord, You do this all for Your own glory! Let my heart cry out that You are most loving, gracious, merciful, long-suffering, abundant in goodness and truth to Your servant!

Notice that one of the most beautiful aspects of this type of prayer is that it forces us to think of God's greatness for its own sake, quite apart from the wonderful things He does *for us.* This is clearly a deeper brand of love. In a way, this is like beginning to learn to love one's spouse for his or her true inner beauty, rather than for the fact that they do nice things for us, such as make us breakfast. John Piper, picking up on the thoughts of his dead mentor Jonathan Edwards, calls this "disinterested love." It is disinterested because it is love for God's intrinsic worth *rather* than a conditional love based on His blessings alone. Piper writes,

> Disinterested love to God is loving God 'for Himself and for his own sake.' In other words, Edwards uses the term 'disinterested love' to designate love that delights in God for his own greatness and beauty, and to distinguish it from love that delights only in God's gifts. Disinterested love is not love without pleasure. It is love whose pleasure is in God himself.[14]

When we love God for His intrinsic worth, our joy in Him is unbounded.

Think about your love for God as expressed in your prayers; do you love Him because God is good, or do you love Him merely because he is *good to you?* Is there a difference?

---

14 John Piper. God is the Gospel. (Wheaton IL: Crossway, 2005) p. 110.

The Confession Chapter Three:

Of God's Eternal Decree

1. God from all eternity did by the most wise and holy counsel of his own will, freely and unchangeably ordain whatsoever comes to pass; yet so as thereby neither is God the author of sin; nor is violence offered to the will of the creatures, nor is the liberty or contingency of second causes taken away, but rather established.

2. Although God knows whatsoever may or can come to pass, upon all supposed conditions; yet has he not decreed any thing because he foresaw it as future, as that which would come to pass, upon such conditions.

3. By the decree of God, for the manifestation of his glory, some men and angels are predestinated unto everlasting life, and others foreordained to everlasting death.

4. These angels and men, thus predestinated and foreordained, are particularly and unchangeably designed; and their number is so certain and definite that it cannot be either increased or diminished.

5. Those of mankind that are predestinated unto life, God, before the foundation of the world was laid, according to his eternal and immutable purpose, and the secret counsel and good pleasure of his will, has chosen in Christ, unto everlasting glory, out of his free grace and love alone, without any foresight of faith or good works, or perseverance in either of them, or any other thing in the creature, as conditions, or causes moving him thereunto; and all to the praise of his glorious grace.

6. As God has appointed the elect unto glory, so has he, by the eternal and most free purpose of his will, fore-ordained all the means thereunto. Wherefore they who are elected being fallen in Adam are redeemed by Christ, are effectually called unto faith in Christ by his Spirit working in due season; are justified, adopted, sanctified, and kept by his power through faith unto salvation. Neither are any other redeemed by Christ, effectually called, justified, adopted, sanctified, and saved, but the elect only.

7. The rest of mankind, God was pleased, according to the unsearchable counsel of his own will, whereby he extends or withholds mercy as he pleases, for the glory of his sovereign power over his creatures, to pass by, and to ordain them to dishonor and wrath for their sin, to the praise of his glorious justice.

8. The doctrine of this high mystery of predestination is to be handled with special prudence and care, that men attending to the will of God revealed in his Word, and yielding obedience thereunto, may, from the certainty of their effectual vocation, be assured of their eternal election. So shall this doctrine afford matter of praise, reverence, and admiration of God; and of humility, diligence, and abundant consolation to all that sincerely obey the gospel.

Prepare in Prayer

Holy Father, as we delve into the mysteries of election in this study, please allow this discussion to deepen our humility, not swell our pride. Without Your grace, we could not read one more sentence. In the name of Jesus we pray, amen.

Into the Scriptures

Read Romans 9 and Ephesians 1.

Reaching Back

There is no question that today's reading from the Confession may be difficult to comprehend intellectually, and also difficult to accept emotionally. Here we find a rather strong articulation of the doctrine of election.[15] Looking back on this generation of Reformed English believers, as well as their American Puritan descendants, may well be a humbling exercise as we

---

15 The doctrine of predestination is asserted most clearly in two places: Ephesians 1 and Romans 9. Nevertheless, the concept of election is laden throughout Scripture. See Deuteronomy 7:6-11; Matthew 22:14; 24:22, 24, 31; Luke 18:7; John 13:18; 15:16; Acts 9:15; 14:28; 13:48; Romans 8:28-29, 33; 11:5-7; 1 Thessalonians 1:4; 2 Thessalonians 2:13; 1 Timothy 2:10; Titus 1:1; 1 Peter 1:1-2; and 1 Peter 2:9.

examine the thoughts and doctrines of a people wholly committed to the sovereignty of God. The Divines as well as their Calvinist Puritan followers were unremittingly committed to the doctrine of God's sovereignty (or Lordship) over all of the cosmos. They relentlessly applied this doctrine to all others, laying a theological foundation for all other teachings upon the concept that God alone is in control of the entire universe, yet in such a way as God is not blamed for sin, nor is the responsibility of human beings destroyed.

By contrast, we live in an age in which individual expression and personal rights are considered our society's highest ideals. Before we can consider the depths of this doctrine, we must first acknowledge our own modern preferences towards individualism, perhaps by repenting of our own radical hold on self-sufficiency.

Look Inward

When you consider the doctrine of election—that God chose you and not the other way around, and not only that but He chose you without condition of your own merit—what does that do to your emotions? Does it cause you to rebel against a Creator-Lord that has that much control of the universe that even the number of the elect cannot increase or diminish aside from His will? Does it cause you to challenge God's fairness or His justice in the manner in which He chose to elect some to salvation, in order to display His mercy, and to pass over others in order to display His justice? If the doctrine of election causes us to recoil because we find that we are not the captains of our own lives, let us probe the inner chambers of our hearts, and ask "why?" If it is somehow egregious to us because we are challenging the right of God Almighty to rule *completely* over His own creation, including His rule over those who are saved and lost, perhaps we are inadvertently challenging God's omnipotence and reign. If this is the case, we must once again fall on our faces in repentance.

Gaze Upwards

We can be sure that we are misunderstanding election *if it does not produce repentance and thankfulness in our hearts*. Coming to the realization that God chose us in Christ before the foundation of the earth is a certain cause for us to express our gratitude for having been chosen and redeemed. In Paul's exposition of election in Ephesians 1, he is full of praise for God's sovereign choice to redeem, exulting by such phrases as "blessed be the God and Father of our Lord Jesus Christ" (1:3), and "to the praise of His glorious grace" (1:6), and again "For this reason (i.e. His glory)...I do not cease to give thanks" (1:15, 16). Let your heart resign itself to thankfulness that you are in Christ, not because of anything you have done to earn it, but rather because of God's choosing you as a vessel to reflect His glory back to Him.

The doctrine of election is one of the most praise-inspiring doctrines in the whole scope of Christian theology, because the whole of it is from God and not of ourselves as Paul writes in Ephesians 2:8-9. Twice in these two verses Paul makes clear that our salvation is "not your own doing" and "not a result of works." If this is the case, then neither our act of the will to accept Jesus Christ, nor our initiative to investigate Him, nor our wisdom in finally doing so, have any weight of credit in our coming to faith. On the contrary, the entire process is *of* and *through* and *to* God. John Calvin writes, "Man has not an atom of cause to boast. The whole work is God's."[16]

But isn't it our "accepting" of Jesus Christ into our hearts that effects salvation? Yes. And no. While it is by faith alone that we are saved, the fact that we were drawn to faith in the first place is again an action which only God can perform. As Jesus teaches in John 6:44, "No one can come to me unless the Father who sent me *draws Him*" (emphasis added), and again in 6:65, "No one can come to me unless it is *granted him by the Father*" (emphasis added). Thus our salvation through and through is the work of God; quite apart from anything and everything we might have done to "earn it."

Praise Him that, in His sovereign plan, He has designed to use broken and frail vessels such as human believers to be redeemed objects of His grace. Worship Him as a God of mercy whose benevolence is also tempered by His administration of perfect justice.

Step Out—Election Reflection

If this doctrine is troublesome to you, be encouraged—being troubled is often a sign that we are growing in our faith. Do not be discouraged that you find yourself kicking against the goads (Acts 26:14), for the Confession will doubtlessly challenge you in many more places to come. If the sovereignty of God is a challenge to your intellect rather than your heart, resolve to delve more deeply into the matter by studying Ephesians 1 and 2, and also Romans 9 more fully. Make a promise to yourself—write it in a journal or

---

16 John Calvin. The Institutes of the Christian Religion. 2.3.6. Edited by Tony Lane and Hilary Osborn. (Grand Rapids MI: Baker Book House, 1987) p. 100.

on your hand if you have to—that you will refuse to settle for worshipping a god that is anything less than the Sovereign God of all that is.

For further work on election, perhaps reading sermons from the early colonial Puritans may be of aid to you. The Puritans were men and women who were consumed with a passionate love for the sovereignty of God. One exemplar of superlative preaching on election is Jonathan Edwards. His sermons *"God's Sovereignty in the Salvation of Men"* and also *"God Glorified in Man's Dependence"* are highly recommended for the purposes of exalting God's Lordship over our souls. So also can we recommend A.W. Pink's very readable The Sovereignty of God, a seminal work on predestination for several generations now. Finally, I would also highly recommend R.C. Sproul's more recent books Chosen by God and What is Reformed Theology? Here this strange and wonderful doctrine of God's sovereign choice is explained in terms that most will find readily digestible.

The fact that God chose the elect is an astonishing evidence of His mercy. Sproul writes,

> That God chooses according to the good pleasure of his will (Ephesians 1:3-5) does not mean that his choices are capricious or arbitrary. An arbitrary choice is one made for no reason at all... In his inscrutable, mysterious will, God chooses for reasons known only to himself. He chooses according to his own pleasure, which is his divine right. If something pleases God, it must be good. There is no evil pleasure in God.[17]

In sum, the doctrine of election causes us to fall on your faces and worship Him as *truly a sovereign God.*

---

17 R.C. Sproul. What is Reformed Theology? (Grand Rapids MI: Baker, 1997) p. 147.

The Confession Chapter Four:

Of Creation

1. It pleased God the Father, Son, and Holy Ghost, for the manifestation of the glory of his eternal power, wisdom, and goodness, in the beginning, to create or make of nothing the world, and all things therein, whether visible or invisible, in the space of six days, and all very good.

2. After God had made all other creatures, he created man, male and female, with reasonable and immortal souls, endued with knowledge, righteousness, and true holiness after his own image, having the law of God written in their hearts, and power to fulfill it; and yet under a possibility of transgressing, being left to the liberty of their own will, which was subject unto change. Besides this law written in their hearts, they received a command not to eat of the tree of the knowledge of good and evil; which while they kept were happy in their communion with God, and had dominion over the creatures.

Prepare in Prayer
God of all creation, maker of Sun, moon, and stars; remind us how small we are in comparison to the works of Your hands. As we think of the handiwork of Your fingers, raise our eyes to Your glory. Amen.

Into the Scriptures
Read Genesis 1 and Psalm 19.

Reach Back
This section of the Confession highlights the creative genius of God. Here, our hearts are drawn to begin to adore God for His beautiful masterwork

in the creation of the universe. The Confession states that it pleased God to create the entire cosmos—from the Earth to electrons, from mountains to molecules, from galaxies to the Galapagos—out of nothing (WCF 4.1)! Here the Confession picks up on the famous Latin phrase "ex nihilo," that is, "out of nothingness." Christian theology has always insisted that only God is eternal. Matter is not.

Longtime professor of theology at Calvin Theological Seminary, Louis Berkhof explains,

> While Greek philosophy sought the explanation of the world in a dualism, which involves the eternity of matter, or in a process of emanation, which makes the world the outward manifestation of God, the Christian Church from the very beginning has taught the doctrine of creation ex nihilo and as a free act of God. This doctrine was accepted with singular unanimity from the start.[18]

This means that God, with His unlimited power, was able to call into existence that which was not. Matter, light, *even time itself* were summoned into existence—not molded and formed from pre-existing "stuff"—and all this by the incredible Word of His power!

Search Inward

Although this section is brief, it beckons us to begin to admire God for His master handiwork. So much of our day is spent in routine patterns and endless habit, that we often forget, proverbially, to "stop and smell the roses." In some sense, we become deadened to the creative artistry of God, much like the curator of a museum might walk though the halls of a gallery day after day, and begin to miss the excitement and power of the artistry as he first enjoyed it. Consider the fact that God, having made the entire Milky Way, stood back and declared it all "very good" (Genesis 1:31). If the creation pleased God, does it also bring joy to *our* senses as well?

The Confession also points out the intense value of human life (WCF 4.2). Like no other object in all of creation, human beings are said to reflect "the image of God" (Genesis 1:27). While theologians have often debated the exact meaning of this phrase, suggestions such as a capacity for moral discernment, a mandate towards dominion over the rest of creation, and the capability to love one another stand out. In any regard, the phrase "the

---

18 Louis Berhof. Systematic Theology. (Grand Rapids, MI: Eerdmans, 1986) p. 126

image of God" ought to convey the preciousness of human life since it mysteriously mirrors the wonder of God's own fingerprint upon our being. Take a few breath prayers to confess those moments when you think or act as though human life was worth less than it was created to be. The poor, the neglected, the homeless, the drug-addicted—all still bear God's image-stamp, and thus are valuable in His sight.

If then, humankind alone out of all of creation is made in the image of God as the Bible declares it to be, how should that notion improve our understanding of the sacredness of human life? Should not this radical thought re-create our understanding of the sanctity of our very lives? And yet, we live in a world where fetuses are considered "medical waste." Suicide bombers explode themselves at bus stations because of national descent. Gang lines are drawn over race, class, and turf. Somehow in the mayhem of human existence, the precious nature of the "image of God," stamped into fragile human flesh, has been lost. It is the duty of the Christian to recover it.

David writes of human formation in the womb,

> For you formed my inward parts; you knitted me together in my mother's womb. I praise you for I am fearfully and wonderfully made. Wonderful are your works; my soul knows it full well. My frame was not hidden from you, when I was being made in secret, intricately woven in the depths of the earth. Your eyes saw my unformed substance; in your book were written, every one of them, the days that were formed for me, when as yet there were none of them (Psalm 139:13-16).

The more we study creation itself, yea even the human body, the more we are prone to incline our faces and hands toward the living architect of them!

Gaze Upward

In today's reading, the Psalmist gives us a tutorial on the manifestation of God's glory through His own creation. David writes, "the sky above proclaims His handiwork. Day to day pours out speech, and night to night reveals knowledge" (19:1). Make some time in your morning or evening devotions to journal about the handiwork of God in nature. Note the extended metaphor in verses 5 and 6 that David uses to describe the sun routing its course. What type of language would you pen to give God glory for other beauteous aspects of creation: a river cascading over a rock face, a spider crafting a symmetrical web, the balance of the solar system? And yet we must be very careful to never give praise to the creation itself, but rather to yield exclusive honor to its Creator as solely worthy of our highest esteem (Romans 1:22-23).

In order to inspire a greater love for the beauties of creation, you may choose to pray through several of the Psalms that focus on the glory of God revealed in nature. Among them are Psalms 8, 19, 29, 33, 89, 93, 96, 98, 121, and 148. The next time you pack a lunch and head to a park, or pitch a folding chair on the sand at the beach, take your Bible along with you and attempt to absorb some of the imagery of these Psalms into your heart.

Step Out—Encountering God in Nature

Looking back again to Jonathan Edwards, we find that the famous pastor often spent hours walking in the woods and riding though nature in order to foster his relationship with God. Interestingly, one of his most spiritual experiences, a personal encounter with a manifestation of Christ's glory, came not during his most rigorous intellectual exercises, but rather during one of those extended times of prayer in the woods.

Edwards' biographer writes,

> He described himself as often lost in contemplations of nature. Before his spiritual transformation, he noted, he had been 'uncommonly terrified' by thunderstorms; afterward they inspired 'sweet and glorious contemplations of my great and glorious God.' It became natural for him 'to sing or chant forth my meditations; to speak my thoughts in soliloquies, and speak with a singing voice.[19]

I find it strangely sad that evangelical Christians today do not appear to be as concerned about the state of the environment as many of our liberal counterparts. Perhaps it is because our eschatology (theology of the end times) allows us to give up too easily. After all, doesn't 2 Peter 3:7 teach that, "By the same word the heavens and earth that now exist are stored up for fire, being kept until the Day of Judgment and destruction of the ungodly?" Indeed. And yet at the same time, I am convinced, God's eschatological

---

19 George M. Marsden. Jonathan Edwards: A Life. (New Haven: Yale University Press, 2003) p. 44.

wrath does not negate the mandate to be stewards of the earth as given to Adam and Eve in Genesis 2:15. More than that, the Bible also describes the eternal state as being the "new heavens *and the new earth*" (Revelation 21:1 emphasis added). How does your treatment of the world around you reflect or deflect from your reverence to God as our Creator and Maker?

Hopefully, you set aside moments, or even hours, to intentionally encounter God in the midst of His creation. As I write this, the northern hemisphere just experienced the peak meteor shower of the year. The other night I did something unusual by wrapping in a blanket, walking out into the crisp December air, and sitting on my porch looking at the stars. As I sat there, it struck me that some of us spend much of our time in crowded markets, urban buildings, and traffic jams. Then, we are baffled as to why we have a hard time approaching God on His own terms.

This may sound radical to you, but perhaps you would do well to call off of work for a personal day to spend walking a field, or traversing a mountain path, or journaling in a park. Perhaps one of the most helpful things that we can do is to seek Him out where His footprints are the most visible, alone in the midst of His unvarnished creation.

The Confession Chapter Five:

Of Providence

1. God, the great Creator of all things, does uphold, direct, dispose, and govern all creatures, actions, and things, from the greatest even to the least, by his most wise and holy providence, according to his infallible foreknowledge, and the free and immutable counsel of his own will, to the praise of the glory of his wisdom, power, justice, goodness, and mercy.

2. Although in relation to the foreknowledge and decree of God, the first cause, all things come to pass immutably and infallibly, yet, by the same providence, he orders them to fall out according to the nature of second causes, either necessarily, freely, or contingently.

3. God, in his ordinary providence, makes use of means, yet is free to work without, above, and against them, at his pleasure.

4. The almighty power, unsearchable wisdom, and infinite goodness of God, so far manifest themselves in his providence, that it extends itself even to the first Fall, and all other sins of angels and men, and that not by a bare permission, but such as has joined with it a most wise and powerful bounding, and otherwise ordering and governing of them, in a manifold dispensation, to his own holy ends; yet so, as the sinfulness thereof proceeds only from the creature, and not from God; who being most holy and righteous, neither is nor can be the author or approver of sin.

5. The most wise, righteous, and gracious God, does oftentimes leave for a season his own children to manifold temptations and the corruption of their own hearts, to chastise them for their former sins, or to discover unto them the hidden strength of corruption and deceitfulness of their hearts, that they may be humbled; and to raise them to a more close and constant dependence for their support upon himself, and to make them more watchful against all future occasions of sin, and for various other just and holy ends.

6. As for those wicked and ungodly men whom God, as a righteous judge, for former sins, does blind and harden; from them he not only withholds his grace, whereby they might have been enlightened in their understandings, and wrought upon their hearts; but sometimes also withdrawals the gifts which they had; and exposes them to such objects as their corruption makes occasion of sin; and withal, gives them over to their own lusts, the temptations of the world, and the power of Satan; whereby it comes to pass that they harden themselves, even under those means which God uses for the softening of others.

7. As the providence of God does, in general, reach to all creatures, so, after a most special manner, it takes care of his Church, and disposes all things to the good thereof.

Prepare in Prayer
Mighty God, as we read, think, and study today, please remind us that without Your providence, having ordered all the events in the past that preceded our lives, we would not have even been born. For this, we give You praise. Amen.

Into the Scriptures
Read Job 1-3 and Romans 1.

Reach Back: What do we really mean when we say things like "God is in control" and "It's in God's hands"? We often use words like these when a friend is looking for a job, or a single person is anxious to find a spouse, or a child becomes sick. And yet in what ways is God really in control of our lives?

Theologian Wayne Grudem writes that the providence of God means,

> God is continually involved with all created things in such a way that He 1) keeps them existing and maintaining the properties with which he created them; 2) cooperates with created things in every action, directing their distinctive properties to cause them to act as they do; and 3) directs them to fulfill His purposes.[20]

Once again in this reading from the Confession, we find that the Divines are pushing the doctrine of the sovereignty of God to its full extension. Here, the writers credit God with being the active Lord over all creation. He is no passive landowner. The Divines are quick to point out that God is not only the giver of divine blessings, but also the *withholder* of blessings both to test the righteous, and to mete out judgment on the unrighteous

---

20 Wayne Grudem. Systematic Theology. (Grand Rapids MI: Zondervan, 1994) p. 315.

(WCF 5.5,6). Admittedly, it is hard to swallow the idea that God would allow His children to suffer, but suffering is never without a perfect purpose (see Philippians 3:10).

Thomas a'Kempis writes, "Prepare yourself to endure many adversities and various kinds of trouble in this difficult life, for that is the way it will be with you wherever you are, and you will find it that way no matter where you hide yourself."[21] Each and every one of us will suffer in this life. The difference is to whom or what we cling when the suffering comes.

Gaze Upwards

So many times, in our childish conceptions of God, we are willing to only credit God for his interventions into human history and our own lives when God brings about pleasurable things. Yet the Scriptures contain a much fuller picture of the sovereignty of God. As the account of Job reveals, God often removes His hand of comfort, even from believers, so that the fullness of their dependence may be revealed in times of duress. And yet, we learn from Job's experience, that Satan's power is severely restricted to the permission of God (Job 1:12, 2:6). The evil one may not even blink without God's permission.

Thus, the Divines' hope to point out in the Confession that temptation, illness, disease and other secondary causes (or "means," WCF 5.3) are not unexpected flare-ups of evil contrary to the will of God, but are in fact, quite mysteriously, ordained in the secret counsel of God's holy and perfect will to bring about God's divine plan for human history and even our own individual lives. Often, it is these very trials that promote the glory of God in our lives as we endure them.

Search Inward

The Confession is very clear, as is Scripture, that God permits evil to exist for a time, but that He is never the first cause of evil (WCF 5.4). He is not the author of evil and does no malevolence, for this would be contrary to His holy nature. "Let no one say when he is tempted," writes James, "'I am being tempted by God,' for God cannot be tempted with evil, and He Himself tempts no one" (1:13). Do you ever mistakenly blame God or despise Him in your heart for the results of your own sin, the sin of another person, or even the fallen nature of creation itself? Ask God to give your

---

21 Thomas a'Kempis. The Imitation of Christ. (North Brunswick NJ: Bridge-Logos Publishers, 1999) p. 102.

heart a proper balance for understanding that He is in control of all things, and yet does no evil of His own accord.

More than that, does your heart give praise to God for the wonderful things that He does *which appear at the time to be difficulties?* Often what we perceive as a hindrance is actually God working on our behalf.

For instance, several years ago my son Elijah went to the doctor for a routine check-up. He had had a severe cough and chest cold. After listening to the lungs, our family doctor called for a chest x-ray. To the doctor's astonishment and ours, a large cyst was discovered in his left, top lung. Though my wife and I wept at the thought of an object the size of a jumbo egg being lodged in our three-year-old's lung, we couldn't help but praise God that the discovery was made. After all, had Elijah not contracted the cold, we would have never known that this cyst was growing inside of him. Having been discovered, the cyst was removed by the careful hand of the surgeon before it caused more problems later in life. After our initial grief, Kelly and I attributed this discovery to God as a serendipity. The providence of God is marvelous, although it is often mysterious.

Step Out—Rejoicing During Trial

In your prayers today, do something quite unnatural to your human inclination by praising God for the greatest struggle that you are engaged in right now. Are you or a loved one ill? Praise God that He has allowed you to suffer for a purpose. Are you struggling with a temptation? Praise God for giving you His Holy Spirit to strengthen you during this time. Are you grappling with the evils of this world such as terrorism, natural disasters, or the death of a loved one? Praise God that, though you do not understand His will, He is still in control of all things. Think back over your life and highlight the times that God has allowed you to go through serious suffering. Note the ways that God has caused you to cling more desperately to Him.

I remember a children's book that I read as a child. The clouds and the sun were having a competition to see who could more easily cause the man to take off his trench coat. The clouds attempted first. They blew and fussed, attempting to rip the coat right off of the man. They could, they supposed, get right underneath the material and tear off the outer coat. But the harder the winds blew, the more the man clung desperately to it. Shouldn't trials, temptations, and times of suffering work that way too? The more ferocious the storm, the more we cling to our robes of righteousness?

Later the Sun made his attempt. In quite an opposite way, the Sun's tactics were subtler. He gently shined on the man's back. The man hardly knew what was happening. Soon he took off the coat and left it behind. Unfortunately he was more exposed to the Sun's dangers as he began to burn. The Sun had won. The man let down his guard. If you are not in a time of hardship now, be careful here too. Often when we feel secure in our selves, perceiving that we are in no state of danger, we are prone to the pitfalls of sin, the temptations of the flesh, and subtle tendencies toward self-reliance and self-sufficiency.

Using the words of the Confession, extol Him for His *"almighty power, unsearchable wisdom, and infinite goodness"* no matter what type of hardship you are going through.

The Confession Chapter Six:

Of the Fall of Man, of Sin, and of the Punishment Thereof

1. Our first parents, being seduced by the subtlety and temptations of Satan, sinned in eating the forbidden fruit. This, their sin, God was pleased, according to his wise and holy counsel, to permit, having purposed to order it to his own glory.

2. By this sin they fell from their original righteousness and communion with God, and so became dead in sin, and wholly defiled in all the faculties and parts of soul and body.

3. They being the root of mankind, the guilt of this sin was imputed, and the same death in sin and corrupted nature conveyed to all their posterity, descending from them by original generation.

4. From this original corruption, whereby we are utterly indisposed, disabled, and made opposite to all good, and wholly inclined to all evil, do proceed all actual transgressions.

5. This corruption of nature, during this life, does remain in those that are regenerated; and although it be through Christ pardoned and mortified, yet both itself, and all the motions thereof, are truly and properly sin.

6. Every sin, both original and actual, being a transgression of the righteous law of God, and contrary thereunto, does, in its own nature, bring guilt upon the sinner, whereby he is bound over to the wrath of God, and curse of the law, and so made subject to death, with all miseries spiritual, temporal, and eternal.

Prepare in Prayer

Dear God, please bring to our attention all of those sinful thoughts, words, and deeds that we have committed which displease You. May we fully and honestly confess our sin before we study this topic. In Jesus' name we pray, amen.

Into the Scriptures

Read Genesis 3 and Romans 3.

Reach Back

This section of the Confession stands staunchly opposed to the culture of our day. Here the Divines unfold their theology of the total depravity of humanity and the full repercussions of the Fall (Genesis 3). Society today tells us that we are whole, that we are good, that we are "normal." As the title of one book suggests, "I'm OK, You're OK."

This, however, is neither the position of Scripture nor the Confession. Scripture teaches, and the Confession rightly explains, that each person has suffered the consequences of the Fall, so that we not only commit actual sins in our lives (and every day!), but we also bear the marks of fallenness on our very souls. As Paul writes in Romans 3:10, "None is righteous, no, not one; no one understands; no one seeks for God. All have turned aside; together they have become worthless." Thus, we are sinful both in essence and action.

When Reformed theologians use the term "total depravity" we do not mean that each of us is as bad as we possibly *could be*. Not many of us for instance have lived as did Hitler. On the contrary, we mean that our fallenness has corrupted every aspect of our human nature: the mind, the soul, the body, the intellect, the emotions, the will; all have been tainted by our proclivity towards sin. In some way, we are like a marble sitting on a desk. No longer are we truly able to move objectively in the sense that we could "roll" in any direction we want. The table is now constantly slanted—away from God. We are now declined towards sin. Every facet of our being suffers this corruption.

In the Confession, this Calvinist document goes even further than our Arminian[22] brothers would by acknowledging that *we would not even be able to receive or to choose Christ* if not for a massive work of grace in our lives prior to our conversion (WCF 6.4).

Christian theologians in general and Reformed theologians in particular have long discussed the doctrine of "original sin." That is, that all human beings, by nature of the fact that we are descendants of Adam, have inherited his proclivity towards sin, initiated at the Fall in the Garden of Eden. John Calvin gives us a helpful summary of the doctrine of original sin,

> The contamination of parents is transmitted to their children so that everyone, without exception, is depraved from the earliest moments. The start of this depravity cannot be discovered until we go back to the first parent of all, as the fountain-head. We must grasp the fact firmly, as we think of human nature, that Adam was not just an ancestor but a root, so that by his corruption the whole human race was justly tainted.[23]

A contemporary theologian, Wayne Grudem, adds this distinction as we consider our fallen nature,

> If this term (original sin) is to be used, it should be remembered that the sin spoken of does not refer to Adam's first sin, but to the guilt and tendency to sin with which we are born. It is 'original' in that it comes from Adam, and it is also original in that we have it from the beginning of our existence as persons, **but it is still our sin**, not Adam's sin, that is meant (emphasis added).[24]

---

22 Arminian theology is named after Jacob Arminius (1560-1609), pastor in Amsterdam and professor of theology at Leiden University. Arminius challenged the Reformed theology of his colleagues and mentors. After his death his followers were proponents of the Remonstrance of 1610, a backlash against the prevailing Calvinism of the day. Arminians, by definition, are those Christian theologians who, like their namesake, de-emphasize God's sovereign election in favor of human free will. Arminians interpret most Biblical passages on election as God merely looking down the corridors of time and foreknowing those who would choose Him. Throughout post-reformation history there have been greater or lesser degress of antagonism between Arminian and Reformed theology.

23 John Calvin. The Institutes of the Christian Religion. 2.1.6. Edited by Tony Lane and Hilary Osborne. (Grand Rapids MI: Baker Book House, 1987) p. 88.

24 Wayne Grudem. Systematic Theology. (Grand Rapids MI: Zondervan, 1994) p. 495.

Thus, we are not able to pawn off the responsibility of our own sin on our ancestors. Each one of us must make a reckoning with God on our own behalf. You cannot atone for my sin; I cannot atone for yours. Both of us are desperate for Christ.

Search Inward

It has been said that the doctrine of the total depravity of sinners is the doctrine that has been proved more consistently by experience than any other doctrine in the Christian faith. Time and time again—generation after generation—have ratified Adam and Eve's sinful rebellion in the Garden of Eden by following suit in further rebellion; both personal and corporate.

One of the first signs of our genuine conversion and regeneration is that we begin to be grieved by our sins and to truly hate them. If we have not yet begun to hate our sin and to despise any thought, word, or deed that brings dishonor to Christ, we only discover how much more we are dependant on God to purge us. Our sin ought to bring pain and remorse to our hearts as we realize, more and more, that our fallen actions bring sorrow to the heart of God who desires nothing less than joyful obedience from His redeemed, covenant people. Today, search your heart to discover whether you have truly begun to despise your sin. While we may be disgusted by sin theoretically, sometimes if we are truly honest, we still cherish our rebellious tendencies in the remote regions of our hearts.

Step Out—Repentant Self-Examination

One of the most ancient and practical elements in spiritual formation is the practice of repentant self-examination (Psalm 139:23-24). This is essentially a guided process of laying our sin bare before God in prayer.

Most of the times that I have attempted repentance and self-examination, my prayers are far too generic. During my missionary service to Africa after graduating from college, I often found myself alone and depressed. Thankfully, I was provided with a wealth of books into which I could delve. Often, I found that the books I enjoyed most were those that I related to in my struggles. My future mother-in-law sent me a copy of the book entitled The Life and Diary of David Brainerd. Brainerd found himself in a situation similar to mine—alone, single, and on the mission field. Only 250+ years and the Atlantic Ocean separated Brainerd and me; he a missionary to the Delaware Indian tribe, I a missionary to the Fang tribe of Central West Africa.

It was in Brainerd's private confessions that my understanding of self-examination and confession emerged. I simply could not believe the depth in which Brainerd could analyze his own soul. Consider this reading marked Friday February 10th of 1744:

> Was exceedingly oppressed, most of the day, with shame, grief, and fear, under a sense of my past folly, as well as present barrenness and coldness. When God sets before me my past misconduct... it sinks my soul into shame and confusion, makes me afraid of a shaking leaf. My fear is such as the prophet Jeremiah complains of (Jer. 20:10). I have no confidence to hold up my face, even before my fellow worms.[25]

And yet as soon as I am tempted to think that Brainerd's confession was nothing more than self-flagellation and unmitigated guilt, he turns the tide toward Christ,

> ...But only when my soul confides in God, I find the sweet temper of Christ, the spirit of humility, solemnity, and mortification, and resignation alive in my soul. But, in the evening, (I) was unexpectedly refreshed in pouring out my complaint to God; my shame and fear was turned into a sweet composure and acquiescence in God.[26]

Though Brainerd is explicit in his confession, he does not resort to unwarranted self-pity. He knows that His redeemer lives (Job 19:25). This is the essence of self-examination. The more honest we can be regarding our own folly, the more of a reality our justification in Christ becomes. This truth of our identity in Christ can only draw us all the more into His gracious arms.

One simple technique that I have adopted in my prayer life, is to write out the Ten Commandments in the flap of my Bible, and assign one or two of the Commandments to each day of the week. On Mondays, for instance, I ask the Spirit of God to search my heart to root out any rogue idolatry in my life, and to instruct me on those thoughts and secret desires I have that violate this commandment. Or on Thursdays, I may confess the seventh commandment to make sure that

---

25 David Brainerd. Ed. by Jonathan Edwards. The Life and Diary of David Brainerd. (Grand Rapids MI: Baker Book House, 1949) p. 153.

26 Ibid.

my mind is pure from adultery, as well as to ask God to increase my love for my wife.

I have found that if I try to confess through all Ten Commandments in a single day, I do the job too swiftly and don't delve deeply enough into the intent of the Commandments. For months, I have found this simple routine to be effective in rooting out the sin in the hidden corridors of my heart. Perhaps it would be helpful for you as well.

The Confession Chapter Seven:

Of God's Covenant with Man

1. The distance between God and the creature is so great, that although reasonable creatures do owe obedience unto him as their Creator, yet they could never have any fruition of him, as their blessedness and reward, but by some voluntary condescension on God's part, which he has been pleased to express by way of covenant.

2. The first covenant made with man was a covenant of works, wherein life was promised to Adam, and in him to his posterity, upon condition of perfect and personal obedience.

3. Man by his fall having made himself incapable of life by that covenant, the Lord was pleased to make a second, commonly called the covenant of grace: wherein he freely offered unto sinners life and salvation by Jesus Christ, requiring of them faith in him, that they may be saved, and promising to give unto all those that are ordained unto life, his Holy Spirit, to make them willing and able to believe.

4. This covenant of grace is frequently set forth in the Scripture by the name of a testament, in reference to the death of Jesus Christ, the testator, and to the everlasting inheritance, with all things belonging to it, therein bequeathed.

5. This covenant was differently administered in the time of the law, and in the time of the gospel: under the law it was administered by promises, prophecies, sacrifices, circumcision, the paschal lamb, and other types and ordinances delivered to the people of the Jews, all fore-signifying Christ to come, which were for that time sufficient and efficacious, through the operation of the Spirit, to instruct and build up the elect in faith in the promised Messiah, by whom they had full remission of sins, and eternal salvation, and is called the Old Testament.

6. Under the gospel, when Christ the substance was exhibited, the ordinances in which this covenant is dispensed, are the preaching of the Word, and the administration of the sacraments of Baptism and the Lord's Supper; which, though fewer in number, and administered with more simplicity and less outward glory, yet in them it is held forth in more fullness, evidence, and spiritual efficacy, to all nations, both Jews and Gentiles; and is called the New Testament. There are not, therefore, two covenants of grace differing in substance, but one and the same under various dispensations.

Prepare in Prayer
Lord Jesus Christ, Son of God, and Savior; we call out to You today to be everything to us. As we study the concept of "covenant," may we be cognizant of the fact that You alone bring us into relationship with the Father. Amen.

Into the Scriptures
Read Genesis 17 and 2 Corinthians 3.

Reach Back
Reformed theology is sometimes called Covenant theology. Covenant theology is an attempt to understand God's history of redeeming His people in the context of two grand covenants by which the Almighty relates to His people.[27] First, however, we would be well served to define a covenant. John Frame the renowned defender of the Reformed faith defines a covenant thus:

> The following seems to me to capture the essential elements of the biblical covenants between God and man. A 'covenant' is a relationship between a 'Lord' and a people whom he has sovereignly called to be his. The people may be called the Lord's vassals or servants. He rules over them by his power and law and brings upon them a unique blessing (or, in some cases, a unique curse).[28]

---

27 Some Reformed theologians would point to *three* covenants: the covenant of redemption between the Father and the Son in eternity past, the covenant of works with Adam, and the covenant of grace in Christ

28 John M. Frame. "Introduction to the Reformed Faith." Cited from http://www. monergism.com/directory/link_category/Reformed-Theology/Essays/. Accessed on February 26, 2009. Page 7. This document is a paper written for his students as an introduction to Reformed theology during the years when professor Frame taught at Westminster Theological Seminary

In another place, Frame writes,

> The covenant is not the result of negotiation; God imposes it
> unilaterally. It is His free gift, His grace, His unmerited favor.
> Then by His power He continues to maintain the covenant and
> brings to bear His sanctions: blessings for obedience, curses for
> disobedience.[29]

Michael Horton says simply, "a covenant is a relationship of 'oaths and
bonds' and involves mutual, though not necessarily equal commitments."[30]

The first covenant, as explained in the Westminster Confession, relates to
God's covenant of works with Adam and Eve in the Garden. In this pact,
God promised life and reward to our first parents, but demanded perfect
obedience from them (Genesis 2:16-17, Galatians 3:10). This covenant
of works was "republished," as it were, at Mount Sinai. The moral law
had the power to point out failures and transgressions, but not to save.
This first covenant was therefore conditioned upon obedience. Having
fallen and broken the covenant stipulations, God's people faced a need of
another saving agenda to supplant the first, which we had dishonored in
our rebellion.

The other great covenant in Scripture is the covenant of grace. Surprisingly
to some, it pervades both New and Old Testaments. (It is not enough to
say that the Old Testament contains the covenant of works, and the New
Testament the covenant of grace). Here, God promises that He will redeem
His people through a Messiah. The sacrificial system, the tabernacle, and
the temple were all types and shadows of His coming mercy in Christ. This
covenant is "unconditional," depending not on man's faithfulness to God,
but on God's faithfulness to man. God's saving agenda to redeem a people
for Himself cannot be thwarted. Christ would certainly come. He would
assuredly be given a people to redeem by the Father. His atonement would
infallibly avail for them, and His resurrection undoubtedly secure their
reward. We see this covenant unveiled in God's "royal grants" to Abraham
(Genesis 12:1-9; 15:1-20) and David (2 Samuel 7:15-16; Psalm 89; Psalm
132), as the "new covenant" promised to Jeremiah, (Jeremiah 31.31) and
most explicitly published as the Gospel in the New Testament.

---

29 John Frame. Salvation Belongs to the Lord: An Introductory to Systematic Theology.
(Phillipsburg NJ: P&R Publishing, 2006) p. 116.

30 Michael Horton. Introducing Covenant Theology. (Grand Rapids MI: Baker) p. 10.

Covenant theology sees God's work in redemption as one grand story, not a chopped up compilation of several unrelated eras. Thus, this way of seeing God's work in human history emphasizes the unity of the people of God, both in the Old and New Testaments. There is one covenant people, related by their common hope in the redeemer, Jesus Christ; the Old Testament saints looking forward to his appearing, the New Testament saints looking back upon the cross. Covenant theology, then, attempts to view God's wonderful saving work in our lives through an overarching, meta-narrative view of redemptive history.

Gaze Upward

While we have discussed at length God's judgment and sternness in regard to sin, let us now begin to develop a fuller appreciation of His mercy. Here, the Confession bids us to consider deeply God's mediatorial mercy by sending His Son Jesus Christ (WCF 7.3). This section of the Confession gives us at least three reasons to cry out in the highest praise to God our Heavenly Father.

First of all, we ought to praise God that He deeply desires to commune with us in the first place. As the Confession rightly states, *"The distance between God and the creature is so great, that although reasonable creatures do owe obedience unto him as their Creator, yet they could never have any fruition of him"* (7.1). Nevertheless, despite this un-navigable gap, God in His mercy initiates a relationship with humankind, and not just any relationship but one founded on promises. The fact that God condescends to make binding covenants with us is a massive testimony to His grace.

Second, we ought to praise the Son Jesus Christ for fulfilling the *first covenant* for us by His perfect obedience to the law. Have you ever stopped to think that Christ demonstrated His love for us, not only by dying for us (Romans 5:8) but also by living perfectly in order to fulfill the covenant of works on our behalf?

Finally, we praise God the Holy Spirit for the supernatural process of applying the covenant of grace to us, thus opening the eyes of our hearts, as it were, in order that we might learn to love the precious sacrifice of the Son. The covenant of grace promises to us that God has done literally *everything* to save us.

Search Inward

The fact that God is a covenant-making God ought to alert us to the way in which we cooperate with our fellow human beings. I often wonder if I honor my own promises in the same way that God expects me to. For instance, a while back I was busy working on a project repairing some drywall. My daughter was begging me to play a game with her that required my sustained attention. Without a second thought, I easily put her off by promising to play "later." This was a promise that I had no plan to fulfill, and therefore was meant to deceive. Though I barely noticed this act of deception at the time I committed it, I later reflected upon God's covenant-keeping character, and I realized the error of my ways.

We enter into covenants with other people more frequently than we realize. Marriage for instance is the greatest of these. As I recently explained to a young couple during their pre-marital counseling, the difference between a contract and a covenant is that in the latter, we owe our obligation to the other party (love, mercy, service, forgiveness) *regardless of whether or not they live up to their part of the agreement.* The love expressed in a marriage is not contingent on conditional factors: *(I will love you IF you continue to wash the dishes, prepare meals for me, satisfy me sexually, or pay the bills on time).* No, unlike a contract that can be terminated at the first hint of failure, a covenant is a binding agreement between two parties that inseparably ties their future together.

Other examples of covenants may include the covenant of parental love for children, the covenant of a local church body to bind itself to Christ and His Word, or even a covenant within oneself to live a moral life such as the one Job imposed upon himself so as not to commit lust in his heart (Job 31:1).

Step Out—The Intention of the Heart

Like the above example with my daughter, I suggest that all of us errantly make these kinds of simple statements that we have no intention of fulfilling. How many times has another believer asked prayer of you, to which you assured that person that you would pray—and yet you never actually prayed for them? If you are like me, this kind of casual neglect is far too frequent to be ignored if we seek to emulate the master Jesus Christ.

This week, be intentional about the promises you make to people. If we truly desire to honor God with our lives, we must be people of our word. If we are the covenant people of God, how much more should we to be people whose lives reflect the integrity of the covenants (or promises) we make?

The Confession Chapter Eight:

Of Christ the Mediator

1. It pleased God, in his eternal purpose, to choose and ordain the Lord Jesus, his only-begotten Son, to be the Mediator between God and men, the prophet, priest, and king; the head and Savior of the Church, the heir or all things, and judge of the world; unto whom he did, from all eternity, give a people to be his seed, and to be by him in time redeemed, called, justified, sanctified, and glorified.

2. The Son of God, the second Person in the Trinity, being very and eternal God, of one substance, and equal with the Father, did, when the fullness of time was come, take upon him man's nature, with all the essential properties and common infirmities thereof; yet without sin: being conceived by the power of the Holy Ghost, in the womb of the Virgin Mary, of her substance. So that two whole, perfect, and distinct natures, the Godhead and the manhood, were inseparably joined together in one person, without conversion, composition, or confusion. Which person is very God and very man, yet one Christ, the only Mediator between God and man.

3. The Lord Jesus in his human nature thus united to the divine, was sanctified and anointed with the Holy Spirit above measure; having in him all the treasures of wisdom and knowledge, in whom it pleased the Father that all fullness should dwell: to the end that being holy, harmless, undefiled, and full of grace and truth, he might be thoroughly furnished to execute the office of a Mediator and Surety. Which office he took not unto himself, but was thereunto called by his Father; who put all power and judgment into his hand, and gave him commandment to execute the same.

4. This office the Lord Jesus did most willingly undertake, which, that he might discharge, he was made under the law, and did perfectly fulfill it; endured most grievous torments immediately in his soul, and most painful sufferings in his body; was crucified and died; was buried, and remained under the power of death, yet saw no corruption. On the third day he arose from the dead, with the same body in which he suffered;

with which also he ascended into heaven, and there sits at the right hand of his Father, making intercession; and shall return to judge men and angels, at the end of the world.

5. The Lord Jesus, by his perfect obedience and sacrifice of himself, which he through the eternal Spirit once offered up unto God, has fully satisfied the justice of his Father; and purchased not only reconciliation, but an everlasting inheritance in the kingdom of heaven, for all those whom the Father has given unto him.

6. Although the work of redemption was not actually wrought by Christ till after his incarnation, yet the virtue, efficacy, and benefits thereof were communicated into the elect, in all ages successively from the beginning of the world, in and by those promises, types, and sacrifices wherein he was revealed, and signified to be the seed of the woman, which should bruise the serpent's head, and the Lamb slain from the beginning of the world, being yesterday and today the same and for ever.

7. Christ, in the work of mediation, acts according to both natures; by each nature doing that which is proper to itself; yet by reason of the unity of the person, that which is proper to one nature is sometimes, in Scripture, attributed to the person denominated by the other nature.

8. To all those for whom Christ has purchased redemption, he does certainly and effectually apply and communicate the same; making intercession for them, and revealing unto them, in and by the Word, the mysteries of salvation; effectually persuading them by his Spirit to believe and obey; and governing their hearts by his Word and Spirit; overcoming all their enemies by his almighty power and wisdom, in such manner and ways as are most consonant to his wonderful and unsearchable dispensation.

Prepare in Prayer
Perfect Christ, we acknowledge that You alone have provided a sufficient sacrifice to pay for our sins. So sinful were we, that we could not have even raised our eyes to Heaven before You called us. Help us to trust fully in the cross. In Your name we pray, amen.

Into the Scriptures
Read John 1 and Philippians 2.

Reach Back

Today's reading may be one of the most important and significant sections of the Confession. Here the Westminster Divines outline their theology of the incarnation; the beauty and perfection of complete divinity enmeshing Christ's full humanity. As Colossians 2:9 describes succinctly, "For in him the whole fullness of deity dwells bodily."

Like the Athanasian Creed[31] and the Nicene Creed[32] before it, the Westminster Confession joins the great heritage of believers who rightly understand Scripture's majestic testimony regarding the two natures of Jesus Christ. Simply stated, the Confession enthusiastically confirms the biblical witness that Jesus Christ is both 100% human and 100% divine. Some of the clearest words concerning the nature of Jesus Christ came from the head of the Latin Church many centuries before the Westminster Assembly gathered. Leo the Great, writing in June of 449, clarifies this distinction, "The properties of each nature and substance (divine and human) were preserved in their totality, and came together to form one person." Anticipating the objection that this would cause God's nature to be weakened in some way, Leo continues, "For that 'emptying of himself' by which the invisible God chose to become visible, and the Creator and Lord of all willed to be a mortal, was an *inclination of compassion not a failure of power*" (emphasis added). Leo concluded regarding these two natures, "The one is resplendent with miracles, the other submits to insults."[33]

That two natures (divine and human) co-exist in the same person, Jesus Christ, has been called the hypostatic union. This is perhaps one of the most important theological convictions of Reformed theology because, as a human, Jesus alone is able to represent humanity before the Father. And yet as God, Jesus alone is flawlessly righteous, able avoid all sin, standing in accord with the unparalleled holiness of the Father. To devalue Jesus' full divinity, would be to undermine the holiness required of the Mediator. To deny His full humanity would be to exclude Him as an adequate representative head of humankind.

---

31 The Athanasian Creed was a fifth-century creed that strongly affirmed the Trinity and the Incarnation of Christ.

32 The Creed of Nicea, 325 AD, refuted the claims of Arius and his followers that Jesus was a creation of God, different from the Father. It affirmed that the Son is "of the same substance" as the Father.

33 "Leo the Great on the Two Natures." In The Christian Theology Reader. Ed. by Alister McGrath. (Malden MA: Blackwell Publishing, 2001) p. 267-268.

Search Inward

Another of the most basic and important facets of spiritual formation is to learn to contemplate the death and resurrection of Jesus Christ. This has been one of the most ancient practices for those saints who desire to know Christ intimately. The Confession states graphically, that "*he was made under the law, and did perfectly fulfill it; endured most grievous torments immediately in his soul, and most painful sufferings in his body; was crucified and died; was buried, and remained under the power of death, yet saw no corruption*" (WCF 8.4).

What does it mean to you that Jesus Christ had to bear the incredible physical pain of crucifixion on your behalf, while at the same time bearing the unbelievable spiritual agony of the guilt and shame of the world? Have you ever contemplated undergoing a cruel death on a Roman cross only to be relieved that the work had been done *in your place* by God's Son?

Gaze Upward

As we desire to grow in the process of spiritual formation, it will be beneficial at times to consult the works and writings of those who have gone before us. Many who have preceded us, such as John Calvin, have spent their entire lives attempting to contemplate this great cosmic exchange: our sin for Christ's righteousness. Understanding how Jesus Christ literally took the physical agony and spiritual suffering in our stead is a must in the process of spiritual formation. Calvin writes:

> To obtain our ransom, it was essential to choose a type of death in which he could deliver us, both by giving himself up to condemnation and also undertaking our expiation. If he had been mown down by assassins or killed in a rebellion, there would have been no satisfaction. But when he stands as a criminal at the bar, and witnesses are brought to give evidence against him and the judge condemns him to death, we see him taking on the character of an offender.[34]

Calvin's ability to illustrate the scene of the crucified and dying Christ is portrayed in striking language as he hopes to communicate the reality of our Savior's wrath-bearing. Again he writes:

> Christ stepped in, took the punishment upon himself and bore

---

34 John Calvin. The Institutes of Christian Religion. 2.16.5. Edited by Tony Lane and Hilary Osborne. (Grand Rapids: Baker Books, 1987) p. 131.

the judgment due to sinners. With his own blood he expiated the sins which made them enemies of God and thereby satisfied him. By his intercessions, he appeased God's anger, and on this basis created peace between God and men, and by this bond secured God's goodwill towards them. As he thinks of all this, of the disaster he had escaped, wouldn't anyone be deeply moved? To sum up, our minds cannot lay hold of life with sufficient eagerness, or accept it with suitable gratitude, unless we have first been made afraid of divine anger and the thought of eternal death. So we are instructed by divine truth to understand that without Christ, God is in some way hostile to us and has to lift his arm to destroy. Then we look to Christ alone for divine favor and fatherly love![35]

Yes, not only does the anger of God against sin rise forth in Calvin's writings, but also the passion and love that Christ felt for the redeemed as He died for them. Over and over again, as a running theme throughout his works, Calvin writes of the unrelenting love of Christ's cross for the salvation of the elect.

Step Out—Being Crucified with Christ

I find it a valuable spiritual exercise to try to comprehend the physical agony that Jesus endured on my behalf, remembering *that I could not have borne this struggle.* Though this may seem strange at first, this exercise is quite biblical. Indeed, part of me has actually died with Christ. The apostle wrote, "I have been crucified with Christ. It is no longer I who live, but Christ who lives in me" (Galatians 2:20).

The exercise of reminding myself that the crucifixion of Christ put to death (or mortifies) our sinful nature is necessary to shedding our fleshly passions. Sometimes, I envision the flogging from Roman soldiers; I try to elicit the feeling of the crown of thorns on His forehead and consider the pain of the crucifixion process itself. While this may seem morbid to some or unnecessary to others, I find it a great motive to praise God that Jesus accomplished this work *on my behalf.* Having then spent time in an agonizing exercise like this one, I am then able to whisper breath-prayers to God throughout the day thanking Him with words like, "You have saved me!" or "It is finished!"

---

35 Ibid. 2.16.2. p. 129-130.

For today's exercise in worship, attempt to prayerfully contemplate the great hymn of Philippians 2:6-12. To the extent that you are able, ask God to allow you to visualize and worship Christ at each stage of the hymn's humiliation and exaltation of Christ.

Begin with verse six by contemplating the fact that Jesus Christ was, from all eternity past, equal with God the Father and God the Spirit in majesty and perfection. Then with verse seven, allow yourself to consider the incarnation of Jesus at His birth. Take time to imagine yourself worshipping at the manger, at the foot of a trough where He would have lay as an infant. Next with verse eight, walk behind Him as he bears the cross up the hill of Calvary to Golgotha, the place of the skull. Fall on your face at the foot of the cross, too ashamed to look up at His face as He bleeds. Finally, in verses 9-10, exalt with the great throng of the redeemed as people from every tribe and nation give praise to their Savior!

The Confession Chapter Nine:

Of Free Will

1. God has endued the will of man with that natural liberty, that it is neither forced, nor by any absolute necessity of nature determined to good or evil.

2. Man, in his state of innocence, had freedom and power to will and to do that which is good and well-pleasing to God; but yet mutably, so that he might fall from it.

3. Man, by his fall into a state of sin, has wholly lost all ability of will to any spiritual good accompanying salvation; so as a natural man, being altogether averse from that good, and dead in sin, is not able, by his own strength, to convert himself, or to prepare himself thereunto.

4. When God converts a sinner and translates him into the state of grace, he frees him from his natural bondage under sin, and, by his grace alone, enables him freely to will and to do that which is spiritually good; yet so as that, by reason of his remaining corruption, he does not perfectly, nor only, will that which is good, but does also will that which is evil.

5. The will of man is made perfectly and immutable free to good alone, in the state of glory only.

Prepare in Prayer
God, before the aid of Your Holy Spirit, the very faculty of our being that allows us to approach You, the volition, was damaged. Please continue to repair our will by the sanctification of the Spirit so that we can see and savor Your glory. In the name of the Son we pray, amen.

Into the Scriptures
Read Romans 6 and 7.

Reach Back
One of the most common objections to the Reformed faith, is that it is said by its opponents to deny any sense of human free will. Calvinism is purported by its detractors to deny human beings any sort of "say" in their lives or destinies, as though human beings are mere robots or automatons, and that history itself is fatalistic. As with most criticisms, this is not entirely correct, and is rather misleading.

As sections one and two in today's reading make clear, human beings *did* in fact have a free will. This free will was given to humanity by God in the Garden. At that time, human beings were completely free to do either good or evil. As we know, our Edenic parents chose to disobey and the consequences were tragic. However, what the Confession also makes clear is that our free will was irreparably damaged, so that the will was, from that time on, inclined towards evil to the extent that man is *"not able, by his own strength, to convert himself, or to prepare himself thereunto"* (WCF 9.3). Thus, the will is now in bondage to sin.

For this reason God's grace is necessary *before* conversion is possible. Regeneration, a complete act of God alone, begins the process of the death of the sinful nature, and the commencement of spiritual life. This is what Jesus called being "born again" (John 3:3). As I stated in the introduction to this work, regeneration is an instantaneous event, whereas sanctification is a process that lasts for the rest of the believer's earthly life.

To recap; the will was completely free in the Garden, then bound to sin due to Adam's fall; regenerated (yet still depraved) at conversion, and will one day be completely renovated at our death, or the Lord's return.

Gaze Upwards
We may feel that hearing of our will's bondage to sin while on this earth is a depressing notion that could lead to self-loathing and even despair. Yet if we are tempted to stop trying altogether, we might be strengthened by Paul's autobiographical comments in Romans 7:13-24. Here Paul is moving through the difficult task of introspection. In one verse, he notes within himself both the desire to obey God, "For I have the desire to do what is right..." and he also acknowledges his depraved inability to achieve it "...but not the ability to carry

it out"(7:18). This section acknowledges that Paul is undergoing a personal war within himself. He says in another place, "I do not understand my own actions. For I do not do what I want, but I do the very thing that I hate" (7:15). Finally, he arrives at the sad conclusion, "Wretched man that I am" (7:24)!

Then in a surprising turn, just as Paul begins to have a true comprehension of the depravity of his will and his inability to carry out his righteous aspirations, he chooses instead to turn away from despair towards the God of his hope. Incredibly, he chooses to praise God despite his total inability by proclaiming, "Who will deliver me from this body of death? Thanks be to God through Jesus Christ our Lord" (7:24-25).

Thus in ironic exultation, the very cause by which he might have fallen into self-depreciation and total lament—his corrupt nature and stubborn will— is transformed into an opportunity to praise God who alone can save him from himself.

Search Inward

The freedom and bondage of the human will is a highly complicated philosophical theme. Some will love the intellectual rigor that this age-old debate provides. If you tend to be of the ilk that loves a highly philosophical inquiry, it will be necessary for you to feed that quest for knowledge on a deeper level. Because the concept of the freedom of the human will is so easily confused and distorted, it may help us again to seek out writers in Christian history that have best tackled this pursuit. Martin Luther's The Bondage of the Will is perhaps the definitive work in this area. A second work by another Reformed author would be Jonathan Edwards' The Freedom of the Will. Both of these works are recommended.

Let us focus for the moment on some distinctions made by Saint Augustine. Augustine made clear that at Creation, mankind was endowed with both the ability not to sin (*posse non peccare*) as well as the ability to sin (*posse peccare*). It was the former, the ability not to sin (*posse non peccare*), which was lost at the fall. The will has been corrupted and therefore is not truly "free." It inclines toward sin. Nevertheless, Augustine looks forward to the day of redemption, made possible through Jesus Christ, wherein our freedom of the will (*liberum arbitrium*) will be fully recreated so that our inability to sin is regained and enhanced. It is in the redemption of all things that Augustine looks forward to yet another "edition" of the human will, the inability to sin (*non posse peccare*) at which the soul is fully glorified and made to honor God in all things. He writes,

Thus the freedom of that city will be one single will, present in everyone, freed from all evil and filled with every good, enjoying continually the delight of eternal joy. Although sins and punishments will be forgotten, this will not lead to forgetting its liberation, or being ungrateful to its liberator.[36]

Step Out—Fasting

How then can we begin to live as though our inclination towards sin is really being crucified, while at the same time acknowledging that Augustine's view of a holy City of God has not yet been reached? To say it another way, are there *things that we can do* to suppress the desire latent inside all of us to stray from God, while at the same time cultivating activities that increase our love and obedience to Him? At this point, we might suggest another one of the ancient spiritual disciplines to assert the soul's dominion over the body.

Jesus had a spiritual practice that He used to sustain Himself, during particularly difficult times, in which the rigors of life and ministry were especially draining. It wasn't something that He drew much attention to. It wasn't something that He made a central focus of His ministry. Nevertheless, He did not shy away from direct teaching about it, especially when this practice became the subject of controversy. It's rarely something we talk about today (we practice it even less). What was it? Fasting.

Jesus' most notable fast was during His desert temptation recorded in both Matthew and Luke. Both accounts are recorded in the fourth chapters of each gospel. Here we see Jesus preparing for His life of ministry. Yet incredibly, instead of fueling up, He fuels down. He drops His dependence on earthy sustenance, and increases His intake of the Word of God. During one crucial moment of temptation from Satan, the devil challenges Him to create His own bread using His divine powers as the Son of God. He refuses, offering instead what some may choose to adopt as a life principle: "Man does not live on bread alone, but on every word that comes from the mouth of God" (Matthew 4:4).

At other points in His ministry, Jesus down-played fasting, essentially stating, "Do it, but don't make a big deal about it" (that's my paraphrase of Matthew 6:16-18). Then He says something that we often skip over, "But *when* you fast..." (NIV, emphasis mine). Did you catch that? Jesus

---

36 "Augustine On Human Freedom," in The Christian Theology Reader. Ed. by Alister McGrath (Malden MA: Blackwell Publications, 2001) p. 399-400.

taught with the assumption that fasting would be a normal discipline in the Christian life. His purpose was not to discourage fasting, but rather to give guidelines for the attitude of the heart.

For the early church, fasting was considered a normal part of the spiritual life, and a formative time. It was done when God called the Church to either great discernment, times of deliberation, or the commissioning of mission workers. Consider Acts 14:23, "And when they had appointed elders for them in every church, with prayer and fasting, they committed them to the Lord in whom they had believed."

Fasting is a gift of God, a tool of spiritual formation, by which we deprive ourselves of some of our human dependencies and needs, so that we may be filled with the Spirit in greater measure, and thereby become sensitive to His call and direction. If you are undergoing a crucial time of discernment and prayer, perhaps this might be a moment when you would consider emptying yourself from your normal human dependencies in order that you may be filled to a fuller measure with an understanding of God's will.

Let me share with you three helpful recommendations.

First, as with all fasts, the point of the exercise is to *replace* what satisfaction you might normally gain through food with the Word of God. Make sure to fuel your body with readings from Scripture and times of extended prayer.

Second, if you have never fasted before, begin modestly. This is a time to diminish your pride, not sustain it. You ought not to attempt something that will be too difficult just to "prove" you can do it. For some, a fast can be as simple as skipping a single lunch break to read the Word. Others may consider fasting for a whole day or more. The time period is not essential. Again, don't try anything that would hurt you.

Third, it might be good for you to consult your physician or nutritionist before beginning a fast. This will be especially important for those with dietary restrictions or other health concerns.

There are specific times in our lives when the people of God must be especially given over to prayer and submission to the will of God. Perhaps for you, this is one of those times.

The Confession Chapter Ten:

Of Effectual Calling

1. All those whom God has predestinated unto life, and those only, he is pleased, in his appointed and accepted time, effectually to call, by his Word and Spirit, out of that state of sin and death in which they are by nature, to grace and salvation by Jesus Christ: enlightening their minds, spiritually and savingly, to understand the things of God, taking away their heart of stone, and giving unto them an heart of flesh; renewing their wills, and by his almighty power determining them to that which is good; and effectually drawing them to Jesus Christ; yet so as they come most freely, being made willing by his grace.

2. This effectual call is of God's free and special grace alone, not from any thing at all foreseen in man, who is altogether passive therein, until, being quickened and renewed by the Holy Spirit, he is thereby enabled to answer this call, and to embrace the grace offered and conveyed in it.

3. Elect infants, dying in infancy, are regenerated and saved by Christ through the Spirit, who works when, and where, and how he pleases. So also are all other elect persons who are incapable of being outwardly called by the ministry of the Word.

4. Others, not elected, although they may be called by the ministry of the Word, and may have some common operations of the Spirit, yet they never truly come to Christ, and therefore can not be saved: much less can men, not professing the Christian religion, be saved in any other way whatsoever, be they never so diligent to frame their lives according to the light of nature, and the law of that religion they do profess; and to assert and maintain that they may is without warrant of the Word of God.

Prepare in Prayer

Lord, when You chose to call us, we listened and came—not because we were good, but because You are good. Your grace was irresistible to us. May Your Word continue to irresistibly draw us closer to You today as we study, amen.

Into the Scriptures

Read Matthew 16:13-20.

Reach Back

One of the reasons that studying Reformed theology makes for such a great experience of spiritual formation is that it is so intensely God-centered. The more we are able to credit God with all honor, glory, and praise in our theology, the more we are able to acknowledge that He is reigning on the throne of our lives as well.

For this reason, the Confession is sure to credit God alone with the salvation of His people at each stage of the journey. In today's reading, which is intricately tied to the previous chapter, we note that the broken and sin-inclined human will is no longer able to choose or discern that which is holy. Thus, prior to our conversion, we were not able to make the final decision to trust in Jesus Christ as our Savior until He prepared us to do so.

Consider, for instance, Peter's confession that Jesus is the Christ (Messiah) in Matthew 16:13-20. After Peter made this bold confession in the face of a plethora of varying opinions, Jesus did not *congratulate* him on a decision well made. Jesus did not chalk this victory up to the freedom of Peter's will. On the contrary, Jesus said clearly, "Blessed are you, Simon son of Jonah, for this was not revealed to you by man, but by my Father in Heaven" (Matthew 16:17, NIV). Peter, who tended to put his foot in his mouth, finally got one right! And yet Jesus gave all the praise to God's grace, and none of it to Peter's will.

In another place, Jesus spoke even more clearly about effectual calling. In John 6, Jesus twice speaks of the impossibility of one coming to God on one's own terms. He says in verse 44, "No one can come to me unless the Father who sent me draws him." Then again, in verse 65 He underscores this thought, "None can come to me unless the Father has *enabled* him" (NIV, emphasis added). Thus on our own journeys of spiritual formation, we must learn to credit God with His work in our lives, even when we think we have accomplished something significant on our own.

Perhaps one of the saddest verses in all of Scripture follows shortly thereafter, "After this many of His disciples turned back and no longer walked with Him" (6:66). Apparently, Jesus' God-centered pronouncement on irresistible call and human inability was too much for some.

Search Inward

Today as you endeavor to make confession before our Holy God, think back on some of the things in your life that you had unwittingly given yourself credit for, instead of giving it to God. Have you credited yourself for your wise choice to become a believer in Christ, instead of acknowledging that He first drew you (John 6:44, 65)? Have you often spoken as though you objectively weighed the factors of whether or not to become a Christian, rather than crediting the Spirit's pull on your life?

Perhaps there are other areas in your life where you have given yourself undue credit: your education, your marriage, your professional life, your health—all may seem to be within our power to control and manipulate—and yet all of these were first given to us as gifts, and then entrusted to our stewardship.

Gaze Upward

Much of living the Christian life is learning to continually look upward toward God, moment-by-moment. We must understand that we are living in His world, rather than He intervening occasionally in ours.

Remember our earlier reference to Copernicus and his revolutionary discovery. The Earth was thought to be the center of the universe. The Sun was described in human language as "rising and setting." (We still use that type of language today). Yet, as we all know, the advent of the telescope revealed that the Sun and stars do not revolve around the Earth, but rather the Earth revolves around the Sun. This discovery startled the world with its topsy-turvy perspective on reality.

In the same way, once we discover that God is the center of the universe—that He calls, converts, and sanctifies us—it is eye-opening to begin to see our lives orbiting around His plan. We were made exclusively to bring glory to Him. He is no mere afterthought; He is the first cause and last end of all things.

Step Out--Journaling

In today's step out exercise, I recommend once again putting pen to paper to make a list of the wonderful ways in which God has worked by His Holy Spirit ahead of your experience. For instance, you may choose to draw up a timeline of your own life, making sure to note the many instances where God guided, protected, saved, or preserved you in order for His divine purposes to be carried out in your life. You may note things in your timeline such as persons He placed in your life at just the right time, accidents from which He spared you, even decisions that He prevented you from carrying out that could have led to disaster. Be sure to jot down the ways God prepared your heart for conversion *before* you believed.

When we put a timeline of our life together, we begin to see the direction that God has been carrying us all along. I often look down at ants or other bugs as they go about their business. I marvel at the crazy, loopy, courses that they take as they go about their daily lives. I often wonder, if they could see their route from another perspective, whether they might save themselves a tremendous amount of time and energy by traveling a straighter course. If you were to draw such a map of your life, do you think you might better see the overarching plan through which God is leading you?

Journaling may just be the exercise that will help you to understand the proper "orbit" of your life around His will. For many generations of believers, this has been found to be the case. Donald Whitney records this observation by Josiah Pratt at an 1803 gathering of evangelicals in London:

> "The practice of keeping a diary would promote vigilance. The lives of many are spent at a sort of hazard. They fall into certain religious habits; and are perhaps under no strong temptations. They are regular at church and sacrament, and in their families. They read the Bible and pray daily in secret. But here it ends. They know little of the progress or decline of the inner man. They are Christians, therefore, of very low attainments. The workings of sin are not noticed, as they should be, and therefore grace is not sought against them; and the genial emotions of grace are not noticed, and therefore not fostered and cultivated. Now a diary would have a tendency to raise the standard to such persons by exciting vigilance."[37]

You see, it is often in the extra regimens such as journaling that we are

---

37 Donald Whitney. Spiritual Disciplines for the Christian Life. (Colorado Springs CO: Navpress, 1991) p. 207.

sure to intentionally recognize God in the center of our universe. The observations, clarifications, and petitions of a personal journal can help us to assure that God's mysterious movements are traced and recorded. Not only this, but journaling helps to safeguard our inner morality from desecrations of conscience. This of course was well known to the Puritans who likewise sought a fully God-immersed lifestyle. Edmund Morgan writes:

> The fact that many Puritans kept diaries of this kind helps to explain their pursuit of social virtue: diaries were the reckoning books in which they checked the assets and liabilities of their souls in faith. When they opened these books, they set down lapses of morality with appropriate expressions of faith. Cotton Mather (for instance) made a point of having at least one good action to set down in his diary on every day of the week.[38]

If you have never attempted the spiritual discipline of journaling before, I recommend these three easy steps to begin.

> 1) Purchase a simple diary or notebook. It may be anything from a leather-bound professional log to a simple spiral notebook. Having a special book just for this purpose will help you to keep yourself accountable. Making a special purchase of this new journal will help you to strengthen your resolve to begin.

> 2) Begin journaling after your normal times of reading the Bible and prayer. Make your journal an extension of your prayers rather than another thing that you "have to do." Write you prayers directly to God as though they were notes or letters addressed to Him. I have found that as I pray, writing on paper or typing on my computer, my mind is forced to think more concretely, in a linear fashion, with less wandering.

> 3) Finally, be as honest as you can. Do not write for any other supposed audience aside from God alone. Should your writings tend to become almost "too personal" go ahead and destroy them if necessary. Pope John Paul II for instance, specifically requested that all of his personal journals be destroyed after he died. This is not to assume that he had anything to hide, but rather simply to protect what is between one man and God. The

---

38 Edmund Morgan quoted in Donald Whitney, Spiritual Disciplines for the Christian Life. (Colorado Springs CO: Navpress, 1991) p. 208.

purpose is not to leave a record of your life behind for others to read, but rather to simply engage God on a more concerted plane of thought. You will find that writing out your thoughts will keep your mind from straying and allow God to remain the fixed, unmovable point of reference for your life.

The Confession Chapter Eleven:

Of Justification

1. Those whom God effectually calls, he also freely justifies: not by infusing righteousness into them, but by pardoning their sins, and by accounting and accepting their persons as righteous; not for any thing wrought in them, or done by them, but for Christ's sake alone; not by imputing faith itself, the act of believing, or any other evangelical obedience to them, as their righteousness; but by imputing the obedience and satisfaction of Christ unto them, they receiving and resting on him and his righteousness by faith; which faith they have not of themselves, it is the gift of God.

2. Faith, thus receiving and resting on Christ and his righteousness, is the alone instrument of justification; yet is it not alone in the person justified, but is ever accompanied with all other saving graces, and is no dead faith, but works by love.

3. Christ, by his obedience and death, did fully discharge the debt of all those that are thus justified, and did make a proper, real, and full satisfaction of his Father's justice in their behalf. Yet inasmuch as he was given by the Father for them, and his obedience and satisfaction accepted in their stead, and both freely, not for any thing in them, their justification is only of free grace, that both the exact justice and rich grace of God might be glorified in the justification of sinners.

4. God did, from all eternity, decree to justify the elect; and Christ did, in the fullness of time, die for their sins and rise again for their justification; nevertheless they are not justified until the Holy Spirit does, in due time, actually apply Christ unto them.

5. God does continue to forgive the sins of those that are justified; and although they can never fall from the state of justification, yet they may by their sins fall under God's Fatherly displeasure, and not have the light of his countenance restored unto them, until they humble themselves, confess their sins, beg pardon, and renew their faith and repentance.

6. The justification of believers under the Old Testament was, in all these respects, one and the same with the justification of believers under the New Testament.

Prepare in Prayer

Heavenly Father, if at any point in the course of this study we begin to feel that we are winning Your affection through our learning, remind us again that we are Yours because of the blood of Christ—not because of anything we have done. In Jesus' name, amen.

Into the Scriptures

Read Romans 3 and 4.

Reach Back

The doctrine of justification was the blade that severed the tie between the Reformers and their Roman Catholic moorings. For this reason, this doctrine demands precision in its explanation and diligence in its defense. Let us speak for a moment, then, on the difference between "infused" righteousness and "imputed" righteousness, for this is a crucial distinction in the Confession. The Confession denies that righteousness is *infused* into the believer in any way. To infuse means to place into, or to put inside. For instance, we might say that a doctor infuses an inoculation into a patient's arm.

When Christ atoned for our sin, He did not infuse His righteousness into our hearts so that we became, practically speaking, 100% holy. We do not walk around town as perfect mortals, as Christ was in His earthly form. We have not become impervious to sin.

Rather, the Confession holds that righteousness was "imputed" to our behalf. Imputation, is best described by the words "considered," or "reckoned," and implies a legal transference on one's behalf. Thus in the legal records of God's "Book of Life," believers are considered in a right standing with God because of the exchange of the righteousness of Jesus Christ for the guilt and shame that our sin merited. He took our shame, and gave us His standing with God. Thus we are treated, pardoned, and cleared from all charges as *though* we had lived the life of Christ.

Why then does the Confession seem to deny "imputation" in section one? For it reads, "not by imputing faith itself, the act of believing, or any other evangelical obedience to them, as their righteousness..." Here, the Confession is using "imputation" in another sense, so as to make clear that it was not our faith (considered as a *work*), or any other act of human goodness, that counts as our righteousness in God's mind. For in the very next line, the Confession stipulates exactly *what* has been imputed to our account: "the obedience and satisfaction of Christ unto them" as righteousness (WCF 11.1).

Thus, neither our obedience to the law, nor any acts of our own goodness—not even our faith *if reckoned as a kind of work*—can justify us in God's eyes. Only a "legal" transfer of Christ's righteousness to our account can bring about God's regarding our lives as acceptable in His sight. For this reason, the Reformers have long held our justification to be something *extra nos* (Latin: outside of ourselves).

Search Inward
Jonathan Edwards gives us a helpful definition of justification. He writes:

> "Justification is not only pardon of sin... but an act or sentence approving of him as innocent and positively righteous, and so having a right to freedom from punishment, and to the reward of positive righteousness... The pardon we have in Christ is a freeing of persons from the punishment of sin, as an act of justice, and because they are looked upon and accepted as having that which is equivalent to innocence."[39]

Notice how, in Edwards' definition, the believer is entirely passive. He does nothing to receive this new reckoning; but he is enabled to live freely *because* of it. Notice also how Edwards points out that Christ's active obedience was also credited to us. Thus, justification is not merely God wiping away all of our sins, He also imputes to us the positive credit of Christ's perfect life. The purpose of most of these 'Search Inward' sections is to give us the opportunity to see flaws in ourselves that we may not have discovered on

---

39 Quoted in Gary Crampton. A Conversation with John Edwards. (Grand Rapids MI: Reformation Heritage Books, 2006) p. 128.

our own. Testifying from my own personal experience, I can say that for years I carried on as though my faith was in fact the "work" that saved me. Had someone asked me, I would have responded faithfully that I could not earn my salvation; nevertheless I believed as though I truly had earned, it by considering my faith the one work that does save. I was wrong.

The pride of presumption is a very subtle sin. Perhaps you have not gone so far as to credit yourself for your own salvation, but now that you have observed yourself growing in the faith, you live and feel as though you are responsible for maintaining it. You may view others as more corrupt than you were, thinking "he could never be redeemed," or "she is beyond help," or "that person could never be saved." If any of these descriptions fit, search inward to recognize that without a divine miracle, you too would have never been considered justified in God's eyes.

Step Out—Scripture Memorization

I have been attempting in the last few sections to recommend to you some of the most timeless applications of spiritual formation. We have spoken so far of confession of sins (chapter six), contemplation (chapter eight), fasting (chapter nine), and journaling (chapter ten). Let us now consider Scripture memorization.

While the reading of Scripture, along with prayer, may be the greatest tools of personal spiritual formation, Bible memorization takes this practice to a new level of difficulty. Matthew Henry, the great Presbyterian commentator once wrote, "The more conversant we are with (the words of Holy Scripture) the more we shall admire them and be affected with them, and may thereby be instrumental to communicate divine light and heat."[40]

Do you consistently and systematically memorize sections of Scripture in order that you may digest them more fully? At first you may make light demands of yourself, such as expanding John 3:16 to include the 17th verse as well. As you build confidence, perhaps you will try a more complex passage. Romans 3:21-25 is likely the most concise statement on justification in Scripture. It reads,

> But now the righteousness of God has been manifested apart
> from the law, although the Law and the Prophets bear witness to

---

40 Matthew Henry. Commentary in One Volume. (Grand Rapids MI: Zondervan, 1960) p. 182.

it—the righteousness of God through faith in Jesus Christ for all who believe. For there is no distinction: for all have sinned and fall short of the glory of God, and are justified by his grace as a gift, through the redemption that came by Christ Jesus, whom God put forward as a propitiation by his blood, to be received by faith.

This is a text that I require the ruling elders serving on our church session to commit to memory. Such memorization, not only allows us to comprehend these complicated doctrines of the faith more fully, but also allows to us rejoice in their freeing power for our lives more completely.

While I was in seminary, I took a class on prayer from a wise, elderly pastor. One day, when discussing Scripture memorization and contemplation, the professor passed out pieces of hard candy for the class to enjoy. The caveat was that we had to suck on the candy as slowly as possible while meditating upon a passage of the Psalms. We were not allowed to chew them and break them apart. As he explained, too many people bite directly into Scripture, break it down quickly, and swallow it in large chunks. This is as bad for our spiritual health as it is for our physical health! On the contrary, he explained, how much better it is for us to savor Scripture's taste, for as long as possible, so that we don't soon forget its sweetness!

If you are particularly challenged by memorization, begin with small portions and work your way up. Instead of the entire passage quoted above, you may resolve to learn just a line or two such as *"for all have sinned and fall short of the glory of God, and are justified by his grace."*

The Confession Chapter Twelve:

Of Adoption

All those that are justified, God does vouchsafe, in and for his only Son Jesus Christ, to make partakers of the grace of adoption: by which they are taken into the number, and enjoy the liberties and privileges of the children of God; have his name put upon them; receive the Spirit of adoption; have access to the throne of grace with boldness; are enabled to cry, Abba, Father; are pitied, protected, provided for, and chastened by him as by a father; yet never cast off, but sealed to the day of redemption, and inherit the promises, as heirs of everlasting salvation.

Prepare in Prayer
God, the brevity and beauty of this section of the Confession is glorious to us. Help us to see what You have done in Christ more clearly, that our joy may be more complete, amen.

Into the Scriptures
Read Romans 8:12-27 and Galatians 4.

Reach Back
Today, it is accepted nearly without challenge that all human beings are the children of God. In one sense this is true, as God is the progenitor of all life. He alone gives life, and has divine prerogative and authority over life as well as death. Today it is seen as generous, tolerant, and enlightened to speak of all people as the children of God, as long as we are not too specific on what we mean by "god."

The Westminster Divines, however, took a more biblical, if less tolerant, approach to understanding the family of God. Why did they do this? For one thing, Jesus spoke rather plainly about the "father" of unbelievers—he is not God but rather the devil. He said,

> Why do you not understand what I say? It is because you cannot bear to hear my word. You are of your father the devil, and your will is to do your father's desires. He was a murderer from the beginning, and has nothing to do with the truth because there is no truth in him (John 8:43-44).

Here Jesus was speaking to as-yet unconverted Jews, whom He clearly loved enough to speak the truth. His desire was not to belittle them, but rather to clearly demarcate the line of the Covenant of Grace.

Rather than assuming that all people are children of God, the Bible speaks of God's family as *specifically* those who have been converted to true worship of God through His Son Jesus Christ; who savor Christ as their treasure above all things. The Apostle Paul in several places uses the word "adoption" to more fully convey the truth that God's people must first be redeemed to Him through conversion, faith, and justification. This is why chapter twelve of the Confession starts out, *"All those who are justified..."* In acknowledging this truth, the authors of the Confession sought to better describe the benefits of love, forgiveness, and acceptance into the family of God that conversion brings.

Gaze Upwards

In my view, this is one of the most beautiful statements of the Confession, and clearly one of its highlights. In this twelfth section on adoption, we can truly see how a deeper understanding in theology inspires us to praise God in ways that we would not be able to do otherwise. What is especially beautiful in this section is the authors' use of the imagery of adoption to convey the grace that would be felt by a pauper that had been adopted by a king!

We have all seen movies that portray the conditions and feelings of self-pity felt by the parentless and orphans. The movie and Broadway play "Annie" for instance, captures the longing of a child for the unconditional love of an accepting father. And yet does not our Heavenly Father do so much more for us than any earthly Daddy Warbucks?

Speaking to His disciples on the night of his arrest, Jesus teaches directly on this subject, as He promises to give them the Holy Spirit, who will fill them and serve as their Comforter in His absence. Jesus declares, "I will not leave you as orphans." (The Greek word for orphans is "orphanos"). "I will come to you. Yet a little while and the world will see me no more, but you will see me. Because I live, you also will live" (John 14:18-19).

The Larger Catechism of the Westminster Confession (included here as Appendix D) has a wonderful description of our new identity as adopted children of God. It asks in Question 74:

> What is adoption? Answer: Adoption is an act of the free grace of God, in and for his only Son Jesus Christ, whereby all those that are justified are received into the number of his children, have his name put upon them, the Spirit of his Son given to them, are under his fatherly care and dispensations, admitted to all the liberties and privileges of the sons of God, made heirs of all the promises, and fellow-heirs with Christ in glory.

Did you notice that both chapter twelve from the Confession and answer #74 from the Larger Catechism repeat the phrase "have His name put upon them?" We remember that in the Scriptures, one's name carried with it the implication of one's character. Isaac was "he laughs" because of his improbable conception, a miracle performed by God in his parents' old age. Jacob was "a deceiver," seeking after his brother Esau's reward—and taking it. Elijah the prophet was "Yahweh is my God," the content and object of his prophetic ministry. What then does it mean to have God's name placed upon us? The humility and exaltation of such a proposition is overwhelming. The important praise-inspiring key to understanding adoption, is not to credit our own virtue which prompted God to select us out from among the riff-raff of the world, but rather to acknowledge God's sheer grace in adopting *any of us at all*.

Search Inward

Take a few moments to re-read section twelve of the Confession. What words and phrases inspire longing in your soul to draw close to God? As you take assurance from these truths, you may look deeper into your own heart and ask yourself, "During what times of my life do I *not* feel the force of these wonderful promises? What actions that I take, or circumstances that may surround me, cause me to lose focus on my identity as a child of God?" Take the following excepts from the Confession and pray them repeatedly—for yourself, for your family, and for other believers with whom you fellowship:

> That we would be vouchsafed in the hands of our loving God

> That we would enjoy the liberties and privileges of being children of God

> That His name would be placed upon us as a seal

> That we would have access to the throne of boldness in prayer

> That we would be chastened and disciplined when needed

Step Out—Suffering Well

One of the true marks of our growth in Christ is our ability to suffer well for the sake of Jesus. You may not think of suffering as a spiritual discipline, but it is. Certainly not one we would choose for ourselves, but it is a discipline none the less. When enduring hardships such as failing health, troubled relationships, or financial need, we must always remember our place in the Kingdom of God. If we are justified through faith in Christ, we have also been adopted into the Family of God. As we learn to cling to God as our most treasured possession, we also must learn to suffer as His children, oftentimes by God's chastening, just as our own children are subject to our loving discipline. To suffer well, I believe, would be to endure all types of hardship while never forgetting, forfeiting, or relinquishing our identity in Christ; and giving thanks for it all.

Dietrich Bonhoeffer memorably wrote in his landmark book, The Cost of Discipleship, "If we would bear the image of his glory, we must first bear the image of his shame. There is no other way to recover the image we lost through the Fall."[41] Bonhoeffer himself was no stranger to suffering and shame, and therefore his words strike us with a certain force. Bonhoeffer, a Lutheran pastor and theologian, ministered in Germany during the rise of Hitler. A respected leader among the Confessing Church, a movement of Christians who endeavored to stand strong for the gospel during a time of massive ecclesiastical compromise, Bonhoeffer spearheaded an

---

41 Dietrich Bonhoeffer. The Cost of Discipleship. (New York NY: Touchstone, 1995) p. 301.

underground training seminary for young pastors. After coming to the United States to teach and preach—the landscape of Germany having become more and more dangerous for Confessing pastors—Bonhoeffer was eventually convinced that it was his duty to return to his homeland in order to continue his efforts. But more than that, he would actively work for the fall of Hitler's evil regime. He was hanged for his efforts. This noble herald of truth would taste suffering's ultimate fate: martyrdom. Still, his words on suffering ring in our ears, "If we would bear the image of His glory, we must first bear the image of His shame."

Perhaps the greatest and most ubiquitous type of suffering in this life is enduring temptation to sin. Here again, the Confession is a masterful encouragement for us, as we cling to the rock that is higher than ourselves. Just as the child of a king would be able to claim safe-passage through the recognition of his noble name, so also the children of God garner strength by claiming the name of the Father which has been sealed upon us. When tempted, think back to the promises named here in the Confession: which promises give us strength to resist? Which promises give us encouragement to obey? Which promises give us motive to please our Father?

In Galatians 4:6-7, the Apostle Paul makes this claim to the name of the Father explicit by stating, *"And because you are sons, God has sent the Spirit of His Son into our hearts, crying, 'Abba Father!'* (Aramaic: daddy) *So you are no longer a slave, but a son, and if a son, then an heir through God."* In this way, we ought always to cling to God as our generous, protective, and caring daddy, calling out for His hand in times of darkness.

The Confession Chapter Thirteen:

Of Sanctification

1. They who are effectually called and regenerated, having a new heart and a new spirit created in them, are further sanctified, really and personally, through the virtue of Christ's death and resurrection, by his Word and Spirit dwelling in them; the dominion of the whole body of sin is destroyed, and the several lusts thereof are more and more weakened and mortified, and they more and more quickened and strengthened, in all saving graces, to the practice of true holiness, without which no man shall see the Lord.

2. This sanctification is throughout in the whole man, yet imperfect in this life: there abides still some remnants of corruption in every part, whence arises a continual and irreconcilable war, the flesh lusting against the Spirit, and the Spirit against the flesh.

3. In which war, although the remaining corruption for a time may much prevail, yet, through the continual supply of strength from the sanctifying Spirit of Christ, the regenerate part does overcome: and so the saints grow in grace, perfecting holiness in the fear of God.

Prepare in Prayer
Oh God, we are so far from perfect! As we read Your Word and listen to Your Spirit's voice, please continue to file off our rough edges so that we may be more and more like Your Son Jesus. Amen.

Into the Scriptures
Read Psalm 51 and Romans 8.

Reach Back

I have already noted in a couple of places, especially in the introduction, that sanctification is not only an important theological concept, but also the stage of our faith journey in which we likely expend the most time and human energy. While election, regeneration, adoption, and justification are either timeless or instantaneous, sanctification is a *stage* of progressive and gradual growth in Christ-likeness that begins at conversion and is not completed until our death, or the Lord's return.

For this reason, historic proponents of Reformed theology have rejected the notions of perfectionism in this life that other Christian traditions have proposed (viz. the Wesleyan tradition). John Wesley, the founder of Methodism, believed that human beings could attain perfection in this life, but admitted that neither he nor anyone he knew had attained this. Reformed theologians on the other hand, such as the Westminster Divines, do not admit to any possibility of human perfection in this life, but rather conceive of sanctification as an unfinished process, a "continual and irreconcilable war" (WCF 13.2).

Gaze Upwards

As we attune our thoughts toward God this day, let us take special notice of the grace and the ministry of the Holy Spirit, whose duty consists of renovating our hearts, more and more, subsequent to our initial regeneration into new life. How often are we conscious that the Holy Spirit of God, the same Spirit that empowered Jesus' resurrection from the dead, also lives inside of us (Romans 8:11)?

Do we often acknowledge His indwelling place in our very souls? If we are honest, we often fail to notice His presence, although He has not once left us once since our conversion (Ephesians 1:13-14). Notice how the Confession places the emphasis on the active work accomplished "by his Word and Spirit dwelling in them" (13.1). Thus, the work of the Holy Spirit is intrinsically tied to His primary implement, the Word of God.

Do you give attention to the gentle ways that the Holy Spirit convicts us of sin (John 16:8-9), warns us of dangerous paths (John 16:13), or even suggests words of encouragement to our minds when needed? Furthermore, it is the special work of the Holy Spirit to direct our minds to what we have *already* been taught through the Holy Scriptures (John 14:26). His influence in our lives is gentle, powerful, convicting, and relentless.

Search Inward

One of the telling phrases from the Confession was this: *"The dominion of the whole body of sin is destroyed, and the several lusts thereof are more and more weakened and mortified"* (13.1). Once again we find that the Confession, like the various creeks, streams, and tributaries of a great river, usually leads us right back to the deeper waters of repentance. For many of the so-called spiritual "giants," confession of sins was regarded as the primary tool of spiritual formation and the straightest road toward godliness. In fact, Dietrich Bonhoeffer called confession, "the God-given remedy for self-deception and self-influence."[42]

I have often found that my own times of confession are far too general. One of the first pieces of advice I received from a wise spiritual mentor in the faith after I came to Christ was to "confess specific sins specifically" (See WCF 15.5). For this reason it is often beneficial to the soul to name and list the specific "lusts thereof" that continually plague us on our journey towards holiness.

Step Out—Mortification of Sin

"Mortification" must sound like an old-fashioned word to modern Christians, but for the Reformers and Puritans, it was a vital aspect of sanctification. In this process, the spirit of the believer is given reign over what the New Testament calls the "flesh." John R. W. Stott defines the Greek word *sarx* this way, "By *sarx* (flesh) Paul means neither the soft muscular tissue which covers our bony skeleton, nor our bodily instincts and appetites, but rather the whole of our humanness viewed as corrupt and unredeemed."[43] It is this vile aspect of our human nature that must relentlessly be put to death by the Spirit. As Paul writes, "For if you live according to the flesh you will die, but if by the Spirit *you put to death* the deeds of the body, you will live" (Romans 8:13, emphasis added).

For today's application, consider the importance of asking for the mortification of specific sins by name. You may first want to list the three to five sins that haunt you most. Do not attempt to cover every conceivable sin in any one setting. We are often blind to most of them, and we are prone to forget some of the others anyway. Then, take those

---

42 Dietrich Bonhoeffer. The Cost of Discipleship. (New York NY: Touchstone, 1995) p. 289.

43 John R. W. Stott. Romans: God's Good News for the World. (Downer's Grove IL: InterVarsity Press, 1994) p. 222.

besetting sins and ask for their death. Visualize them being taken captive by Christ, or starved to death. You may pray something like this:

> "Oh God, put to death my jealous envy of my sister!"
>
> Or, "God please crush the pride within me that desires to advance beyond my co-workers."
>
> Or again, "Merciful Father, do not let my sexual lust breathe for another day."

By naming specific sins specifically, you will find that you are making greater advances in sanctification than if you were to generically say, "God forgive all of my sins."

The colonial and early American Puritans knew much about the mortification of the sinful nature. The wonderful book entitled The Valley of Vision contains many anonymous prayers from prior generations that "modern Puritans" can pray directly, or use as a model to write their own. As we close this chapter on sanctification, let us pray one such of these anonymous prayers:

> O divine lawgiver,
>
> I take shame to myself for open violations of thy law, for my secret faults, my omissions of duty, my unprofitable attendance upon means of grace, my carnality in worshipping Thee, and all the sins of my holy things.
>
> My iniquities are increased over my head; my trespasses are known in the heavens, and there is Christ gone also, my advocate with the Father, my propitiation for sins, and I hear His word of peace.
>
> At present it is a day of small things with me, I have light enough to see my own darkness, sensibility enough to feel the hardness of my heart, spirituality enough to mourn my want of a heavenly mind; but I might have had more, I ought to have had more, I have never been straightened in Thee; Thou hast always placed before me an infinite fullness, and I have not taken it.

I confess and bewail my deficiencies and backslidings; I mourn my numberless failures, my incorrigibility under rebukes, my want of profiting under ordinances of mercy, my neglect of opportunities for usefulness. It is not with me as in months past; O recall me to Thyself, and enable me to feel my first love.[44]

44 The Valley of Vision: A Collection of Puritan Prayers and Devotions. (Carlisle PA: The Banner of Truth Trust, 2005) p. 80.

The Confession Chapter Fourteen:

Of Saving Faith

1. The grace of faith, whereby the elect are enabled to believe to the saving of their souls, is the work of the Spirit of Christ in their hearts; and is ordinarily wrought by the ministry of the Word: by which also, and by the administration of the sacraments, and prayer, it is increased and strengthened.

2. By this faith, a Christian believes to be true whatsoever is revealed in the Word, for the authority of God himself speaking therein; and acts differently, upon that which each particular passage thereof contains; yielding obedience to the commands, trembling at the threatenings, and embracing the promises of God for this life, and that which is to come. But the principle acts of saving faith are, accepting, receiving, and resting upon Christ alone for justification, sanctification, and eternal life, by virtue of the covenant of grace.

3. This faith is different in degrees, weak or strong; may be often and many ways assailed and weakened, but gets the victory; growing up in many to the attainment of a full assurance through Christ, who is both the author and finisher of our faith.

Prepare in Prayer
God, so often we find that our faith seems too small! And yet You have told us that faith as small as a mustard seed is living and growing, beautiful in Your eyes. Holy Father, increase our understanding that what You have given us is all-sufficient! Amen.

Into the Scriptures
Read Hebrews 11.

Reach Back

The doctrine of justification by faith alone was the key assertion on which the Reformation hung. It was because of the corruption of this Biblical truth that Martin Luther was compelled to nail The 95 Theses to the door at Wittenberg. Perhaps there is no other doctrine of the Christian faith that is more crucially important, both for our salvation and our daily life, as we seek to live in peace and obedience to God. Faith, which is a gift of God, is described rightly here by the Confession as being "the work of the Spirit of Christ" in our hearts. Consider for a moment the precise wording of Ephesians 2:8-9, "For it is by grace you have been saved through faith. And *this* is not your own doing; it is the gift of God, not a result of works, so that no one can boast" (emphasis added).

In this statement by Paul, what is the antecedent of the word "this" in the second sentence? To ask the question another way, to what is Paul referring when he says "and *this* is not your own doing?" Is it the grace spoken of in the first sentence? No, rather it is the faith by which we have been saved! Yes, faith is a gift!

Faith is given to believers as the first of many extravagant gifts. God actually *empowers* us to believe when we were unable to do so before! This is the reason why the Confession describes this process with the words *"the elect are enabled to believe to the saving of their souls"* (WCF 14.1).

Gaze Upwards

Read aloud the definition of faith given in Hebrews 11:1 and 6, *"Now faith is the assurance of things hoped for, the conviction of things not seen... And without faith it is impossible to please Him, for whoever would draw near to God must believe that He exists and that He rewards those who seek Him."*

Have you ever mistakenly searched for faith, only to discover that something in your heart was missing, flat, or numb? Perhaps that is because faith is much more than a "feeling." Many of us remember fondly the first time we fell in "love." We long for that kind of emotional electricity with God. And yet we do not often "feel" that kind of passion for our faith. On the other hand, faith is also much more than some kind of cold doctrinal orthodoxy, where we must simply sign our names to the bottom of a statement of theological propositions. The power of faith is contained not in our being swept up by a rapturous feeling, nor in the accuracy of our ability to describe it, *but rather by the beauty and glory of the One in whom our faith is placed.*

Hebrews 12:2 describes Jesus as both the "author and perfecter of our faith" (NIV). The radical implication of these words is that our faith is given by Jesus Christ (the author), rests upon Him as the object of our faith, and also relies upon Him to see to it that we persevere until the end (the perfecter). A. W. Tozer, commenting on this verse, writes, "From all this, we learn that faith is not a once-done act, but a continuous gaze of the heart at the Triune God."[45] A master of making the complex simple, Tozer adds, "Faith is... by its very nature scarcely conscious of its own existence. Like the eye which sees everything in front of it and never sees itself, faith is occupied with the object upon which it rests and pays no attention to itself at all."[46]

Search Inwards

In today's reading, the Confession uses three strong verbs to describe the kind of response that faith inspires in our lives; "yielding... trembling...and embracing" (WCF 14.2). Let's take each of these in turn:

Yielding: Normally when we think of yielding we think in terms of traffic. This may not be so far from the truth. Just as a failure to yield on the highway may result in a serious crash, so also a failure to yield to God's commands will often result in a collision of priorities, values, and purpose resulting in damage done to our spiritual walk. At the same time that faith requires us to cling to Jesus Christ as our rock, it also necessitates that we release our grip on self-reliance. Dietrich Bonhoeffer writes,

> If we would follow Jesus we must take certain definite steps. The first step, which follows the call, cuts the disciple off from his previous existence. The call to follow at once produces a new situation...Unless a definite step is demanded, the call vanishes into thin air, and if men imagine that they can follow Jesus without taking this step, they are deluding themselves like fanatics.[47]

Trembling: How often have you considered trembling before God? We are inundated with descriptions of God as though He were our buddy, grandfather, or simply "the man upstairs." True faith ought to result in our trembling at His power, majesty, and holiness, even though we have already been saved from His wrath, and will suffer no condemnation under His

---

45 A. W. Tozer. The Pursuit of God. (Camp Hill PA: Christian Publications, 1993) p. 84.

46 Ibid p. 84-85.

47 Dietrich Bonhoeffer. The Cost of Discipleship. (New York NY: Touchstone, 1995) p. 62-63.

mighty fist (see Romans 8:1). When confronted by the reality of God's holy beauty in his beatific vision of the God, Isaiah the prophet rightly shrieked, "Woe is me! For I am lost; for I am a man of unclean lips, and I dwell in the midst of a people of unclean lips; for my eyes have seen the King, the Lord of hosts!" (Isaiah 6:5). Surely He is no God with which to trifle!

Embracing: Finally, embracing is the most affectionate of the three active verbs in today's reading. We tend to think of embracing as something confirming, uplifting, and infilling. And indeed it is. Just as we ought to melt in the warm embrace of a lover, a parent, or one of our own children, so too we may be filled with delight in the embracing of God's promises as we find ourselves secure in His everlasting arms.

Step Out—Yielding; Trembling; Embracing

Take some time to look reflectively at your own life today. What evidence is there of your yielding to God's commands? As we mentioned above, yielding is a lot like driving, in that it often requires us to slam on the brakes, in a jolting and violent way, in order to refrain from colliding with something potentially dangerous to our souls. If there is an action in your life that requires immediate change—ask God for the power to make that change as soon as possible. Erwin Lutzer, the pastor of historic Moody Church in Chicago once quipped, "If you have a chasm to jump over in your life, it is much better to do it in one large leap than two shorter jumps!"

Next, what evidence is there of your trembling at His power? Do you ever stand in awe of His power as though you were standing in front of an incredible force that could completely overwhelm you? Or do you speak and think of God as though He were a much lesser deity than He truly is? The Apostle Paul urged believers to "work out your own salvation with fear and trembling" (Philippians 2:12). I would submit that far too many believers today work under the operating assumption that God is much closer to an elderly grandfather in demeanor than the Holy God who inspired books like Ezekiel and Nahum and Joel. If you have not read these books recently, perhaps they will refresh your view of God's power.

Finally, what evidence is there of your embracing God's promises? Recently I have spent much time reading the Chronicles of Narnia aloud to my daughter Soriah. We often sit for hours reading the pages of these great and fantastical allegories of spiritual truth. As her father, I deeply enjoy reading the voices of characters like Lucy, Peter, Digory Kirke, and of course Aslan the Lion! Often I will stop what I am reading and ask her questions just to make sure she understands what we are reading. At the end of one chapter I asked, *'Soriah, what do you enjoy most about reading this book?'* Soriah simply replied, *'Oh Daddy! I just love being with you!'* True faith—faith that justifies— certainly means yielding to God's commands and trembling at his power. But if it does not also include the mere enjoyment of God's presence, then we do not have it, and it does not have us.

The Confession Chapter Fifteen:

Of Repentance Unto Life

1. Repentance unto life is an evangelical grace, the doctrine whereof is to be preached by every minister of the gospel, as well as that of faith in Christ.

2. By it a sinner, out of the sight and sense, not only of the danger, but also of the filthiness and odiousness of his sins, as contrary to the holy nature and righteous law of God, and upon the apprehension of his mercy in Christ to such as are penitent, so grieves for, and hates his sins, as to turn from them all unto God, purposing and endeavoring to walk with him in all the ways of his commandments.

3. Although repentance should not be rested in as any satisfaction for sin, or any cause of the pardon thereof, which is the act of God's free grace in Christ; yet is it of such necessity to all sinners, that none may expect pardon without it.

4. As there is no sin so small but it deserves damnation; so there is no sin so great that it can bring damnation upon those who truly repent.

5. Men ought not to content themselves with a general repentance, but it is every man's duty to endeavor to repent of his particular sins, particularly.

6. As every man is bound to make private confession of his sins to God, praying for the pardon thereof, upon which, and the forsaking of them, he shall find mercy: so he that scandalizes his brother, or the Church of Christ, ought to be willing, by a private or public confession and sorrow for his sin, to declare his repentance to those that are offended; who are thereupon to be reconciled to him, and in love to receive him.

Prepare in Prayer

God, even the title of this chapter of the Confession convicts us! Help us continue to repent that nothing may ever come between us. You alone are our source of life! In Jesus' name we pray, amen.

Into the Scriptures

Read Psalm 5 and James 5.

Reach Back

This section of the Confession is instrumental in teaching and applying the doctrine of repentance. Repentance is not the same thing as mere confession of sins, even though they are cut out of the same cloth. If confession is acknowledgement of our sins in the presence of God or other human beings, especially those that we have offended, repentance takes confession one step further by turning away from sin and setting forth on a more perfect path. Literally in the Greek language of our New Testament, metanoia (repentance) means a changing of the mind.

One of the things that this section makes clear is that "repentance be not rested in as any satisfaction for sin" (WCF 15.3). This means that our mere entrance into the mindset of repentance does not cancel out the weight of our sin in the eyes of God. But doesn't our repentance in some way signal and trigger God's forgiveness? Yes and no. 'Yes,' because it is the human response that God demands of us in order for us to obtain forgiveness. But 'no' because it does not force God into the position of obligation to give us forgiveness, nor does it actually absorb the wrath (or penalty) of our sin— only the blood of Christ can do that. God does not *have to* forgive us merely because we have repented.

Clearly then, the satisfaction for our sins rides not upon our tears of sorrow (however authentic they may be), but upon the cross beams of Jesus' death in our place through His substitutionary atonement. As one wise theologian said, "even our tears of repentance must be washed in the blood of Jesus Christ." So then, it is Christ's death on the cross that *guarantees* our forgiveness, rather than our ability to wail and moan at our errors. Yet it is our repentance that demonstrates that we are "purposing and endeavoring to walk with Him in all the ways of His commandments" (WCF 15.2).

Gaze Upwards

What kind of God do we serve that commands, no *demands*, our constant and immediate repentance? Only a God who exudes and overflows with holiness and justice! The fifth Psalm declares,

> Give ear to my words, O Lord; consider my groaning. Give attention to the sound of my cry, my King and my God, for to you do I pray. O LORD in the morning you hear my voice; in the morning I prepare a sacrifice for you and watch. *For you are not a God who delights in wickedness; evil may not dwell with you* (5:1-4 emphasis added).

In this Psalm, we see quite a bit about the nature and character of God as it regards our repentance. First and most obviously, God does not tolerate our wickedness in any way. Many of us suffer from far too weak of a conception of God at this point. C.S. Lewis wrote,

> We want, in fact, not so much a Father in Heaven as a grandfather in heaven—a senile benevolence who, as they say, 'liked to see young people enjoying themselves,' and whose plan for the universe was simply that it might be truly said at the end of each day, 'a good time was had by all'.[48]

As Lewis points out in jest, it is far too common to assume that we live under the soft touch of the sort of god who does not seem to care about sins like greed, lust, sloth, idolatry and the like. We would far prefer a god whose highest hope is that everyone was able to do precisely the things they liked to do. But this is not our God. We have a much higher and majestic God than that.

Secondly, we see a God who condescends to hear our prayers. Just as any father is stern and severe in His demands for obedience in His children, how much more does God rush to our side when we fail! Notice how the Psalm writer describes his own repentance as "groaning," and "the sound of my cry." Praise God that He listens to the whimpers of His children.

Search Inwards

When is the last time that you can say with integrity that you "groaned" over your sin? Does it produce remorse in your heart? Does it produce hatred for

---

48 C. S. Lewis. The Problem of Pain. (New York NY: Touchstone, 1996) p. 35-36.

sin's place in your life? Or perhaps your repentance consists rather of a desire not to be punished by divine methods for the *consequences* of your sin. Sometimes a watered-down version of repentance results in us playing a spiritual game of "hide the crumbs under the rug." We do this merely to avoid the penalty for our sin, rather than digging deeply enough to really change our desires.

Once, I spoke with a student in the youth group who had been caught repeatedly using drugs, both by his parents, and by the police. When asked about this behavior (we had a well-established friendship) he ardently admitted that he wanted to stop—but not because he loathed the action, but only because he did not want to be punished by having his drivers license taken away. I told him that until he wanted to glorify God *more* than he wanted to abuse these substances, he would find it impossible to quit.

Repentance is intrinsically tied to faith. In fact, it is impossible to have the one without the other. John Frame says it like this,

> You can see, then, that repentance and faith are inseparable. They are two sides of a coin. You cannot turn from sin without turning to Christ or vise versa. Turning from sin points you in the direction of Christ. You don't need to turn twice, only once. Faith and repentance are the same thing, viewed positively and negatively. Neither exists before the other, and neither exists without the other.[49]

Stepping Out—Public Confession

Many Protestants are generally unfamiliar with the concept of making confession to a pastor, to the congregation, or to other believers. In fact, many relish the theological truth that we need not exclusively do any of these in a spoken manner to find the grace of God's forgiveness. But perhaps in our desire to distance ourselves from our Roman Catholic past, we have seriously weakened the practice of confession.

Richard Foster, the Quaker and author of the book that set many pastors and churches on fire for the spiritual disciplines, writes in his ground-breaking work, Celebration of Discipline:

---

49 John Frame. Salvation Belongs to the Lord: An Introduction to Systematic Theology. (Phillipsburg NJ: P&R Publishing, 2006) p. 197.

Confession is a difficult discipline for us because we all too often view the believing community as a fellowship of saints before we see it as a fellowship of sinners. We feel that everyone else has advanced so far into holiness that we are isolated and alone in our sin. We cannot bear to reveal our failures and shortcomings to others. We imagine that we are the only ones who have not stepped onto the high road of heaven. Therefore, we hide ourselves from one another and live in veiled lies and hypocrisy.[50]

Of course, we are *not* the only imperfect ones. Were we to open ourselves to a righteous humility from time to time, the Spirit would be available to do more work than we ever thought possible.

The Epistle of James makes it clear that we need not abandon this practice of public confession. James writes, "Confess your sins to one another and pray for one another, that you may be healed. The prayer of the righteous person has great power as it is working" (5:16). This potent teaching on repentance makes it clear that there ought to be times when we make verbal confession in the presence of our brothers and sisters in Christ. This may be the case especially:

When sin is committed against another brother or sister in the faith. If this is the occasion, we will need to come to him or her directly in order to obtain his or her pardon and release.

When sin is a public matter that directly involves the whole of the church. An individual found embezzling money from the church operating funds for example, would require such public acknowledgement.

When egregious sin is committed by a leader of the church such as a pastor, elder, teacher, or worship leader.

When our lives are detracted by a besetting sin that cannot be broken out of by normal methods of confession and repentance.

To demonstrate the power of public confession, let me finally mention that in 1995 a massive student-led revival began on the campus of Wheaton College. This revival resulted in the spreading of the renewal fervor to several other campuses. Many, many students came to Christ and rededicated their lives to His Lordship. Students waited in long lines to get to the microphone to testify about what the

---

50 Richard Foster. Celebration of Discipline. (New York NY: Harper San Francisco, 1998) p. 145.

Holy Spirit was doing in their lives. What could cause thousands of students to rededicate their lives to Jesus in worship services that lasted throughout the night, and even resulted in canceled classes? It all began as several student leaders made public acknowledgement of their sins, admitted their deep failures, and sought public restoration. Perhaps God will withhold His blessings from our lives until we do the same.

The Confession Chapter Sixteen:

Of Good Works

1. *Good works are only such as God has commanded in his holy Word, and not such as, without the warrant thereof, are devised by men out of blind zeal, or upon any pretense of good intention.*

2. *These good works, done in obedience to God's commandments, are the fruits and evidences of a true and lively faith: and by them believers manifest their thankfulness, strengthen their assurance, edify their brethren, adorn the profession of the gospel, stop the mouths of the adversaries, and glorify God, whose workmanship they are, created in Christ Jesus thereunto, that, having their fruit unto holiness, they may have the end, eternal life.*

3. *Their ability to do good works is not at all of themselves, but wholly from the Spirit of Christ. And that they may be enabled thereunto, besides the graces they have already received, there is required an actual influence of the same Holy Spirit to work in them to will and to do of his good pleasure; yet are they not hereupon to grow negligent, as if they were not bound to perform any duty unless upon a special motion of the Spirit; but they ought to be diligent in stirring up the grace of God that is in them.*

4. *They, who in their obedience, attain to the greatest height, which is possible in this life, are so far from being able to supererogate and to do more than God requires, that they fall short of much which in duty they are bound to do.*

5. *We can not, by our best works, merit pardon of sin, or eternal life, at the hand of God, because of the great disproportion that is between them and the glory to come, and the infinite distance that is between us and God, whom by them we can neither profit, nor satisfy for the debt of our former sins; but when we have done all we can, we have done but our duty, and are unprofitable servants: and because, as they are*

good, they proceed from his Spirit; and as they are wrought by us, they are defiled and mixed with so much weakness and imperfection that they can not endure the severity of God's judgment.

6. Yet notwithstanding, the persons of believers being accepted through Christ, their good works also are accepted in him, not as though they were in this life wholly blameless and unreprovable in God's sight; but that he, looking upon them in his Son, is pleased to accept and reward that which is sincere, although accompanied with many weaknesses and imperfections.

7. Works done by unregenerate men, although for the matter of them they may be things which God commands, and of good use both to themselves and others; yet, because they proceed not from a heart purified by faith; nor are done in a right manner, according to the Word; nor to a right end, the glory of God; they are therefore sinful and can not please God, or make a man meet to receive grace from God. And yet their neglect is more sinful, and displeasing unto God.

Prepare in Prayer
God, we know that without You, nothing that we can ever say or do is "good" enough. And yet, because of the blood of Your Son, we are made complete in Your eyes, as righteous as Christ. We marvel in Your presence today! Amen.

Into the Scriptures
Read Matthew 6:1-4 and John 15.

Reach Back
Many of us suffer from a deeply distorted view of the moral value of our "good deeds." We tend to fall into one of two great errors. Either 1) we correctly diagnose the great moral failure intrinsic to our human nature and then incorrectly conclude that God *cannot* or *will not* use us positively for His glory, or else 2) we errantly begin by underestimating our sinful nature and then spring into arrogant works of self-righteousness. Neither the Confession nor the Scriptures themselves will support either of these false ideas.

On the contrary, the Confession is clear that for believers, *"their ability to do good works is not at all of themselves, but wholly from the Spirit of Christ"*

(WCF16.3). Thus, the Westminster Confession maintains a perfect balance between our human inability to do anything of value on account of our fallen nature, and the amazing reality of the Holy Spirit working through our lives.

Consider again the possibilities of the Spirit-filled believer. When abiding in the love and power of Jesus Christ (cf. John 15) our fallible and feeble attempts of obedience are converted into, *"the fruits and evidences of a true and lively faith: and by them believers manifest their thankfulness, strengthen their assurance, edify their brethren, adorn the profession of the gospel, stop the mouths of the adversaries, and glorify God"* (WCF 16.2).

This mysterious conversion happens only as God views our corrupted attempts as righteousness *"through Christ."* It is as though God now views our actions through the lens of the righteousness and goodness of Christ Himself. Thus *"their good works also are accepted in him,"* and yet, *"not as though they were in this life wholly blameless and unreprovable in God's sight; but that he, looking upon them in his Son, is pleased to accept and reward that which is sincere"* (WCF 16.6).

Search Inward

When we take reflective time to look into our own hearts, we discover that many of us have taken sort of a "checking account" view of our good deeds (our works). We have come to believe that our lives are akin to the balancing of a financial account. God first of all eliminated all of the red ink in our account by forgiving us in Christ. We then suppose that the rest of our lives we are making deposits into our account in order to "pay back" our Creditor. Right?

But stop for a moment and contemplate your best deed of service. Pick your very best one. Perhaps a ministry that you have started, a class that you have taught, a young person in whom you have invested, a mission you have supported, or even a degree you have earned. Can you select even one deed that you have done with the purest of motives? Is there not a hint of self-service in even the best of our actions? Do we not often serve in order to be noticed, or study in order to be recognized? Do we not pray to be considered holy, and weep in order to be seen as compassionate? Do we not teach in order to be considered wise, and give in order to be considered generous?

Despite our very best attempts to act nobly, Jesus Christ clearly says, "If a man remains in me and I in him, he will bear much fruit; *apart from me you can do nothing*" (John 15:5, NIV, emphasis added). It seems that no sooner does the Spirit calls us and equip us for service "in the vine," then our own pride and desire for recognition grow up as a weed around it and choke the life out of it.

Step Out—Secrecy

The remedy for this constant and perpetual desire to be recognized for our goodness is the New Testament practice of secrecy. While serving God in secret has its own temptations (our secrecy becomes another credit for our internal boasting) its advantages outweigh its dangers. For this reason, Jesus Christ, in the Sermon on the Mount bid His hearers to serve God without any view of human recognition. "Beware of practicing your righteousness before other people in order to be seen by them, for then you will have no reward from your Father who is in Heaven" (Matthew 6:1). What, no reward? Jesus continues, "But when you give to the needy, do not let your left hand know what your right hand is doing so that your giving may be in secret. And your Father who sees in secret will reward you."

John Calvin, commenting on this passage from Matthew writes, "We ought to be satisfied with having God for our only witness, and to be so earnestly desirous to obey him, that we shall not be carried away by any vanity. It frequently happens that men sacrifice to themselves rather than to God."[51]

One time when I was in seminary, a secret benefactor emerged to help with my education. This generous person gave money to our church treasurer with the specific purpose of helping me complete my graduate degree. The caveat was that I was never allowed to know the giver's identity. The beauty of the gift, of course, was that I never knew who to thank for it. For this reason I realized that I must treat each and every person in the congregation *as though they were the giver of the gift*. I soon found that my appreciation for my church family grew as a result; for all I knew, any one of them could have been the giver. Secrecy, then, protects the giver from an inflated sense of self-importance, as well as perpetuates the generosity and thanksgiving of the gift.

---

51 John Calvin on Matthew 6:1-4. Calvin's Commentaries: Volume XVI. Translated by the Rev. William Pringle. (Grand Rapids MI: Baker Books, 1999) p. 310.

When is the last time that you have done something righteous *in secret?* The wonder of secrecy is that it brings joy to the Father's heart. Secrecy purifies the motives as Purell purifies the hands. By doing works of compassion namelessly, we "sanitize" our gift and prevent ourselves from passing along our germs of self-righteousness. Secrecy helps us to defer our reward for obedience until eternity. Rather than "cashing in our chips" now, and taking an immediate reward of human respect and honor, secrecy allows us to delay our reward until the day that the investment matures in heaven.

Here are a few ways that you can practice the discipline of secrecy this month:

> Write an anonymous letter of encouragement to someone in your family, workplace, small group, or Sunday School class. Tell them exactly what you appreciate about them and then watch their smile perk up throughout that day. It can be fun to hide in "stealth mode!"

> Send a donation or gift to a missionary or soldier on the field that you know is hurting or lonely. If you cannot think of one or don't know one personally, send a donation to a mission cause anyway. You don't even have to know the person to affect them!

> The next time you are tempted to complain about a bad day at work, a headache, or the traffic, keep that complaint "secret" so as not to vocalize your resentment or pain. Sometimes a held back complaint is an effective way to restrain the cantankerous heart.

> Send a care-package to a college student. Instead of taking personal credit for it, sign it from your Bible Study group, your church family, or simply "someone who loves you."

If you put your mind to it, I am sure you can come up with some even better forms of secrecy than I have given above. But don't just think about it, do it! What can you do for the Kingdom of God, just between you and Him, so that not even your left hand knows what your right hand is doing?

The Confession Chapter Seventeen:

Of The Perseverance of the Saints

1. They whom God has accepted in his Beloved, effectually called and sanctified by his Spirit, can neither totally nor finally fall away from the state of grace; but shall certainly persevere therein to the end, and be eternally saved.

2. This perseverance of the saints depends, not upon their own free-will, but upon the immutability of the decree of election, flowing from the free and unchangeable love of God the Father; upon the efficacy of the merit and intercession of Jesus Christ; the abiding of the Spirit and of the seed of God within them; and the nature of the covenant of grace; from all which arises also the certainty and infallibility thereof.

3. Nevertheless they may, through the temptations of Satan and of the world, the prevalence of corruption remaining in them, and the neglect of the means of their perseverance, fall into grievous sins; and for a time continue therein: whereby they incur God's displeasure, and grieve his Holy Spirit; come to be deprived of some measure of their graces and comforts; have their hearts hardened, and their consciences wounded; hurt and scandalize others, and bring temporal judgments upon themselves.

Prepare in Prayer
God, our greatest comfort in this life is that nothing can separate the Saved from the Savior. May we live so that Your grace is affirmed and never denied; for *Your* saving work never fails! Amen.

Into the Scriptures
Read John 6:22-40 and John 10:22-42.

Reach Back

The doctrine of the "perseverance of the saints" is another of the keystone teachings of the Reformed theological tradition, although it could more accurately be called the "perseverance of Jesus Christ." In the acronym T.U.L.I.P[52] which has come to define the systematic theology known as Calvinism, the fifth and final designation "P," is reserved for this important pastoral encouragement. Simply stated, the perseverance of the saints is the biblical teaching that once a person has truly been born again, and has entrusted his or her life to Jesus Christ, that person is kept in His grace and cannot fall away. In our day, it has become more common to teach this truth by simply saying, "once saved, always saved."

The Apostle Paul, writing to the church of believers in Rome boldly stated,

> In all these things we are more than conquerors through Him who loved us. For I am sure that neither death nor life, nor angels nor rulers, nor things present nor things to come, nor powers, nor height nor depth, nor anything else in all creation will be able to separate us from the love of God in Christ Jesus our Lord (8:37-39).

Search Inward

Most Christians have doubted their salvation from time to time. Some have been raised in churches where the pastor encouraged them to "get saved" every single week! Many have even spent nights awake wondering if they will really be saved at the end of their lives. Even Christians who have known Jesus for years have fallen into the trap of doubting their salvation. "After all," they wonder, "would God really save a wretch like me, who continues to fail day after day?"

And yet the simple truth of the Bible is, "absolutely yes!" Consider the direct teaching of Jesus in the Gospel of John,

> And this is the will of Him who sent me, that I should lose nothing of all that He has given me, but raise it up on the last day. For this

---

52 T.U.L.I.P. is the compact way to summarize the Reformed teaching on soteriology. It stands for Total depravity (that every human being is thoroughly corrupted by sin); Unconditional election (that God chose believers by His own will and volition without the condition of our merit); Limited atonement (that Jesus Christ's death was intended to ransom believers, the elect, and not unbelievers, reprobate); Irresistible grace (that the Holy Spirit so moves in the hearts of the elect that they cannot, or will not, resist His love once He reveals Himself to them); and Perseverance of the Saints ("once saved, always saved").

is the will of my Father, that everyone who looks on the Son and believes in Him should have eternal life, and I will raise him up on the last day (6:39-40).

We can notice several things from the above quotation. 1) The foundation of our perseverance is rooted in the Father's will. Thus, perseverance is intrinsically tied to God's eternal decrees (see WCF chapter three). 2) The burden and responsibility for redeeming the lost has been entrusted into the Son's hands. Christ is our infallible redeemer. 3) The Son exudes the greatest confidence that He will not fail in the slightest degree in carrying out the Father's plan. Again in John 10, Jesus teaches that He will not let any believer out of the grip of grace, *"I give them eternal life, and they will never perish, and no one will snatch them out of my hand. My Father, who has given them to me, is greater than all, and no one is able to snatch them out of the Father's hand. I and the Father are one* (John 10:28-30).

Gaze Upwards

The doctrine of the perseverance of the saints is likely one of the most praise-inspiring teachings of the Scriptures. The fact that God saves us despite our ongoing sin is a testament to the amazing love of the Father. The reality of our salvation fully depends upon Christ and not us. It is His love that binds us fast to the throne of grace. It is His hand that grips us tightly in His care. It is His relentless pursuit of fallen sinners that guarantees our inheritance.

Perhaps most clearly in this doctrine, we see the vast difference between the Reformed faith and that of our Arminian brothers and sisters. Ours is so completely God-centered that we ascribe not one ounce of praise to ourselves, but have every reason to praise God for His greatness.

1. We deny that we could keep ourselves on the path of rightness were it not for His constant hand of guidance. We praise God that He loves deeply enough to protect and guide us.

2. We deny that we must remain obedient or risk falling into the fires of hell. We praise God that *He* works obedience in our lives through His Spirit.

3. We deny that we are able to keep ourselves in a position of favor with

God. We praise God that we don't *have* to. We have already been adopted as His children. God will not disown us.

Imagine for a moment that you are a parent of a two-year old. (Some, like me, will not have to pretend!) If your two-year old was playing in the front yard and began wandering towards the street, your eyes would trace her every move. If she came perilously close to the edge of the street, your body would instinctively kick into high gear. If she took one more step while a vehicle was approaching, you would do everything in your power to prevent catastrophe. What parent wouldn't? In the same way, Christ refuses to let us "run into the road." As an infallible parent, God will not and *cannot* fail in saving us from perdition.

Step Out—Perseverance

If it is the nature of Jesus Christ to persevere in saving sinners, even though we often trip all over ourselves, how much more then ought Christians to learn perseverance in this life as well!

I remember when I was twelve I joined a hard-pitch baseball team. Most of the kids on the team were older than me by one or two years, and I could hardly keep up with them. I was rarely able to get on base (except for being walked as a hit batsman!) Unfortunately, as some of the parents fought over which kids would get more playing time, the coach fell out of favor with an influential group of parents. The team imploded. Most of the players quit, supported by their pouting parents. Both coaches dropped out too. Finally, we ended up with seven players and just a few committed parents. *And yet my mom and dad would not let me quit the team.* We could barely field a squad against some monstrous opponents, but I was never allowed to quit a sport or team once I committed. That lesson has always stuck with me.

Believers clearly don't follow Jesus' example in perseverance closely enough. Here, I am not talking about salvation but rather perseverance in our daily lives. If Jesus Christ would not give up on the disciple Peter even though he denied *even knowing* the Lord—what does that say about the way we so easily give up on:

> Students who don't measure up to our standards
> Churches which do not provide the programs we want
> Denominations that crumble in their hierarchy
> Ministries that don't seem to hold our interest anymore

Friends who insult us repeatedly
Small groups that get boring
Pastors who make mistakes or overlook our needs...

The list could go on and on. As a pastor, nothing brings me greater joy than serving my congregation. But as we have tried to build our church through evangelism and discipleship, I must say that one of the greatest disappointments of church leadership in the 21st century is the varied reasons people walk away from the Church: musical preferences, gossip, personal offences (real and perceived), even boredom.

What a deep irony it is that the same Lord who refuses to give up on His people, must bear with a people that so easily walk away from His Church! Let us resolve to be Christian people of an indefatigable spirit in the same way that Jesus Christ Himself perseveres in loving and saving us.

The Confession Chapter Eighteen:

Of the Assurance of Grace and Salvation

1. Although hypocrites, and other unregenerate men, may vainly deceive themselves with false hopes and carnal presumptions: of being in the favor of God and estate of salvation; which hope of theirs shall perish: yet such as truly believe in the Lord Jesus, and love him in sincerity, endeavoring to walk in all good conscience before him, may in this life be certainly assured that they are in a state of grace, and may rejoice in the hope of the glory of God: which hope shall never make them ashamed.

2. This certainty is not a bare conjectural and probable persuasion, grounded upon a fallible hope; but an infallible assurance of faith, founded upon the divine truth of the promises of salvation, the inward evidence of those graces unto which these promises are made, the testimony of the Spirit of adoption witnessing with our spirits that we are the children of God; which Spirit is the earnest of our inheritance, whereby we are sealed to the day of redemption.

3. This infallible assurance does not so belong to the essence of faith but that a true believer may wait long and conflict with many difficulties before he be partaker of it: yet, being enabled by the Spirit to know the things which are freely given him of God, he may, without extraordinary revelation, in the right use of ordinary means, attain thereunto. And therefore it is the duty of everyone to give all diligence to make his calling and election sure; that thereby his heart may be enlarged in peace and joy in the Holy Ghost, in love and thankfulness to God, and in strength and cheerfulness in the duties of obedience, the proper fruits of this assurance: so far is it from inclining men to looseness.

4. True believers may have the assurance of their salvation shaken in many ways, diminished, and intermitted; as, by negligence in preserving of it; by falling into some special sin, which wounds the conscience, and grieves the Spirit; by some sudden or vehement temptation; by God's withdrawing the light of his countenance and suffering even such as fear him to walk in darkness and to have no light: yet are they never utterly destitute of that seed of God, and life of faith, that love of Christ and the brethren, that sincerity of heart and conscience of duty, out of which, by the operation of the Spirit, this assurance may in due time be revived, and by the which, in the meantime, they are supported from utter despair.

Prepare in Prayer

Like a small child that continually needs affirming love, so also we need to be reminded of Your unfailing mercies. Show us again today, as we study, that Your grace is a sure foundation. In Christ's name we pray, amen.

Into the Scriptures

Read Psalm 77 and Hebrews 6.

Reach Back

Can a believer ever truly know that he or she is saved? Can one who is a redeemed child of God ever lose this status? These are the primary questions considered in chapter 18 of the Confession. This section picks up where the last chapter left off. Again, the Confession focuses our attention on the assurance and surety of our salvation in Jesus Christ. Here it is called God's "infallible assurance" (WCF 18.3) since it rides on God's promises alone.

Charles Hodge, the great Reformed Princeton theologian wrote in his three-volume systematic theology:

> It is only the lamentable mistake that God loves us for our goodness, that can lead any one to suppose that His love is dependant on our self-sustained attractiveness, when we should look to His fatherly love as the source of all goodness, and the ground of the assurance that He will not allow Satan or our own evil hearts to destroy the lineaments of His likeness which He has impressed on our souls.[53]

In explaining why a true believer can never fall from grace, Hodge also spells out six reasons why once we are saved we shall ever be so:

---

53 Charles Hodge. Systematic Theology. Volume III. (Peabody MA: Hendrickson, 2003) p. 112

1) The Law. Christians have been delivered from the power of the Law, namely, its ability to condemn us (cf. Romans 7).

2) The Spirit. God has given us the Holy Spirit who "secures not only the life of the soul, but also the ultimate and glorious life of the body."[54]

3) Sonship. Christians have been fully adopted as children of God and as such receive all the benefits of His doting love (cf. WCF 12).

4) Purpose. No person, force, or mistake can override God's eternal purpose in redemption (see Romans 8:28 and 38). To do so would be to rip us from Christ's hand.

5) Love. "A love so great as the love of God to his people cannot fail of its object."[55]

6) Immutability. God's nature and His promises are unchanging.

Thus Hodge concludes, "(Our perseverance) is due to the purpose of God, to the work of Christ, to the indwelling of the Holy Spirit, and to the primal source of all, the infinite, mysterious, and immutable love of God. We do not keep ourselves; we are kept by the power of God."[56] For these reasons, Reformed churches have always taught that their people can *know* they are saved, and *rest* in their assurance.

Gaze Upwards

For this section's reading we have selected Hebrews 6. Ironically, we must note that the first part of this biblical passage is one of the passages cited by theologians who assert that true believers *can* in fact fall from grace and lose their salvation (against the WCF). These theologians would point to verses 1-6 to suggest that a believer can lose their salvation by a final act of volitional sin. But is this person described in verses 1-6 truly a believer? In verse 4, it says that this person has been enlightened "once"; has merely "tasted" the heavenly gifts, and again in verse 5 "tasted" the goodness of the Word of God. These temporal

---

54 Ibid p. 111.
55 Ibid p. 112.
56 Ibid p. 113.

indications seem to depict a person who has not fully and finally trusted in Jesus Christ.

The most difficult part of Hebrews 6 to understand is what the author meant by those having "shared in the Holy Spirit." Theologian Wayne Grudem unpacks this challenging phrase,

The text also further says that these people 'have become partakers of the Holy Spirit' (Heb. 6:4). The question here is the exact meaning of the word *metochos*, which is here translated 'partaker'...For example, the context shows that in Hebrews 3:14 to become a 'partaker' of Christ means to have a very close participation with Him in a saving relationship. On the other hand, *metochos* can also be used in a much looser sense, simply to refer to associates or companions. We read that the disciples took in a great catch of fish so that their nets were breaking, 'they beckoned to their *partners* in the other boat to come and help them' (Luke 5:7)...By analogy, Hebrews 6:4-6 speaks of people who have been 'associated with' the Holy Spirit, and thereby had their lives influenced by him, but it need not imply that they had a redeeming work of the Holy Spirit in their lives, or that they were regenerated.[57]

What then do we learn of God's promises from Hebrews 6? When we read the context of the passage in its entirety, we learn from verses 13-20 that salvation does not depend upon our human ability to avoid perdition, but rather upon God's *own integrity* as a covenant maker. Here, we read that God swears by His own name that His promises are true and trustworthy since, "he had no one greater by whom to swear" than Himself (6:13). The author of Hebrews writes further, "So when God desired to show more convincingly to the heirs of the promise the unchangeable character of His promise, He guaranteed it with an oath" (6:17). The resulting confirmation for our faith is that God has finally and irrevocably accepted Jesus Christ's atonement of our sins as our great high priest. He has done this so unchangeably that He cannot lose any one that He has saved. Thus our promise of salvation is secure, for "it is impossible for God to lie" (Hebrews 6:18).

Step Out—Thanksgiving
Sometimes this world is so full of pain, full of doubt and uncertainty, that we feel we have little to rejoice in. As I write today, I am reminded of the grief I felt for an attendee of my home church who was recently married. They

---

57 Wayne Grudem. Systematic Theology. (Grand Rapids MI: Zondervan, 1994) p. 797-798.

were an extraordinarily happy couple on their wedding day. And yet two months after the wedding bells rang and the rice was thrown, the husband was in a terrible car accident and suffered a serious head injury. He is now unable to speak as he once was.

Although this world is so full of debilitating sadness, nevertheless we can give thanks to God for the greatness of our final deliverance from this world. A.W. Tozer, the great Chicago pastor writes,

> The man who has God for his treasure has all things in One. Many ordinary treasures may be denied him, or if he is allowed to have them, the enjoyment of them will be so tempered that they will never be necessary to his happiness. Or if he must see them go, one after one, he will scarcely feel a sense of loss, for having the Source of all things, he has in One all satisfaction, all pleasure, all delight.[58]

Because God is our all-surpassing treasure, Christians are enabled to endure any number of difficulties and hardships in this life, knowing that the one pure delight, our relationship with our Redeemer, is unbreakable.

As the Confession says, *"True believers may have the assurance of their salvation shaken in many ways...by God's withdrawing the light of his countenance and suffering...yet are they never utterly destitute of that seed of God...(and) are supported from utter despair"* (WCF 18.4).

Today, make it your aim to perfect the art of thanksgiving; especially as it pertains to the surety of your final deliverance from this temporary world of grief. God has promised and will give you the salvation that He has offered in Jesus Christ. For today's practice in spiritual formation, make a list of all of the letters in the alphabet from A to Z. Then take a half-hour to write out one thanksgiving for each letter. You may balance your list with both theological and practical thanksgivings. Make sure to list the important people in your life under the letters of their first names.

If this particular practice does not appeal to you, try doing a rewriting of the 136th Psalm in your own words, substituting items of thanksgiving from your own life for those of the Psalm writer. When we copy and assimilate Scripture into our hearts, we find that our natural ability to give thanks to God in all situations is increased.

---

58 A. W. Tozer. The Pursuit of God. (Camp Hill PA: Christian Publications, 1993) p. 19-20.

By recounting the ways that God has blessed us "with every spiritual blessing in Christ Jesus" (Ephesians 1:3) we will find our hearts swelling and overflowing with thanksgiving no matter how dark a situation in which we may find ourselves.

As we close this section on assurance, let us take courage from the words of Jonathan Edwards:

> You will certainly be accepted of the Father if your soul lays hold of Jesus Christ. Christ is chosen and anointed of the Father, and sent forth for this very end, to save those that are in danger and fear; and he is greatly beloved of God, even infinitely, and he will accept those that are in him. Justice and the law will not be against you, if you are in Christ; that threatening...will not touch you. The majesty and the honor of God are not against you...If you come to Christ it will be a sure sign that Christ loved you from all eternity, and that he died for you; and you may be sure if he died for you, he will not lose the end (purpose) of his death, for the dispensation of life is committed unto him.[59]

59 Jonathan Edwards. "Safety, Fullness, and Sweet Refreshment in Christ." In Sermons of Jonathan Edwards. (Peabody MA: Hendrickson, 2005) p. 27.

The Confession Chapter Nineteen:

Of the Law of God

1. God gave to Adam a law, as a covenant of works, by which he bound him and all his posterity to personal, entire, exact, and perpetual obedience; promised life upon the fulfilling, and threatened death upon the breach of it; and endued him with power and ability to keep it.

2. This law, after his Fall, continued to be a perfect rule of righteousness; and, as such, was delivered by God upon mount Sinai in ten commandments, and written in two tables; the first four commandments containing our duty toward God, and the other six our duty to man.

3. Besides this law, commonly called moral, God was pleased to give to the people of Israel, as a Church under age, ceremonial laws, containing several typical ordinances, partly of worship, prefiguring Christ, his graces, actions, sufferings, and benefits; and partly holding forth diverse instructions of moral duties. All which ceremonial laws are now abrogated under the New Testament.

4. To them also, as a body politic, he gave various judicial laws, which expired together with the state of that people, not obliging any other, now, further than the general equity thereof may require.

5. The moral law does forever bind all, justified persons as well as others, to the obedience thereof; and that not only in regard of the matter contained in it, but also in respect of the authority of God the Creator who gave it. Neither does Christ in the gospel any way dissolve, but much strengthen, this obligation.

6. Although true believers be not under the law as a covenant of works, to be thereby justified or condemned; yet is it of great use to them, as well as to others; in that, as a rule of life, informing them of the will of God and their duty, it directs and binds them to walk accordingly; discovering also the sinful pollutions of their nature, hearts, and lives; so as, examining themselves thereby, they may come to further conviction of, humiliation for, and hatred against sin; together with a clearer sight of the need they have of Christ, and the perfection of his obedience. It is likewise of use to the regenerate, to restrain their corruptions, in that it forbids sin, and its warnings serve to show what even their sins deserve, and what afflictions in this life they may expect for them, although freed from the curse thereof threatened in the law. The promises of it, in like manner, show them God's approbation of obedience, and what blessings they may expect upon the performance thereof; although not as due to them by the law as a covenant of works: so as a man's doing good, and refraining from evil, because the law encourages to the one, and deters from the other, is no evidence of his being under the law, and not under grace.

7. Neither are the aforementioned uses of the law contrary to the grace of the gospel, but do sweetly comply with it: the Spirit of Christ subduing and enabling the will of man to do that freely and cheerfully, which the will of God, revealed in the law, requires to be done.

Prepare in Prayer
Lord, like a perfect doctor, Your Law diagnoses exactly where we are ailing. Today, as we study these sacred texts from Scripture, show us where Your healing touch is required. In Jesus' name we pray, amen.

Into the Scriptures
Read Exodus 20 and Leviticus 19-20.

Reach Back
It is quite common today for churches to declare themselves "New Testament Churches." We desire to be a Spirit-filled people; a community consumed and impassioned by the Resurrected Christ. The Gospels, for many, are deliciously easy to read—stories of Jesus' life and ministry, healings and miracles, fish and bread, soils and seeds. And yet the Old Testament is often a "different animal." For one thing, the concept of the sacrificial system is strange, bizarre, even barbaric to our modern and sophisticated lives. In the book of Leviticus for example we read of bloody sacrifices of bulls and goats, stonings and capital punishment, festivals and ceremonies, all of which may make us feel that we have just stamped our passport into a foreign and alien land.

And yet the same Jesus who teaches us passionately to love the Lord our God with all of our hearts and to love our neighbors as ourselves, also declares that He did not come to remove one jot or tittle (dotting of an "i" or a crossing of a "t") from the Law, but rather to fulfill it (Matthew 5:17-20).

The first thing that we need to know about the Law is that it is not consigned only to the Old Testament, just as grace is not consigned only to the New. "Law" is properly any command that is required of *us* (imperatives), while grace is anything God has done *for us* (indicatives). Any confusion here, and we will soon be on the road to legalism (salvation by law-keeping) or antinomianism (despising moral restraints altogether).

Further, the Westminster Confession helps us as believers today to become discerning with regard to the distinctions between God's moral law, ceremonial law, and civic (or judicial law). Let's start with the latter. The civic laws were those that were required of Israel as a nation, as a theocracy. These regulations are concerned primarily with social and criminal laws, as well as with regulations regarding Israel's governance. These, the Confession says, have "expired" as believers today are not expected to stone disobedient children for instance (Leviticus 20:9), or wage wars against the Philistines (see WCF 19.4).

Secondly the ceremonial law, the Confession says, has been "abrogated" (19.3). This is not to say that it has been set aside, *but rather that it has been fulfilled and bettered in the New Covenant.* For instance, we no longer need to make animal sacrifices as the OT book of Leviticus instructs us, for the NT book of Hebrews is clear that Jesus Christ has become the final priest and sacrifice, fulfilling the requirements of sacrifice and atonement.[60] Thus the necessities of slaying bulls, sprinkling blood, and offering grain have been fulfilled and perfected in the sacrifice of Jesus Christ.

The moral law, expressed most concisely in the Ten Commandments, is that which has been written upon our hearts; timeless principles that reflect the very nature of God Himself. These will not be abrogated and they still make serious demands of us today. The Sermon on the Mount (Matthew 5-8) is Jesus' commentary on the moral law. It has not slackened as some suggest, but is intensified even to the level of the secret thoughts and motivations! For instance, Jesus teaches us that restraining oneself from murder or adultery is not enough. The purposes of the Commandments

---

60 See especially Hebrews 7-10.

are greater still—to warn us against hatred and lust *as corrupting forces within the heart.*

Thus, like caution signs on a dangerous pass, the moral law has the power to warn us about the catastrophic repercussions of driving off the cliff, but they cannot save us once we fall. For salvation, we need *grace*, we need *the cross.*

Gaze Upwards

John Calvin wrote that the Law has at least three purposes for believers today. First the Law warns us, like a mirror, of the blemishes and ugly spots in our lives. Calvin writes, "When we look in the mirror we notice any dirty marks on our faces; so in the Law we are made aware first of our helplessness, then of our sin, and finally the judgment."[61] How else will believers learn to discover the corruption of our thinking and the selfishness of our pursuits without an absolute standard by which to gauge our lives? When we see these repulsions in our lives, we are driven to grace in the cross of Christ.

Second, the Law is helpful in that it restrains societal evil. The core content of the Old Testament law is built with the foundational purpose that it would provide structure to community living. "(People under the Law) refrain from outward action," Calvin writes, "and inwardly check the viciousness which would otherwise burst out... because, restrained by fear or shame, they dare not act on impulse."[62] So then, nobody can steal their neighbor's horse or Porsche, make an unwanted sexual conquest, or kill their obnoxious archenemy—without paying a severe price back to the community.

But third, and Reformed theology highly emphasizes this aspect, Calvin taught that the Law helps us to discover what pleases and honors our holy God, and to motivate us to live pleasing lives in the sight of our Master and Sovereign. If resolving to "love the LORD your God with all your heart and with all your soul and with all your might" (Deut 6:5) becomes the consuming passion of our lives, the Law instructs us about *how* to go about setting up such a God-honoring lifestyle. Calvin states, "(The Law) is the best means for them to learn

---

61 John Calvin. The Institutes of the Christian Religion. 2.7.7. Edited by Tony Lane and Hilary Osborne. (Grand Rapids MI: Baker Books, 1987) p. 109.

62 Ibid 2.7.10. p. 110.

daily with greater certainty, what the will of the Lord is which they long to follow."[63]

Step Out—Obedience

We do not often think of obedience as a concept or a discipline that is "for us." No, we prefer to think of this as the kind of exercise that a *child* ought to be schooled in. Obedience, we reason, is for the recalcitrant, the wayward, and the ornery. Yet we often forget that our lives tend to be a bit like wax statues: despite God's constant molding and fashioning of our lives, we tend to slump back down in the sun to the most comfortable shape. Donkeys don't like whips, horses despise their bridles, Christians tend to shrink back from obedience.

In our day, we have difficulty with anyone or anything that has authority over us: Speed limits are made for *other* people (just don't race down *my* street where *my* children play). Tax laws are made for the real cheaters (not a common Joe like me who is just trying to make a buck). Church discipline is for the youth, and the rowdy children (But *I* won't be subject to my elders or pastor. I'm every bit as wise as they are).

And yet obedience is a theme that runs throughout both Testaments like the threaded binding of a book, holding the entire structure together. Consider your attitude towards obedience today: Do you respect the word of your boss, or do you despise him at the water-cooler conversation? Do you honor the desires of your spouse, or do you lord over him or her? But most importantly, is the Law of God producing righteous fear in your life? Does it inspire you to seek out ways to please God as your Master and Friend? Or are you, like an undisciplined sheep, merely kicking against the goads of the Shepherd?

---

63 Ibid 2.7.12. p. 112.

The Confession Chapter Twenty:

Of Christian Liberty and Liberty of Conscience

1. The liberty which Christ has purchased for believers under the gospel consists in their freedom from the guilt of sin, the condemning wrath of God, the curse of the moral law; and in their being delivered from this present evil world, bondage to Satan, and dominion of sin, from the evil of afflictions, the sting of death, the victory of the grave, and everlasting damnation; as also in their free access to God, and their yielding obedience unto him, not out of slavish fear, but a childlike love, and a willing mind. All which were common also to believers under the law; but under the New Testament the liberty of Christians is further enlarged in their freedom from the yoke of the ceremonial law, to which the Jewish Church was subjected; and in greater boldness of access to the throne of grace, and in fuller communications of the free Spirit of God, than believers under the law did ordinarily partake of.

2. God alone is Lord of the conscience, and has left it free from the doctrines and commandments of men which are in any thing contrary to his Word, or beside it in matters of faith or worship. So that to believe such doctrines, or to obey such commandments out of conscience, is to betray true liberty of conscience; and the requiring an implicit faith, and an absolute and blind obedience, is to destroy liberty of conscience, and reason also.

3. They who, upon pretense of Christian liberty, do practice any sin, or cherish any lust, do thereby destroy the end of Christian liberty; which is, that, being delivered out of the hands of our enemies, we might serve the Lord without fear, in holiness and righteousness before him, all the days of our life.

4. And because the powers which God has ordained, and the liberty which Christ has purchased, are not intended by God to destroy, but mutually to uphold and preserve one another; they who, upon pretence of Christian liberty, shall oppose any lawful power, or the lawful exercise of it, whether it be civil or ecclesiastical, resist the ordinance of God. And, for their publishing of such opinions, or maintaining of such practices, as are contrary to the light of nature, or to the known principles of Christianity, whether concerning faith, worship, or conversation; or, to the power of godliness; or, such erroneous opinions or practices, as either in their own nature, or in the manner of publishing or maintaining them, are destructive to the external peace and order which Christ has established in the Church, they may lawfully be called to account, and proceeded against by the censures of the Church, and by the power of the civil magistrate.

Prepare in Prayer
God, help us to see that You have given us liberty in Christ to pursue pure joy at His side. Help us also to never cause another believer or "little one" to stumble as we pursue Your presence. Amen.

Into the Scripture
Read Romans 14 and Galatians 5.

Reach Back
Throughout Christian history, there has always been a struggle to find the delicate balance between avoiding the entrapment of legalism on one hand (the error that we become righteousness by obeying certain laws or requirements) and antinomianism (the error of living apart from the Law so as to feel no restraints on one's behavior) on the other. Our compass for navigating this narrow pass is what the Confession calls "Christian Liberty." If there is a simple way to summarize the complex argument regarding a Christian's freedom in Christ given in Chapter 20 of the Confession it is this: When the fulcrum of the scale is set directly on the aim of glorifying God with one's life, the perfect balance will be struck.

Many groups of Christians have reduced the Christian faith to a matter of strictly keeping rules. These are often unbiblical or supra-biblical rules established by firm-handed community oversight. Scores throughout Christian history have made the faith all about living under and obeying the right sets of rules.

> From those in the New Testament age who insisted that a person must be circumcised in order to be saved;

To those in Martin Luther's age who suggested that salvation could only be gained by properly observing the Mass, buying indulgences, or honoring the relics;

To those in the 1940's and 50's of the last century who suggested that a person watching a movie or swimming in mixed company may be putting their soul in jeopardy.

To the opposing extreme, others such as the church in Corinth attempted to throw off any and all obligations to live the holy life based on an erroneous interpretation of a believer's freedom in Christ. (See 1 Corinthians chapters 5 and 6. Here, one man attempted to express his freedom by having intercourse with his father's wife!) We see these same repackaged concepts flying around and impacting the culture of our day as the standards of marriage and fidelity are continually under assault in many Christian denominations.

Gaze Upwards

Our reading from Romans 14 as well as the Confession both suggest that, when a believer makes the love of God and the goal of glorifying God the center of his or her life, that person will quite naturally avoid the two opposite errors of legalism and antinomianism. If having a loving relationship with our Creator continues to be our goal, we will avoid reducing that relationship to rule keeping. At the same time, striving towards a life that honors God's holy nature will keep one's life on the path of righteousness.

The conscience, then, is not a manipulative wedge by which we avoid living under the restrictions of the holy life. Rather, it is a gift by which we allow our own spirit to feel love for God, and to help determine our course of action, based on the higher principle of the glory of God. So then, in the example given in Romans 14 regarding one's dietary restrictions, Paul's counsel can be summed up succinctly by saying that since "none of us lives to himself, and none of us dies to himself" therefore "if we live, we live to the Lord, and if we die, we die to the Lord" (vs.7-8).

Search Inward

Let us say, for example, that you are struggling with a moral dilemma that is not clearly resolved in Scripture such as the drinking of alcohol. On this matter much of Christendom is divided. Those who abstain (many Baptists,

Pentecostals, and those of the holiness movement) have good reason to do so. Many who partake (many in Lutheran, Reformed, and Catholic traditions) may have good reasons as well.

Suppose that a few of your unbelieving co-workers have asked you to come out to an after-work party and have a drink with them to celebrate a wedding engagement. While you do not normally drink alcohol, you are not sure if you would do more harm than good to have a glass of red wine with them. You are aware that the Scriptures, especially in the Proverbs (e.g. 20:1), give us ample warnings that alcohol can be troublesome and downright dangerous. Yet at the same time, you are not sure that it is intrinsically evil since Christ used wine as a symbol of His own blood (Luke 22:14-23), and Paul counseled Timothy to drink wine for his stomach (1 Timothy 5:23). To make this decision, the believer must ask a series of questions based on the highest priority of the glory of God.

> Would I damage my Christian witness to unbelievers by partaking, or would I better be able to live "incarnationally" among my unbelieving friends by not appearing as a prude?
>
> Would drinking damage my relationship with God by bending or hurting my conscience, or would I be celebrating my freedom in Christ, as Jesus Himself celebrated at the wedding in Cana (John 2)?
>
> Would my conscience be broken by this choice, such that I feel that I have transgressed an inner conviction that God has laid upon my heart, or would I be graciously celebrating God's gifts of bounty (i.e. food, drink, and the wedding engagement)?
>
> Is my hesitance based on my legalism, fear of others' opinions, or is it based on an earnest desire to please God?

In all such difficult choices, the honor of God's name must be our priority as well as our final standard.

Step Out—Discernment
The practice that I have outlined above—making our moral choices based on a resolute determination to glorify God with our lives—is often called the process of discernment. Discernment is as much a learned and disciplined

practice of spiritual formation as it is common sense empowered by the Holy Spirit. I am convinced that far too many believers live out their days without asking themselves the kinds of hard questions that were presented in the above example.

Paul speaks of this term "discernment" in precisely the same context, that of living a pure life, when he writes to the Philippian believers, "And it is my prayer that your love may abound more and more with knowledge and all discernment so that you may approve of what is excellent, and so be pure and blameless for the day of Christ" (Philippians 1:9). I find it interesting that Paul prays for an *increased measure* of this gift for his beloved church. It is almost as though he is saying "the more your love for God increases, the more your discernment will increase; the more your discernment will increase, the more pure your lifestyle will become."

The Confession Chapter Twenty-one:

Of Religious Worship and the Sabbath-Day

1. The light of nature shows that there is a God, who has lordship and sovereignty over all; is good, and doeth good unto all; and is therefore to be feared, loved, praised, called upon, trusted in, and served with all the heart, and with all the soul, and with all the might. But the acceptable way of worshipping the true God is instituted by himself, and so limited by his own revealed will, that he may not be worshipped according to the imaginations and devices of men, or the suggestions of Satan, under any visible representation or any other way not prescribed in the holy Scripture.

2. Religious worship is to be given to God, the Father, Son, and Holy Ghost; and to him alone: not to angels, saints, or any other creature: and since the Fall, not without a Mediator; nor in the mediation of any other but of Christ alone.

3. Prayer with thanksgiving, being one special part of religious worship, is by God required of all men; and that it may be accepted, it is to be made in the name of the Son, by the help of his Holy Spirit, according to his will, with understanding, reverence, humility, fervency, faith, love, and perseverance; and, if vocal, in a known tongue.

4. Prayer is to be made for things lawful, and for all sorts of men living, or that shall live hereafter; but not for the dead, nor for those of whom it may be known that they have sinned the sin unto death.

5. The reading of the Scriptures with godly fear; the sound preaching, and conscionable hearing of the Word, in obedience unto God with understanding, faith, and reverence; singing of psalms with grace in the heart; as, also, the due administration and worthy receiving of the sacraments instituted by Christ; are all parts of the ordinary religious worship of God: besides religious oaths, and vows, solemn fasting, and thanksgivings upon special occasion; which are, in their several times and seasons, to be used in an holy and religious manner.

6. Neither prayer, nor any other part of religious worship, is now, under the gospel, either tied unto, or made more acceptable to, any place in which it is performed, or towards which it is directed: but God is to be worshipped everywhere in spirit and in truth; as in private families daily, and in secret each one by himself, so more solemnly in the public assemblies, which are not carelessly or willfully to be neglected or forsaken, when God, by his Word or providence, calls thereunto.

7. As it is of the law of nature, that, in general, a due proportion of time be set apart for the worship of God; so, in his Word, by a positive, moral, and perpetual commandment, binding all men in all ages, he has particularly appointed one day in seven for a Sabbath, to be kept holy unto him: which, from the beginning of the world to the resurrection of Christ, was the last day of the week; and, from the resurrection of Christ, was changed into the first day of the week, which in Scripture is called the Lord's Day, and is to be continued to the end of the world as the Christian Sabbath.

8. This Sabbath is to be kept holy unto the Lord when men, after a due preparing of their hearts, and ordering of their common affairs beforehand, do not only observe an holy rest all the day from their own works, words, and thoughts about their worldly employments and recreations; but also are taken up the whole time in the public and private exercises of his worship, and in the duties of necessity and mercy.

Prepare in Prayer
Father I thank You, that as a wise parent counsels his children, so also You make us sit down and rest awhile. Despite our desire to run and to work, help us to rest often in Your presence. Amen.

Into the Scriptures
Read Deuteronomy 5 and Matthew 12:1-14.

Reach Back
When discoursing upon the reason why God created the world in the first place, the Reformed pastor and scholar Jonathan Edwards speculated that the single most important reason God did so was that His glory would be enjoyed. He writes, "It seems to be a thing in itself fit and desirable that the glorious perfections of God should be *known*, and the operations and

expressions of them seen, by *other* beings besides himself."[64] Thus, Edwards was convinced, worshipping in the splendor of God's glory is the primary reason God created human beings at all. Because of His surpassing worth, the glory of God must be rejoiced in by other beings. He continues,

> And certainly, the most excellent actual knowledge and will that can be in the creature is the knowledge and love of God. And the most true and excellent knowledge of God is the knowledge of His glory or moral excellence, and the most excellent exercise of the will consists in esteem and love, **and a delight in His glory** (emphasis added).[65]

For this reason—delighting in God's glory—Reformed people hold worship, especially as a gathered people on Sabbath days, in supreme regard.

The Reformed tradition from whence this Confession is derived depends upon the foundational theological grounding that the worship of God ought to be solemn, reverent, orderly, and majestic. As such, worship in Reformed churches has been grounded in what is called the "regulative principle." The regulative principle is the idea that humans may not invent the methods by which we worship (idolatry), but rather we are given them in Scripture alone (see WCF 21.1). In our particular stream of Christian faith, the service of worship is structured intentionally to include prayer, praise in song, confession of sins, the reading of Scripture, the preaching of the Word, and often the receiving of the two sacraments of baptism and the Lord's Supper. The Confession is clear that true worship does not depend upon a particular building or location, but rather takes place any time true faith is applied to the adoration of God. Thus, Reformed worship is designed to bring the human soul to a place of humiliation before the Holy God.

Gaze Upwards

Perhaps one of the reasons that Reformed believers most often worship in a beautifully structured service of worship is that Creation itself is designed by God to have a rhythm and cadence as opposed to a random or unstructured form. Consider the Earth's regular procession around the

---

64 Jonathan Edwards. The End for Which God Created the World. reprinted within God's Passion for His Glory: Living the Vision of Jonathan Edwards by John Piper. (Wheaton IL: Crossway, 1998) p. 148.

65 Ibid p. 172.

sun, the moon's circuitous path around the Earth, or the changing of the tides and seasons: all depend upon a design of temporal regularity as though God Himself stood in front of the orchestra of His creation keeping time as *maestro*. A rhythm of regularity is found even on the molecular level of the universe. Electrons collect obediently and in orderly fashion around protons and neutrons. Likewise, on a vastly larger scale we again see this pattern—the galaxies themselves are in regular motion and fluid movement in the midst of the universe! Should we peer into our own chests, we would see the same creation order exemplified. Our own hearts, aortas and cardiac tissue, keep regular time, sustaining our lives in perfect melody as our lungs play the harmony with in and out swishes of air.

Rather than opting for a formless or impromptu order of worship, the Reformed tradition has preferred a service of worship that dependably moves from confession, to the reading and preaching of the Word, to the sacraments, to praise in song as regularly, dependably, and harmoniously as the maple leaves change colors each autumn.

This is not to say that one particular style of worship is the best. We are not here arguing for traditional worship versus contemporary worship, or liturgical worship forms against charismatic worship services. What is suggested, however, is that God's own design, which He has sewn into the universe, tends to suggest order, complexity, and beauty. Just as an artist's work teaches the observer something about the artist's own personality, life, or thought, so also Creation reflects on many levels the creative genius inherent in God's own being. Our worship should reflect this pattern as well.

Search Inward

In one day at the office I may typically receive up to ten phone calls, several text messages on my phone, one or two drop-ins to visit me at the office, and around 30 emails. (I know many readers will find these numbers low compared to their own places of work.) At the same time, with the help of my wife, I must balance my home life; schedule doctor's visits, monitor the children's school assignments, and keep tabs on family activities, and other calendar chaos. All this is to say that our modern lives are filled with hectic activity. One of our deepest needs, whether felt or unnoticed, is to attain peace. Sabbath worship is designed for that very purpose.

Because the Lord knows the business of our lives, He intentionally designed a regular Sabbath rest, wherein we have the delight (yes the pleasure!) of setting aside all of our hurriedly paced activities to focus exclusively on His glory, for one day out of the week. This is the creation and worship cycle. Again we find this principle at work: the Sabbath day is designed to reflect the creation order itself, just as God called the universe into existence in six days and then rested for one (see Exodus 20:1-21). Thus, worship parallels creation.

Do you find the requirement to drop all that you are doing to worship the Lord in a day of corporate prayer, quietness, and tranquility threatening to your pace of life, or do you find it a welcome relief to the burden of the workplace and the home? Like the Israelites making bricks without straw in the land of Egypt, we too often feel as though our work is endless, meaningless, and more than we can bear. The purpose of Sabbath is to replace our turmoil with restorative rest in God's peace. God gives the gift of Himself to his exhausted people, because He knows that only He Himself can bring satisfaction to a wearied soul. Psalm 65:4 says, "We shall be satisfied with the goodness of your house, the holiness of your temple."

Consider that God has commanded you to rest in His presence. I often command my own children to take naps in the afternoon between heavy sessions of playing (children's work). I know that without proper rest, the children destroy themselves by pestering each other, crying, losing their temper, and eventually collapsing in disgust. We are also like that. Without proper resting in the presence of the Holy, we are reduced to the worst version of ourselves. God has not *suggested* that you rest, He has commanded it.

Step Out--Observing Sabbath

Entering into a Sabbath rest is so much more than "doing church." For many American families, the Sunday routine may occur something as follows: The parents wake up first and quickly scamper to shower, shave, and iron. After some brief personal grooming, the children are quickly hustled into their Sunday clothes. Breakfast is thrown together and the dishes are left on the table with cereal absorbing the remaining milk. The family arrives, perhaps late, at church and quickly disperses, each to their own classroom. Committee meetings are often scheduled for Sunday mornings since "everyone will be here anyway." Next, almost incidentally, "worship" occurs for a little over an hour, and then the family reconvenes at the parking lot. Now the real day begins! Perhaps baseball or football tickets have been purchased. Dad will need to gas up and get downtown before the first quarter starts. He may not be seen again today. Many families even shuttle the teens off to practices, leagues, and soccer games! Later, the teens have to be pestered about completing their homework for the better part of the evening. (They couldn't do it on Friday, of course, *that* was the school dance). Finally the family finishes the day exhausted and drops into bed, after all, Monday is just a few hours away now.

The Scriptures and the Confession offer a radically different view of Sabbath. For one thing, the primary verb that qualifies the day, "rest," is elusive. It takes preparation and forethought to attain rest. Ironing and such must be done the night before—*"the ordering of the common affairs beforehand"* (WCF 21.8). Practices and meetings ought to be unheard of on the Sabbath. After all, the whole point to set aside the weary "extras" of our lives for one full day of contemplation and spiritual recharging.

How often has it occurred for you that you have arrived at the worship location early to pray for the pastor, his message, or the congregants' hearts that will be hearing the Word of God shortly? After all, the Confession says, *"This Sabbath is to be kept holy… after a due preparing of their hearts"* (WCF 21.8). Notice also that the Confession does not condense worship to the one-hour meeting of the service. The Westminster also states that private prayer, family devotions, and the worshipping of God ought to occur *everywhere*. These are as integral to the Sabbath rest as the praise and worship service.

When some simple steps of heart preparation can be taken ahead of time, the worship service provides a deeper avenue of adoration than when it is stumbled into. Even a few moments of reflective anticipation can soften the heart to the content of the sermon or the lyrics of the songs in exponential ways. For most, the very distractions that clutter the rest of their day actually serve to undercut our sacred time together as the People of God. Unintentionally, many worshippers have a hard time settling in to the mood of worship before much of the service has already slipped away. If these centering and meditative moments with Jesus can be attempted *before* holy worship begins, the spiritual harvest will be abundant.

What if your Sabbath rest looked closer to this: Mom and Dad wake up early, not to pick out clothes (those have been pressed and laid out the night before), but rather to read a Psalm and ask God to prepare the family's heart for worship. The children are woken, dressed, and fed as usual. The cereal bowls are *still* left out (same as above)—piling dishes don't matter today. Mom and dad usually attend a small group discussion class while the children head off to Sunday School, but today they opt out and sit quietly in the Sanctuary to read the passages of Scripture printed in the bulletin, and to pray for those that will be sitting in the same pew. After the main worship service, the family drives home, each taking a turn telling what Miss Kristina or Mr. Field taught in Sunday School. Dad may make the simplest lunch possible: grilled cheese and soup, all on paper plates. The littlest one prays over the "feast." No one dashes off for another engagement. These are precious moments. Phone messages and emails pile up helplessly as the family enjoys playing badminton in the back yard all together. The phone is off the hook. By three, mom's cell phone is vibrating again but she's nowhere near it to hear the message tone—she's reading in the lawn chair. After supper the family eats watermelon, has a seed-spitting contest, and shares stories about what God is doing in their lives. They walk off their dinner in a simple stroll around the block. The sun is setting on a long restful day. Soon it's bedtime. This is Sabbath.

The Confession Chapter Twenty-two:

Of Lawful Oaths and Vows

1. A lawful oath is a part of religious worship, wherein upon just occasion, the person swearing solemnly calls God to witness what he asserts or promises; and to judge him according to the truth or falsehood of what he swears.

2. The name of God only is that by which men ought to swear, and therein it is to be used with all holy fear and reverence; therefore to swear vainly or rashly by that glorious and dreadful name, or to swear at all by any other thing, is sinful, and to be abhorred. Yet, as, in matters of weight and moment, an oath is warranted by the Word of God, under the New Testament, as well as under the Old, so a lawful oath, being imposed by lawful authority, in such matters ought to be taken.

3. Whosoever takes an oath ought duly to consider the weightiness of so solemn an act, and therein to avouch nothing but what he is fully persuaded is the truth. Neither may any man bind himself by oath to any thing but what is good and just, and what he believes so to be, and what he is able and resolved to perform. Yet it is a sin to refuse an oath touching any thing that is good and just, being imposed by lawful authority.

4. An oath is to be taken in the plain and common sense of the words, without equivocation or mental reservation. It cannot oblige to sin; but in any thing not sinful, being taken, it binds to performance, although to a man's own hurt: nor is it to be violated, although made to heretics or infidels.

5. A vow is of the like nature with a promissory oath, and ought to be made with the like religious care, and to be performed with the like faithfulness.

6. It is not to be made to any creature, but to God alone: and that it may be accepted, it is to be made voluntarily, out of faith and conscience of duty, in way of thankfulness for mercy received, or for obtaining of what we want; whereby we more strictly bind ourselves to necessary duties, or to other things, so far and so long as they may fitly conduce thereunto.

7. No man may vow to do any thing forbidden in the Word of God, or what would hinder any duty therein commanded, or which is not in his own power, and for the performance of which he has no promise or ability from God. In which respects, monastical vows of perpetual single life, professed poverty, and regular obedience, are so far from being degrees of higher perfection, that they are superstitious and sinful snares, in which no Christian may entangle himself.

Prepare in Prayer
God as we study today, show us some areas in which we have failed to live up to the motto, "My word is my bond." Like Christ, let our lips always be pleasing to You as we speak. Amen.

Into the Scriptures
Read Matthew 5:33-37 and James 3.

Reach Back
In the day this Confession was written, there was no little debate about the moral legitimacy of taking oaths and vows. In fact, if you can believe it, it was one of the raging moral controversies of the day. On one hand, Reformed believers were well aware of the Roman Catholic Church's propensity for vow taking. Catholic believers took a variety of vows that, to the perception of the Westminster Assembly, were dubious. Vows to perpetually remain in poverty, to refrain from creation's design for married life through celibacy, and other ascetic extremes were thought to be unnecessary inventions of the papacy. Some monks lived their lives in self-abasing punishment. One monk for example, was said to have lived out most of his adult years on top of a pillar and even would replace maggots in his rotting flesh when they inadvertently fell out!

On the opposite extreme, the Westminster writers saw another movement afoot; a refusal to make any formal public professions of sincerity. This position was gaining ground in many Anabaptist quarters. This refusal to take public oaths or vows was based largely on the text from Matthew which was recommended in the reading for this chapter. Still today there are some Christian groups such as the Society of Friends (Quakers) and the Mennonites that will not take oaths. This other extreme, the Divines thought, could undermine much of the public social contract. Without the taking of vows, the legal process was thought to be undermined. Personal contracts such as work agreements, marriage contracts, weights and measures, and other societal obligations would no longer be binding or applicable.

The writers of the Confession sought a moderating position. On one hand, they felt that some of the vows of the Roman Church led many believers towards an excessive asceticism, limiting the freedoms that believers—even pastors and preachers—were graciously called to enjoy. On the other hand, they rejected the notion that vows are intrinsically evil (so the Anabaptists) inasmuch as the Scriptures record and even require the making of vows in some instances (Numbers 6; Psalm 22:25; 61:5-8). Even Jesus gave public testimony in the accepted format of His day (John 8:12ff).

Look Inward

The intent of this passage from the Confession bears the same intent as the biblical passages in today's reading. Both the above passages of Scripture and the Confession are designed to help believers make sure that our public statements are in accord with the heart. For as Jesus wisely taught His disciples, "The good person out of the good treasure in his heart produces good, and the evil person out of his evil treasure produces evil, for out of the abundance of the heart his mouth speaks" (Luke 6:43-45). This is the reason that Jesus gave such a stern warning to His disciples about speaking rashly and taking unnecessary vows during His discourse on the Sermon on the Mount (Matthew 5:33-37). Hastily taken promises, no matter to whom or what we swear to, may only serve as occasions for the rotten content of our hearts to be revealed.

James also warns us about the dangers of the tongue on the loose. He states that the tongue "is set among our members, staining the whole body, setting on fire the entire course of life, and set on fire by hell" (James 3:6). In other words, the tongue is like a lit flame that burns and scorches wherever it goes. For most, it is a nearly uncontrollable force that causes damage wherever it goes.

The Old Testament contains an unusual story about the hero Samson. In one adventure recorded in Judges 15, this great warrior takes 300 pairs of foxes, ties their tales together in couplets of woe, lights them on fire and turns them loose in the grain fields of the Philistines. Each pair, wrestling and wrangling to get free, torches the entire crop of Samson's enemies. For many of us, our own tongues and mouths are much like those fire-taled creatures! Our gossip, curses, untruths, and deceptions can do more damage to a church, a family, or a relationship than Samson's fiery cunning.

Gaze Upwards

We serve a God who is willing to put His own name and renown on the line for His gospel. He declares the efficacy of the promises He makes through the gospel of Jesus Christ, as He has nothing higher to swear by than by His own name. "For when God made a promise to Abraham, since he had no one greater by whom to swear, he swore by Himself, saying, 'Surely I will bless you and multiply you' (Hebrews 6:13). While God is able to make and keep an oath based on His own glory, human beings ought to be much more reluctant to do so. This is true for no other reason than that we subject ourselves to the wrath of God if we prove to be false in our account. Perhaps we would do better to honor the words of Jesus and simply let our "yes" be yes, rather than to incur further guilt by placing the honor of God's own name as the guarantor of our statements. Let no Christian be found guilty of dishonoring our great God and Savior by an oath we cannot fulfill.

Stepping Out—Silence

For many Protestants the value of "vows of silence" has been lost entirely, ironically due to the reformers' hesitancy to take these kinds of vows as mentioned above. And yet how greatly would our lives benefit from such a practice when attempted in measured allowances! The practice of self-imposed silence need not take the shape of a life-long vow as some of the monastics have made in the past, but rather can take the form of days or hours of simple quietude. Richard Foster writes about the experience of the practice of stillness, "In the midst of noise and confusion we are settled into a deep inner silence. Whether alone or among people, we always carry with us a portable sanctuary of the heart."[66]

---

66 Richard Foster. Celebration of Discipline. (New York NY: HarperCollins, 1998) p. 96-97.

The benefits of such a practice are many. 1) First, silence allows us to more patiently listen for the voice of God as He speaks to us in our times of prayer. Many of us often wonder *why* God does not speak to us more clearly—as alarms go off, cell phones ring, computers whirl, cars whiz by, and the TV blares in the background! 2) Secondly, silence allows us to become much better listeners. Perhaps if we submitted ourselves to secret days of intensified listening (even if we allowed ourselves to speak when socially required) we would become much better listeners to our spouses, children, and co-workers. Our silence need not serve as a boundary to our everyday communication, but rather as an enhancement. Again Foster writes, "Without silence there is no solitude. Though silence sometimes involves the absence of speech, it always involves the act of listening."[67] 3) Finally, silence allows us to have a greater measure of awareness to the pure sounds of Creation: the winds, the chattering of squirrels, the laughter of children in the neighbor's yard, the gentle drops of rain as a storm approaches. All of this and more become available to our senses, and instill an appreciation for God's work in and around us.

---

67 Ibid p. 98.

The Confession Chapter Twenty-three:

Of the Civil Magistrate

1. God, the Supreme Lord and King of all the world, has ordained civil magistrates to be under him over the people, for his own glory and the public good; and to this end, has armed them with the power of the sword, for the defense and encouragement of them that are good, and for the punishment of evil-doers.

2. It is lawful for Christians to accept and execute the office of a magistrate when called thereunto; in the managing whereof, as they ought especially to maintain piety, justice, and peace, according to the wholesome laws of each commonwealth, so, for that end, they may lawfully, now under the New Testament, wage war upon just and necessary occasions.

3. The civil magistrate may not assume to himself the administration of the Word and sacraments, or the power of the keys of the kingdom of heaven: yet he has authority, and it is his duty, to take order, that unity and peace be preserved in the Church, that the truth of God be kept pure and entire; that all blasphemies and heresies be suppressed; all corruptions and abuses in worship and discipline prevented or reformed; and all the ordinances of God duly settled, administered, and observed. For the better effecting whereof, he has power to call synods, to be present at them, and to provide that whatsoever is transacted in them be according to the mind of God.

4. It is the duty of the people to pray for magistrates, to honor their persons, to pay them tribute and other dues, to obey their lawful commands, and to be subject to their authority, for conscience' sake. Infidelity, or difference in religion, does not make void the magistrate's just and legal authority, nor free the people from their obedience to him: from which ecclesiastical persons are not exempted; much less has the Pope any power or jurisdiction over them in their dominions, or over any of their people; and least of all to deprive them of their dominions or lives, if he shall judge them to be heretics, or upon any other pretense whatsoever.

Prepare in Prayer

God, today's section in the Confession reminds us how limited we are as human beings. There are many others whose influence is greater than our own. When we are not in accord with the desires of our civic leaders, show us how all things are guided towards Your great ends. In Jesus' name we pray, amen.

Into the Scriptures

Read Romans 13 and 1 Peter 2:13-25.

Reach Back

In a like manner to the previous chapter, where Reformed believers sought to underscore a Christian's moral responsibility regarding oaths and vows, so also this chapter of the Confession is devoted to understanding another set of obligations where faith intersects with public life. Foundationally, the Westminster Divines chose as a matter of course a theology of *engagement* rather than *withdrawal* from the public sphere. In this chapter, the writers recommend several ways that a believer can justifiably participate in the civil realm without usurping our primary obligations to the Church and to Jesus Christ as our "first love" (Revelation 2:4).

Here, the Confession exhorts believers to participate in government, and to submit to its authority under God, inasmuch as the believer participates with the express desire to expand God's Kingdom on earth while compromising none of *the Church's* authority and power. Of paramount importance is the fact that a government need not be an overtly Christian enterprise as a prerequisite to involvement. Thus participation *in*, reformation *of*, and even confrontation *with* institutional society all correspond with Christ's commission to make disciples of all nations. The Reformed perspective sees societal involvement *not* as an evil to be feared, nor a duty to be occasionally considered, but rather as an obligation for all believers, in order to further the just requirements of the law of God, and "to do justice, and to love kindness, and to walk humbly with your God" (Micah 6:8).

Gaze Upwards

The glorious doctrine of the sovereignty of God is once again on display in this section. Romans 13 teaches clearly that every person must "be subject to the governing authorities. For there is no authority except from God, and those that exist have been instituted by God" (v. 1). God, then, is seen as ruling over all human affairs including at an international level. The Apostle Paul writes, "For the (the civil authority) is the servant of God, an avenger who carries out God's wrath on the wrongdoer" (v. 4). And yet Scripture does not deny that quite often civil governments do stray far from their God-ordained calling to serve as the restrainer of human evil on earth. The governmental powers of Assyria, Babylon, and Rome (about which Paul was writing) for instance, serve as negative examples of civil power and demonstrate that, perhaps more often than not, the societal administrators of human affairs fall reprehensibly short in every generation.

If many nations (perhaps all) fail so miserably, how then are the civil authorities "the servant of God?" And how is it that those nations, which so vehemently rebel against God, can be said to be "instituted by God"? The only answer must be found in the mystery of the sovereignty of God. Solving these dilemmas is a lot like asking why God allows evil to exist at all in the first place. With our limited human knowledge, we can only assume that God allows evil to reign temporarily in this life for His own divine purposes. Perhaps it is so that believers will be sanctified through their trials in this life. Perhaps it is so God's mercy can be fully on display through His Calvary grace. Certainly the existence of sin as it manifests itself in faulty human governance is an outcropping of humanity's corporate failure in the Garden of Eden.

Nevertheless, in the same way that "the rain falls upon both the just and the unjust" (Matthew 5:45), governments may be viewed as a "common grace" that is available for both the righteous and the unrighteous. In a similar way that natural forces like the rain impact both believers and unbelievers, human institutions of government serve as an umbrella over, and are composed of, many types of persons: Christians, atheists, Muslims, Jews, Hindus, the non-religious etc. Further, even the most faulty governmental systems provide at least some measure of benevolence for their people, even if it is the bare minimum of protection from foreign invaders, or the providing of limited (albeit corrupt) forms of transportation, commerce, or education.

Finally, the Scriptures are also clear (see the prophetic passages in Ezekiel 25-32 for instance) that all governments will have to face the wrath and judgment of a God who is both sovereign over human affairs and *dreadfully holy as well*. While many believers around the world suffer horribly at the hands of their rulers, we can take solace in the thought of the Psalmist who writes, "Arise, O Lord! Let not man prevail; let the nations be judged before you!" (9:19; see also Isaiah 2:4).

Search Inward

When considering the text of 1 Peter 2, it becomes apparent that our views of human authority can often reveal corruptions and flaws in our own character. Perhaps our propensity to complain and deride our leaders reveals a certain lack of honor for other people. Peter simply recommends, "Honor everyone. Love the brotherhood. Fear God. Honor the emperor" (1 Peter 2:17). There is something about politics that seems to bring out the worst in all of us. Maybe it is the fact that our leaders are considered nearly celebrities without feelings, families, or freedoms of their own. Often the way we speak about our leaders, especially the ones we do not agree with, reveals hardness, hatred, jealousy, and discord in our own hearts. On the contrary, Peter's letter teaches us that our cooperation with and participation in civil affairs ought to produce servanthood (2:13-16), honor (2:17) and endurance (2:18-25).

Step Out—Civil Service

Jonathan Edwards wrote:

> In some sense the most benevolent, generous person in the world seeks his own happiness in doing good to others, because he places *his* happiness in *their* good. His mind is so enlarged as to take them, as it were, into himself. Thus when they are happy, he feels it; he partakes with them, and is happy in their happiness. This is so far from being inconsistent with the freeness of beneficence, that, on the contrary, free benevolence and kindness consists in it (emphasis added).[68]

What does Edwards mean? His thesis is that true joy can be found in serving humanity when one's own joy is swallowed up in the well-being of another. The motive of serving (personal joy) is found *within* the blessing that his service brings about for the life of another person. To say it another way, to love Jesus is to serve Him; to serve Him is to serve others. God Himself declares, "'I am the LORD who practices love, justice, and righteousness in the earth. For in these things I delight,' declares the LORD (Jeremiah 9:24). If God Himself rejoices in bringing about love, justice, and righteousness, then we throw ourselves in the accomplishment of His delight when we serve in these ways.

---

68 Jonathan Edwards, quoted by John Piper in Desiring God: Meditations of a Christian Hedonist. (Sisters OR: Multnomah Publishers, 2003) p. 110.

Since true joy can be obtained in pouring oneself out for others, the Confession upholds and praises civil service. Specifically, the Confession mentions the following ways that believers can participate in civil affairs with clean hearts and clear consciences:

1. By working towards the Kingdom ends of peace and justice on the earth. In this way believers stand in line with the great "social justice" advocates of their day: the Old Testament prophets such as Amos, Isaiah, Joel and others who decried unjust social barriers in their own contexts. In our American culture, working towards fair wages and educational opportunities for all, maintaining fair justice systems, and opposing evils such as abortion and pornography are all valuable contributions to civil life.

2. By participating in *just* wars (WCF 23.2). Here, one could wish that the Confession spoke further on defining the parameters of a "just war."

3. By protecting true and spiritual worship (WCF 23.3). Believers must be especially vigilant to work towards the goal of the freedom of Christian believers to engage in public and private worship without the undue limitations of governmental interjection. (In America, believers would do well to pray for their brothers and sisters abroad who do not have these precious freedoms).

4. By praying for our civil leaders who are under tremendous pressure to make complicated and crucial decisions that affect many thousands of people (WCF 23.4). This is perhaps one of the most profound ways that believers can affect the world around them. It must not go without saying that voting is a moral imperative for free people. We must vote for those individuals that will best promote the kingdom fruits of love, joy, peace, patience, kindness, goodness, gentleness and self-control (Galatians 5:22) as well as for policies, laws, and statutes that best embody these ideals.

5. By paying our taxes promptly and with joyful hearts (WCF 23.4). These taxes serve to provide our own people with roads, schools, educators, libraries, and a defense force for our protection, among other things. The giving of our taxes should be done gladly and honestly.

6. Finally, as an act of worship, we are called to submit ourselves willingly to the authority of the governmental leaders *to the extent that their policies do not cause a believer to sin or compromise her conscience* (see Acts 5:29). Ultimately, however, as Peter and the other apostles learned, our highest loyalty must always be to the King of Kings.

The Confession Chapter Twenty-four:

Of Marriage and Divorce

1. Marriage is to be between one man and one woman: neither is it lawful for any man to have more than one wife, nor for any woman to have more than one husband at the same time.

2. Marriage was ordained for the mutual help of husband and wife; for the increase of mankind with a legitimate issue, and of the Church with a holy seed; and for preventing of uncleanness.

3. It is lawful for all sorts of people to marry who are able with judgment to give their consent. Yet it is the duty of Christians to marry only in the Lord. And, therefore, such as profess the true reformed religion should not marry with infidels, Papists, or other idolaters: neither should such as are godly be unequally yoked, by marrying with such as are notoriously wicked in their life, or maintain damnable heresies.

4. Marriage ought not to be within the degrees of consanguinity or affinity forbidden in the Word; nor can such incestuous marriages ever be made lawful by any law of man, or consent of parties, so as those persons may live together, as man and wife. The man may not marry any of his wife's kindred nearer in blood than he may of his own, nor the woman of her husband's kindred nearer in blood than of her own.

5. Adultery or fornication, committed after a contract, being detected before marriage, gives just occasion to the innocent party to dissolve that contract. In the case of adultery after marriage, it is lawful for the innocent party to sue out a divorce, and after the divorce to marry another, as if the offending party were dead.

6. Although the corruption of man be such as is apt to study arguments, unduly to put asunder those whom God has joined together in marriage; yet nothing but adultery, or such willful desertion as can no way be remedied by the Church or civil magistrate, is cause sufficient of dissolving the bond of marriage; wherein a public and orderly course of proceeding is to be observed; and the persons concerned in it, not left to their own wills and discretion in their own case.

Prepare in Prayer

God, no matter what our marital state may be at the moment, let our greatest love always be reserved for You. May we never lose our "first love." In Christ's name we pray, amen.

Into the Scriptures

Read Genesis 2 and Ephesians 5.

Reach Back

On the matters discussed above in chapter twenty-two pertaining to marriage and divorce, the Confession is shockingly relevant. It is with stark clarity—increasingly uncommon in our day—that the Confession stands unflinchingly upon the biblical understanding of marriage. In almost every one of the situations prohibited above, our culture is moving towards an "anything goes" policy in regard to sexual union— especially the stipulation that marriage *must* be limited to one man and one woman (WCF 24.1). Just a cursory glance at the items listed above reveals how cutting the Confession remains: the forbidding of a plurality of sexual partners (WCF 24.1), a condemnation of intermarriage between Christians and unbelievers (WCF 24.3), a rounding denunciation of adultery and fornication outside the marriage covenant (WCF 24.5), a formidable caution against divorce for mere irreconcilable differences (WCF 24.6); all of these warnings sting like salt in a wound to a culture that embraces any and all forms of sexual expression. Our modern American notion, that the only restriction on human sexuality is that it must be between consenting partners, is clearly exposed to be far off the mark, and dreadfully dangerous.

We note here that marriage is another form of "common grace" given by God to all of mankind (WCF 24.3). That is, unbelievers too are given this gift; it is not restricted by God for believers only. Just as God allows all of humanity to eat from the fields of the earth, to be fed by its waters, to enjoy fresh air, and to produce offspring, so also God allows even the unconverted to be enfolded in the grace of matrimony. Nevertheless, the biblical admonition that believers ought not to be unequally yoked together with unbelievers (2 Corinthians 6:14) in marriage is maintained.

While much has been written on the sanctity of Christian marriage that cannot be reproduced here as a matter of space considerations, it is the opinion of this writer that the Confession is refreshing, challenging, and thoroughly welcome as a critique to the mindless rhetoric that is consistently spewing from our television sets, magazine racks, and internet pages. If ever there was a practical, down-to-earth doctrine that ought to set apart the lives of Christian believers from contemporary society, our doctrine of marriage should be the one. Above all, marriage ought to be the most defended and highly regarded of human institutions since it is expressly compared with the relationship of Jesus Christ to His Church (Ephesians 5:22-23).

Gaze Upwards

What does the gift of marriage teach us about the nature of God? According to Ephesians 5:25-33 it teaches us much. In this passage, Paul instructs husbands that their love for their wives ought to be like that of Jesus Christ. While many believers today shrink at the thought of wives being instructed to "submit" to their husbands as commanded in vs. 22, it is the men who are given the more difficult charge! They are commanded to love their wives "as Christ loved the Church." Here in a metaphor from holy matrimony, Paul teaches us several things that Jesus Christ did for us that are to be modeled by Christian husbands:

1) "He gave Himself up for her..." Jesus Christ gave up his own physical body on the cross and endured unimaginable spiritual agony as He bought the redemption of the elect through His atoning death on the cross. In the same way, not only should husbands be literally willing to die for their wives, but they ought to be ready to give up many of their comforts, desires, and aspirations in order to sustain their wives' willing affection. A husband's ultimate goal is his wife's protection and betterment.

2) "...That He might sanctify her." Jesus died not only to save the Church, but also to make believers holy and to draw them closer to God. While Jesus' death imputed His own righteousness to the Church—as though clothing her in His own garments of holiness—it is also His desire to teach the church to *live in a holy manner* as well. Husbands are likewise commanded to put their wives' spiritual health on the top of their list

of absolute priorities. It is to be among his utmost responsibilities to ensure that his wife, as well as any children, are growing in their faith daily, especially in their knowledge of the Word (vs. 26) in order that their spiritual growth is steadily climbing like beautiful flowers in a garden trellis.

3) "...that He might present the Church to Himself in splendor, without spot or wrinkle...and without blemish." Lastly, Jesus Christ undertook to present His bride, the Church, as beautiful and radiant. His goal is to remove any impurities, inconsistencies, and imperfections in her character. This is a quite a challenge for husbands as this takes the infilling of the Holy Spirit to accomplish. Thus, earthly husbands cannot fulfill this task as fully as can Jesus Christ with His Church. Husbands cannot purify their wives directly, but only serve as open vessels which the Spirit can use in His work. Nevertheless, husbands can beautify their wives by uplifting them, complementing them, treating them as valuable beyond limit, and by refusing such condescending behavior as cutting remarks, biting criticism, and inflexible perfectionism.

Step Out—Purity of Heart

John Ortberg, in his book The Life You've Always Wanted, records some strange facts about food and contamination. He notes that the Food and Drug Administration has certain requirements for exactly how many contaminants are acceptable and how much is "too much." For example,

> Apple Butter: If the mold count is 12 percent or more, if it averages four rodent hairs per 100 grams or more, if it averages five or more whole insects (not counting mites, aphids, or scale insects) per 100 grams, the FDA will pull it from the shelves... Coffee Beans: (Caffeine addicts beware!) Coffee beans will get withdrawn from the market if an average of 10 percent or more are insect-infested or if there is one live insect in each of two or more immediate containers...Mushrooms: Mushrooms cannot be sold if there is an average of 20 or more maggots of any size per 15 grams of dried mushrooms.[69]

This disgusting illustration brings me to some interesting questions: How pure is your thought life? How many lustful thoughts would it take for you

---

69 John Ortberg. The Life You've Always Wanted. (Grand Rapids MI: Zondervan, 1997) p. 168-169.

to consider your mind "impure?" Clearly, God expects more than this type of accounting practice when it comes to the spiritual purity of our hearts and minds.

Not only is our theology of marriage an essential element that ought to set Christians apart from our unbelieving world and irreligious neighbors, but the marriage covenant itself can be seen as a reforming discipline of spiritual formation! Nothing brings about humility, confronts our self-centeredness, forces us to rely upon another human being, and draws to the surface our character flaws, like the institution of marriage. Marriage encourages fidelity and sexual purity as both partners restrain their lusts and commit their physical expressions of love for the other person. Marriage forces us to be cognizant of the immediate needs of another human being besides ourselves. Marriage allows us to come to the throne of grace in a lasting Christian fellowship of two. Marriage forces us to bite our tongue when we are tempted to speak. In fact the spiritual disciplines requisite in marriage are innumerable.

How do you view your relationship with your spouse as a mile-marker of your spiritual growth? Do you see your various trials and disagreements with him or her as obnoxious obstacles, or is it possible to see those same challenges as God's chisels to remove your impatience, dullness of heart, and self-centeredness? Do you appreciate your spouse for the benefits that he or she brings upon you (i.e. a paycheck, a reliable meal, a clean house) or have you learned to love another person for their own intrinsic worth?

But now, what of single believers? Yes, they too can strive towards purity of heart as they keep themselves pure for a potential future mate, or else submit themselves to an exclusive relationship with Jesus Christ. The Apostle Paul for instance, wrote to the Corinthian believers that singleness was a *gift from God* that allowed an individual to remain uncommonly devoted to the service of the Lord (1 Corinthians 7). Paul is in excellent company alongside his master Jesus Christ; both chose to remain single so that their hearts could focus exclusively on the glory of God. For those who have not yet found a mate, or who perhaps due to the sovereign plan of God *will not*, purity of heart is a spiritual goal that ranks among the most decorated values of the Christian life.

The Confession Chapter Twenty-five:

Of the Church

1. The catholic or universal Church, which is invisible, consists of the whole number of the elect, that have been, are, or shall be gathered into one, under Christ the head thereof; and is the spouse, the body, the fullness of Him that fills all in all.

2. The visible Church, which is also catholic or universal under the gospel (not confined to one nation as before under the law), consists of all those throughout the world that profess the true religion, together with their children; and is the Kingdom of the Lord Jesus Christ; the house and family of God, through which men are ordinarily saved and union with which is essential to their best growth and service.

3. Unto this catholic and visible Church, Christ has given the ministry, oracles, and ordinances of God, for the gathering and perfecting of the saints, in this life, to the end of the world; and does by his own presence and Spirit, according to his promise, make them effectual thereunto.

4. This universal Church has been sometimes more, sometimes less, visible. And particular Churches, which are members thereof, are more or less pure, according as the doctrine of the gospel is taught and embraced, ordinances administered, and public worship performed more or less purely in them.

5. The purest Churches under heaven are subject both to mixture and error: and some have so degenerated as to become apparently no Churches of Christ. Nevertheless, there shall be always a Church on earth, to worship God according to his will.

6. There is no other head of the Church but the Lord Jesus Christ: nor can the Pope of Rome[70] in any sense be head thereof; but is that Antichrist, that man of sin and son of perdition, that exalts himself in the Church against Christ, and all that is called God.

Prepare in Prayer

God, as we study today, let certain names and faces of those with whom we worship rise to our awareness. As we study the doctrine of the "Body of Christ," let us be mindful of those who need You in this very hour. Amen.

Into the Scriptures

Read Romans 16 and 1 Corinthians 12:12-31.

Reach Back

Dietrich Bonhoeffer once said, "By pursuing sanctification outside the Church we are trying to pronounce ourselves holy."[71] What did he mean by that? He meant, in the very least, that we continually need other believers to uphold us in our common pursuit of God through His Son Jesus Christ. If we forsake this gift, we are displaying our spiritual arrogance.

To understand the significance of the Church, we must prune off several layers of misunderstanding before we can drink of its sweetness. First of all, the Church Universal is not simply a building. While most of us speak of going "to church," it is more accurate to say that *we are the Church.* The Church is composed not of blocks and mortar, glass and drywall, but of human beings: souls who delight in their Lord Jesus Christ above all things. Secondly, the Church is not limited to any one particular or local worshipping body, as authentic and sincere as they may be. The word "church" should not be used exclusively to identify one locality of believers among others. The Confession here is very clear that the Church Universal is "the whole

---

70 We note the strictness by which the Westminster Confession labels the Pope of the Roman Catholic Church as the "antichrist." Here we must understand the historical vehemence with which our forbearers scored the abuses of Roman teaching. Since we have chosen to adhere to the original text of the WCF as closely as possible, we have left this reference intact to make the reader aware of its original wording. Readers should note that the WCF has been amended by several of the denominations that still use this confession to this day. Among those who adhere to an *amended* version of the Confession, removing or altering this phrase, are the Presbyterian Church (USA), the Evangelical Presbyterian Church, the Orthodox Presbyterian Church, and the Presbyterian Church in America.

71 Dietrich Bonhoeffer. The Cost of Discipleship. (New York NY: Touchstone, 1995) p. 280.

number of the elect" (25.1). This number would include not only those who are alive today, *but also those who have already passed on to eternity.* Many feel confident that their own particular denomination comprises the fullest expression of the "Church." They propose that "true Christians" are those who are Roman Catholic, or Baptist, or Presbyterian, or Eastern Orthodox, or Pentecostal, or whatever. *This brand of sectarianism is emphatically denied by the writers of the Westminster Confession.*

The Church, while often used synonymously for a denomination, is much greater than a single strand of Christian heritage. While many sects of Christianity would put just such a proposition forward regarding the superiority of their own label, Reformed Christianity is not among them. The Westminster Confession is very clear that the Church—the Body of Christ—is the total number of all true believers, past, present, and future, and stands above geography, history, language, tradition, heritage, and worship style.

The Westminster Confession draws a helpful distinction between the church visible and the church invisible. This distinction enables us to remember that there are many who may participate openly or "visibly" in and among the church *who have never truly loved the Lord God as their Savior and Redeemer.* Never having confessed their sins or sought conversion, they stand alone upon their own merit and will reap the eternal consequences that their sins demand. It is to these types of people that Jesus said "go away from me, for I never knew you" (Matthew 7:21-23). At the same time, there may be many people among the truly redeemed that were rejected by the established church of their day. These will doubtlessly stand among the saved in the Day of Judgment. One might think of martyrs such as John Wycliffe and John Huss—the latter of which was burned at the stake—who were rejected by the visible church of their day for taking unpopular stands that today we would consider not only orthodox but essential.

The word that we use today, "church," is the term that is usually used to translate the Greek word "ekklesia," which literally means "the called out ones." Thus, when God considers the whole sum of believers, He sees the entire corpus of the redeemed (those whom He has called) and marks them as His beloved. This vision is pictured beautifully in Revelation 7:9-10 which reads,

> After this I looked, and behold, a great multitude that no one could number, from every nation, from all tribes and peoples and

languages, standing before the Lamb, clothed in white robes, with palm branches in their hands, and crying out with a loud voice, 'Salvation belongs to our God who sits on the throne, and to the Lamb!'

Search Inwards

St. Augustine is often cited as the one who said something like, "The church may be a whore, but she is still my mother." Why would one of the theological fathers of the Christian faith say something dreadful like that? For one thing Augustine was well aware of the fact that the Church has always found ways to stain the robes of faithfulness that she wears. She is never perfect. She rarely evangelizes the way that she ought. She hardly defends her doctrines the way she ought. She barely cares for the hurting and the wounded the way she ought. And in many ways, that is exactly what is to be expected! After all, if the Church is composed of *people* as we mentioned above, then we cannot expect her to be perfect at all. There is no better epistle in the New Testament to demonstrate this fact than the Corinthian correspondence. Here we see a local church in Corinth with a myriad of problems: sexual immorality, raucous proceedings at the Lord's Table, disordered worship; Corinth had them all! And yet in the twelfth chapter of his first letter, Paul describes the Body of Christ, the Church with the beautiful language of the human body. Each believer represents an instrumental and integrated part of the whole. And yet, when all of the various components work harmoniously, the Body is a wonder of wonders.

Since the Confession is clear to point out that "union with the Church is essential to (our) best growth" (WCF 25.2) it is a tragedy that so many believers are so condemnatory towards the church. Many view the church as irrelevant, outmoded, and boring. In response to this conception, numerous "parachurch" ministries have sprung up to replace traditional membership in churches. Many more even view the Church as an obstacle to be avoided on their path towards authentic spiritual growth! True, she may be broken in so many ways. She may never have the right programs that we desire, her services may be offered at all the wrong times, the music will often not be the style we prefer, the pastors will doubtlessly be prone to error—and yet she is still our mother.

Look into your own heart and find some of the areas where you may have been overly hurtful or critical of your own local church. Have you spoken against the pastor unjustly for his teachings, manners, timeliness, or communication gaps? Have you treated the staff as though they were your servants, just waiting for your next order to be handed down? Have you red-penned the 1% of errors in the bulletin and neglected the 99% of accurate content? Have you been unfair about the church's worship services, or music styles, or children's programs? If so, take some time this week to fall onto your face in worship of the God of the Church. After all, the church may have failed you in innumerable ways, but has she not also preached the gospel to you? Translated and read the Bible to you? Baptized you and your children? Catechized your teens and young people? Has she not preserved the Creeds on your behalf? Has she not sent missionaries oversees when you yourself did not go? Study the book of 1 Corinthians a little more deeply this week, and you may find that the words of Augustine are relevant in your own situation: each church may be corrupt to some degree, but she is still our mother.

Step Out—Intercessory Prayer
Romans chapter sixteen is a beautiful passage, not for its depth of content, but because it is so earthy and so grounded. Most of the chapter is a list of people and acquaintances that Paul knew; it even sounds like a church directory! There is "Phoebe a servant of the church..." and also "Prisca and Aquila, my fellow workers in Christ Jesus." There is "Andronicus and Junia, my kinsmen and my fellow prisoners..." and also "Persis who has worked hard in the Lord." All told, there are some 26 individuals named specifically by the Apostle. And the stunning fact is this—Paul has not even visited this church before!

Are you able to articulate the individuals in your fellowship who serve so whole-heartedly for the Lord in the same way that Paul has done for the church in Rome? Can you name the leaders of your church who need your prayer and service? Notice the way Paul prayerfully but specifically moves through the people of the church, noting their special gifts, talents, and abilities, as well as their primary contributions to the church. This is a model for the type of person-to-person relationships we ought to have within our own congregations.

Whenever we pray specifically and individually for our brothers and sisters in Christ, this is called "intercessory prayer." Simply defined, intercessory prayer is the lifting up of the specific needs of the people of God to His throne of grace. Many people throughout Christian history have found that the best way to do intercessory prayer is by making lists of those around us and praying through those lists daily or weekly. For instance, we might choose to keep a pad of paper near our computer and simply write down the challenges, joys, and concerns of those near to our hearts as we receive their email correspondences. For myself, I purchased a black hardbound journal that I keep on my desk in which to write down requests to pray through on regular intervals.

The more specific we can make our requests, the more intimately we can acquire the heart of Jesus for His hurting people. General prayers such as "God bless the sick and hurting" can be improved many times over by entering into the struggles of those who are actually hurting, by rehearsing these requests daily. General requests like "God bless the missionaries" are fine, provided that from time to time we enter in to the pain and pleasure of specific missionaries whom we know in the field. Remember: the point of prayer is not so that we can inform God of what is going on down here on Earth. He already knows that; He is omniscient. The point of prayer is so that His own people can learn to develop the heart of Jesus for His Kingdom.

The Confession Chapter Twenty-six:

Of the Communion of the Saints

1. All saints that are united to Jesus Christ their head, by his Spirit and by faith, have fellowship with him in his graces, sufferings, death, resurrection, and glory: and, being united to one another in love, they have communion in each other's gifts and graces, and are obliged to the performance of such duties, public and private, as to conduce to their mutual good, both in the inward and outward man.

2. Saints by profession, are bound to maintain a holy fellowship and communion in the worship of God, and in performing such other spiritual services as tend to their mutual edification; as also in relieving each other in outward things, according to their several abilities and necessities. Which communion, as God offers opportunity, is to be extended unto all those who, in every place, call upon the name of the Lord Jesus.

3. This communion which the saints have with Christ, does not make them in any wise partakers of the substance of the Godhead, or to be equal with Christ in any respect: either of which to affirm, is impious and blasphemous. Nor does their communion one with another as saints, take away or infringe the title or property which each man has in his goods and possessions.

Prepare in Prayer

God, this section of the Confession reminds us just how important the fellowship of the believers is for our lives. Please do not let us forget that we cannot walk the journey of faith alone. In Jesus' name we pray, amen.

Into the Scriptures

Read Psalm 133 and Philippians 1.

Reach Back

We noted in the last chapter that the Church consists of *people* rather than property. Here, the Westminster Confession stresses the mutual joys, as well as the mutual obligations, that Church membership entails.

First for the joys. While it will never be perfectly accomplished here on earth, the Church is primarily a place of Christian love. There ought to be no place else in the world where believers feel the mutual support of other sojourners as they do in the Church. Believers pray for each other, grieve with each other, visit each other when sick, and celebrate together the joys in life such as baptisms, weddings, graduations, and new births. More than that, in the fellowship of believers we enjoy each other's gifts, talents, and abilities. Inasmuch as each person in the fellowship shares different "graces"—some preach, some pray, some sing, many teach, still others paint, act, dance, or play music—the Body of Christ becomes a living tapestry of human faith and benevolence. This is true not only in good times but also during times of trial. In the midst of suffering and hardship, the Body of Christ is at its most intimate. Special giftings in mourning and comforting can be found within the united fellowship of believers as reliably as the spring brings rain. All of these blessings are summed up on the words "they have the communion of each other's gifts and graces" (WCF 26.1).

And yet the Church also shares a mutual *responsibility* for each other's well being. Believers are expected to support each other, defend each other, pray for each other, and even rebuke each other. Like a steel chain that is only strong when each link does its share of the burden bearing, the Church is at its most effective when each individual lives up to his or her own responsibility for the health of the body. In the New Testament, there are more than 15 specific responsibilities commanded for the Body of Christ to perform on behalf of the whole. We can think of them as the "one anothers" of Scripture. A partial list is included below:

> Love: No one has ever seen God; if we love one another, God abides in us and his love is perfected in us (1 John 4:12. cf. 1 Thessalonians 3:12).

> Humility: Likewise, you who are younger, be subject to the elders. Clothe yourselves, all of you, with humility toward one another, for God opposes the proud but gives grace to the humble (1 Peter 5:5).

Service: As each has received a gift, use it to serve one another, as good stewards of God's varied grace (1 Peter 4:10).

Hospitality: Show hospitality to one another without grumbling (1 Peter 4:9).

Confession: Therefore, confess your sins to one another and pray for one another, that you may be healed (James 5:16).

Meekness: Do not grumble against one another, brothers, so that you may not be judged; behold, the Judge is standing at the door (James 5:9).

Encouragement: Let us consider how to stir one another to love and good works, not neglecting to meet together, as is the habit of some, but encouraging one another, and all the more as you see the Day drawing near (Hebrews 10:24-25).

Teaching: I myself am satisfied about you, my brothers, that you yourselves are full of goodness, filled with all knowledge and able to instruct one another (Romans 15:14).

Patience: So then, my brothers, when you come together to eat, wait for one another (1 Corinthians 11:33).

Comforting: Aim for restoration, comfort one another, agree with one another, live in peace; and the God of love and peace will be with you (2 Corinthians 13:11).

Kindness: Be kind to one another, tenderhearted, forgiving one another, as God in Christ forgave you (Ephesians 4:32).

Submission: ...submitting to one another out of reverence for Christ (Ephesians 5:21).

Admonishment: Let the word of Christ dwell in you richly, teaching and admonishing one another in all wisdom, singing psalms and hymns and spiritual songs, with thankfulness in your hearts to God (Colossians 3:16).

Building up: Therefore encourage one another and build one another up, just as you are doing (1 Thessalonians 5:11).

Doing good: See that no one repays anyone evil for evil, but always seek to do good to one another and to everyone (1 Thessalonians 5:15).

Search Inward

I remember a time when my wife Kelly and I badly needed a new vehicle. Our old family van was beaten and bruised. With scores of miles etched on the odometer, the poor mule was dented and road weary. One individual from our church even noticed the tread on the tires dissipating and decided to act. He shared the concern for our vehicle with his small group. Another man in the study spoke up and mentioned that he was intending to sell his mildly used van later that month. All of the sudden an idea was born: what if the whole Bible study chipped in and purchased the newer model from him? And so the plan sprung into action. Within a few weeks, several thousand dollars had been gathered, and the church purchased our family a newer vehicle when we needed it most and could afford it the least! This was truly a time when the love of the church was as real to us as the air we breathe.

Look into your own heart for a moment. When was the last time that you participated in this kind of a benevolent scheme? Have you ever concocted a plan of service that could be described, not as a "random act of kindness" as the popular bumper sticker says, but rather a *calculated* act of kindness?" Look over that list of the "one anothers" of Scripture a second time. Could there be several commands listed there that you need to apply immediately and intentionally in the next week? Think first about widows and the elderly in your congregation. A visit to their home or hospital room could mean more than you know. Think secondly about single mothers. Could you help them with cleaning their gutters or trimming their trees? Painting their house, or tuning their vehicle? Think thirdly of the young people; which of them could use your mentorship?

But the deeper question to consider is this: what is it inside of your heart that holds you back from doing these things naturally and freely? If the Spirit reigns inside of your heart, shouldn't these types of actions become second nature to you? If there is something that causes you to hold back the floodgates of your participation in the Body of Christ, confess it now to the Lord.

Gaze Upwards

What can the nature of God teach us about Christian fellowship? Surprisingly much! Christian fellowship on earth ought to reflect the perfect unity of the Trinity in the heavenly places. In fact we learn directly from the persons of the Trinity several specific ways that we can honor each other and lift each other up. Notice the ways in Scripture that each person in the godhead (Father, Son, and Holy Spirit) honors the others. For instance the Father loves the Son (John 15:9) and glorifies Him (John 17:5), the Son obeys the Father and glorifies Him in return (John 14:13, 31; 17:1), the Spirit is sent by the Father and the Son and yields glory to both (John 14:16, 26; 15:26). In this marvelous, eternal relationship we see the manner in which each person of the Trinity is prized by the others for His intrinsic worth, yet all the while maintaining the distinctions that make each unique.

Step Out—Admitting Brokenness

Perhaps one of the reasons that Christian fellowship is perceived by some to be bland, shallow, and superficial is the failure for believers to share the reality of their *brokenness* with one another. Far too often believers are concerned with protecting their reputation among their peers rather than actually sharing their sufferings as one body.

Remember that the Body of Christ is just that, a body. We have all had the experience of suffering through a physical wound somewhere—a sore in our mouths, a twisted ankle, or even kidney stones. Let's use the example of a paper cut for discussion. Isn't it amazing how the whole body must work together to compensate for the wounded part? Instantly, the brain sends signals for the other parts to help alleviate the trauma. The nerves send signals back to the brain to report the pain. White blood cells are commissioned to fight any infection. Soon we begin to notice how the rest of the fingers on the hand must compensate for that wounded one's usual work load—even if the hurt one is just the pinky! The body does not cut off the wounded part, but rather rushes to its aid! Since Paul's favorite metaphor for the fellowship of believers is the body, how much more should the Body of believers rush to lift one another up when hurting or wounded.

Whether our wounds are spiritual, emotional, or physical, believers ought to be willing to *share* their deeper sufferings instead of covering them up. I knew of a family of believers who found out that their teen daughter was pregnant. Unfortunately, rather than seeking the comfort, forgiveness, and confraternity of the Body of Christ, the domineering father chose to conceal the sin by commanding for the daughter to have an abortion. His reputation was far too valuable to accept the embarrassment a child out of wedlock might bring. He chose a worse sin to plaster up another. Thus, by hiding the wound rather than dressing it, the pain grew much deeper and the hurting of the entire family became worse than before. The family has been trying to hide this growing, open cavity of suffering ever since.

Are you trying to hide your suffering with "lipstick and rouge" rather than seeking the healing presence of the fellowship? If so, you will find that the pain will only grow worse due to neglect. When we treat the *symptoms* (the outward, unavoidable expressions) of our suffering by hiding or denying them, rather than the treating the *cause* (the root or the source) by restoring our relationships with others and with God, we will find ourselves on a terrible downward spiral. Search your own life today. What have you been trying to hide, rather than letting the rest of the body begin to heal? Perhaps you might seek out an older mentor in the faith with whom you can share your battle scars. Admitting our brokenness to one another goes a long way in strengthening the Body of Christ.

The Confession Chapter Twenty-seven:

Of the Sacraments

1. Sacraments are holy signs and seals of the covenant of grace, immediately instituted by God, to represent Christ and his benefits, and to confirm our interest in him: as also to put a visible difference between those that belong unto the Church, and the rest of the world; and solemnly to engage them to the service of God in Christ, according to his Word.

2. There is in every sacrament a spiritual relation, or sacramental union, between the sign and the thing signified; whence it comes to pass that the names and effects of the one are attributed to the other.

3. The grace which is exhibited in or by the sacraments, rightly used, is not conferred by any power in them; neither does the efficacy of a sacrament depend upon the piety or intention of him that does administer it, but upon the work of the Spirit, and the word of institution, which contains, together with a precept authorizing the use thereof, a promise of benefit to worthy receivers.

4. There be only two sacraments ordained by Christ our Lord in the gospels, that is to say, Baptism and the Supper of the Lord: neither or which may be dispensed by any but a minister of the Word, lawfully ordained.

5. The sacraments of the Old Testament, in regard of the spiritual things thereby signified and exhibited, were, for substance, the same with those of the New.

Prepare in Prayer

God, we praise You today that You have given us the dual gifts of the Lord's Supper and Baptism. We pray that today's study will prepare us to receive these gifts with greater reverence the next time we celebrate them in Church. In Jesus' name we ask these things, amen.

Into the Scriptures
Read Matthew 28:18-20 and Luke 22:14-23.

Reach Back
We will be very careful here to define and expand the Westminster Confession's understanding of the sacraments. R.C. Sproul contributes to our understanding of the term,

> The word *sacrament* historically was used for something sacred. The Latin term *sacramentum* was used to translate the New Testament word for mystery. In a broad sense all religious rites and ceremonies were called sacraments. In time, the *sacrament* took on a more precise and narrow meaning. A sacrament became defined as a *visible sign* by which God offers His promise of grace in an outward form. Outward signs seal and confirm the covenant promises of God.[72]

In step with the Reformed tradition's understanding of a "sacrament," the Confession carefully describes baptism and the Lord's Supper as "signs and seals" which signify spiritual realities much greater than the earthly means used to communicate them. Both baptism and communion (Reformed theology holds to only *two* sacraments) use earthly symbols— water, bread, and wine—to convey the spiritual graces that have been given to the Church through the life, death, and resurrection of Jesus Christ. Because God created the world and declared it good (Genesis 1:31) it pleased Him to use these created elements as tangible seals of God's actions in salvation through Christ.

The word "seal" is instructive. It could mean both the wax end-cap used to enclose a proper document or scroll (such as a king might use to ensure the safe delivery of an official document) or else the signet stamp of his majesty's authority upon that document. In both cases, we find the metaphor valid: baptism and communion have been instituted personally by the Lord Jesus Christ (see the readings for today); they bear His

---

72 R. C. Sproul. *Essential Truths of the Christian Faith.* (Wheaton IL: Tyndale House, 1992) p. 223.

divine authority, and convey the reality of salvation through physical reminders of His own works on our behalf.

The Westminster Confession is right to point out that the sacraments are not made effective by the elements themselves (as though they were some powerful amulets). Nor are they made effective by the words of the administrator of the sacrament, as though they were some magical incantation that had to be performed exactly. Nor is their power found in the holiness of the pastor or priest who performs the ceremony. No, the power in the sacraments is in the actions of *God alone* who affects His saving plan through the Holy Spirit and through Christ.

Sproul continues, "The sacraments are nonverbal forms of communication. They were never intended to stand alone without reference to the Word of God."[73] For this reason on the occasions that we celebrate the sacraments of the Lord's Table and Baptism, we must be careful that vigilant preaching and teaching of their Scriptural meaning attends the event itself.

Gaze Upwards

The fact that God has given us the gift of the sacraments ought to again alert us to His mercy. Of all of the holy characteristics that comprise God's personality, (justice, love, transcendence, eternality, self-existence, omnipotence, immutability etc.) His mercy and imminence are prominently displayed in the sacraments. Every time that we baptize an infant or adult convert into the Body of Christ, or partake of the Lord's Supper by consuming bread and wine, we are reminded of the fact that we have a God who not only stands above His creation and is timeless, but who also *condescends to the pitiable condition of His fallen creatures.* In baptism, the covenant community is reminded that Jesus Christ has died and risen to new life and offers the gifts of forgiveness, justification, and eternal life to all those that respond to His gracious call to "follow me" (John 1:43). In the Lord's Supper we are invited to take an intimate look at the suffering Christ endured to attain our salvation through His death on the cross. Here, we contemplate both His broken body and His bloody outpouring in the act of atonement on the cross. As we participate in these great acts of mercy, being cleansed by the waters of baptism (and even enjoying the experience of others being so washed) and also by physically consuming the elements of the Lord's

---

73 Ibid.

Table, let us never forget to praise God for His condescending mercy that approaches us when we could not approach Him.

Search Inwards

What thoughts, feelings, and emotions go through your mind as you participate in the Lord's Supper, or perhaps watch a baptism occur in your congregation? Do you make any extra preparations for your heart that you would not do on a regular Sunday? As you prepare your heart to receive the bread and cup, do you confess your known sins, as Paul instructs? For as Paul writes, "Let a person examine himself, then, and so eat of the bread and drink of the cup" (1 Corinthians 11:28). As you walk forward to the table to receive these gifts, you may choose to recount the path to Calvary that Christ took on your behalf. As you receive each element, the bread first and then the wine, contemplate what each represents.

As you watch a baptism unfold in your worshipping community, do you renew for yourself the vows that the candidate before you has taken? What response do you owe to the candidate now that he or she has made this commitment in front of the people of God? Think of the water: what does it represent? Imagine the Holy Spirit washing over the people as the water is administered to the candidate. Thank God for the death and resurrection that happens as we are born again to new life in conversion (John 3:1-8).

We must avoid the danger of allowing the symbols to become meaningless in our own lives. For this reason, we must consciously refuse to allow them to be emptied of their spiritual value. We empty them when we routinely step through them like hoops. We honor them when we allow our spirits to meet Christ at the sharing of the sacraments.

Step Out—Covenant Renewal

Both sacraments today have this in common: they are occasions of covenant renewal for the gathered people of God. It the past fifty years of evangelicalism, it has become commonplace to speak of a "personal relationship with God." While Christianity is without any doubt a personal relationship with God through Christ, it is actually much more than that. It is also a *corporate* relationship with God.

While many expressions of Christianity today emphasize the deeply pious import of the sacraments—some make them downright *individualistic*—

Reformed Christianity sees both of the sacraments as much more than any one individual person expressing his or her faith. We view these occasions as corporate expressions of dependence, adoration, worship, and thanksgiving to the Redeemer.

If one were to undertake a serious study of the covenants of Scripture, he would find that each of the primary covenants in the Bible are made with specific reference to a gathered community. The covenants of God with Noah, Abraham, Moses, David, and the New Covenant (without any exception) always come with language that includes the whole family. They consistently refer to "descendants," "generations to come," "children," "offspring," "seed," or other such terminology.[74] The signs that baptism and the Lord's Supper replaced from the Old Testament (circumcision and the Passover respectively) were also viewed in Israel's history as occasions of *corporate* or national covenant renewal. In other words, every time the outward sign is experienced as a community, the entire corpus of worshippers is affirming once again, "You will be our God and we will be Your people."

Michael Horton writes,

> The problem with the pietistic version of the Lord's Supper (the individualistic view) is that in its obsession with the individual's inner piety, it loses much of the import of the feast as the sacred meal that actually binds us to Christ **and to each other**...It is no wonder, then, that there is diminished interest in frequent communion (emphasis added).[75]

As we receive each of the sacraments, a meal that has been prepared for the Church and a washing that has been done for us, both of which point us to the grace of Christ, let us not forget that these signs also point strongly to the new community God has made out of us. God has taken a bunch of broken individuals, and made them into a new family. At the Table and the Font we renew His covenant of grace each time we share the elements before us. We will speak more about this in the next two chapters.

---

74 A sampling of this "generations to come" language for each of the major covenants can be found in texts such as the following: Genesis 3:15; 6:18-22; 9:8-17; 15:9-21; 17:1-27; Exodus 19-24; 2 Samuel 7:5-16; Psalm 89:30; 132:12, Jeremiah 32:39; and Acts 2:39.

75 Michael Horton. Introducing Covenant Theology. (Grand Rapids MI: Baker, 2006) p. 160.

The Confession Chapter Twenty-eight:

Of Baptism

1. Baptism is a sacrament of the New Testament, ordained by Jesus Christ, not only for the solemn admission of the party baptized into the visible Church, but also to be unto him a sign and seal of the covenant of grace, or his ingrafting into Christ, of regeneration, of remission of sins, and of his giving up unto God, through Jesus Christ, to walk in newness of life: which sacrament is, by Christ's own appointment, to be continued in his Church until the end of the world.

2. The outward element to be used in the sacrament is water, wherewith the party is to be baptized in the name of the Father, and of the Son, and of the Holy Ghost, by a minister of the gospel, lawfully called thereunto.

3. Dipping of the person into the water is not necessary; but baptism is rightly administered by pouring or sprinkling water upon the person.

4. Not only those that do actually profess faith in and obedience unto Christ, but also the infants of one or both believing parents are to be baptized.

5. Although it be a great sin to condemn or neglect this ordinance, yet grace and salvation are not so inseparably annexed unto it as that no person can be regenerated or saved without it, or that all that are baptized are undoubtedly regenerated.

6. The efficacy of baptism is not tied to that moment of time wherein it is administered; yet, notwithstanding, by the right use of this ordinance, the grace promised is not only offered, but really exhibited and conferred by the Holy Ghost, to such (whether of age or infants) as that grace belongs unto, according to the counsel of God's own will, in his appointed time.

7. The sacrament of Baptism is but once to be administered to any person.

Prepare in Prayer

God, while the moment of our baptism may seem like eons ago, please let Your Spirit remind us how surely Your promises still stand over our lives. In His name we pray, amen.

Into the Scriptures

Read Romans 6:1-14 and Colossians 2.

Reach Back

The meaning of baptism is complicated. At the simplest level, baptism points to the "immersion" of God's covenant people into the renewing love and grace of Christ. But like an onion, the layers must be peeled back to get a fuller understanding of its significance.

According to Scripture the primary meaning (significance) of baptism is a participation in the death and resurrection of Jesus Christ. Paul states in Romans, *"We were buried therefore with him by baptism into death, in order that, just as Christ was raised from the dead by the glory of the Father, we too might walk in newness of life"* (Romans 6:4). As we have stated, the definition of a sacrament is "an outward sign and seal of an inward grace." Thus baptism is a participation of dying to the old self (the immersion into water) and the raising of the new self in Jesus Christ in eternal life (the raising out of the water).

More than that, in Paul's letter to the Colossians, Paul draws a comparison between circumcision, the sign of the Old Covenant, and baptism, the sign of the new covenant. In this passage Paul states,

> ...in him (Jesus Christ) you were circumcised with a circumcision made without hands, by putting off the body of the flesh, by the circumcision of Christ, having been buried with him in baptism, in which you were also raised with him through faith in the powerful working of God who raised him from the dead (Colossians 2:11-12).

Thus baptism is a sign and seal of a person being incorporated into the covenant people of Jesus Christ. Just as circumcision was the outward sign of God's people in the old covenant, so also baptism is a sign of a person's incorporation into the people of God in the new covenant.

So then, baptism is clearly and indisputably a sign and seal of:

Regeneration
Death and resurrection
Participation in the Body of Christ
And belonging to the covenant people of God.[76]

Gaze Upwards

The Greek word for baptism is "baptizo." It literally means to immerse; to submerge; or to douse. As we consider this picture of one being covered

---

76 What about infant baptism? For centuries this has been one of the most hotly contested debates within Christendom. But let us remember that this debate is precisely that—*within Christendom*. It is an in-house debate amongst believers and ought not to divide those who love and glorify the Lord Jesus Christ. Sadly, time, study, and a great amount of healthy debate has not been able to overcome this obstacle for some.

Do we have any positive examples of infants being baptized in the New Testament? Probably. The closest thing we have is the account of household baptisms such as those of the household of the Philippian jailer in Acts 16. Such households were likely to have had children, possibly infants, and are our closest biblical links to infant baptisms.

Several more things can be said in favor of infant baptism: Infant baptism quickly became the practice of the early church, and has been practiced throughout most of Christian history. Thus it has the weight of tradition. The greatest theologians of Christian history (i.e. Augustine, Awuinas, Luther, Calvin, and Edwards) *all* practiced infant baptism. This does not prove the case, but certainly weighs in its favor. Furthermore, the recordings of baptisms in the NT were of the *first generation of believers* and thus would logically be converted adults. So it makes sense that we would have few instances of infant baptism in the New Testament. Finally, the early church debated the efficacy of baptisms made by "impious priests" and came to the determination that the efficacy of baptism does *not* depend upon the righteousness of the administrator or the receiver of the sacrament or any other factor, save the promises of God Himself. This means that, even if the administrating pastor is a total charlatan, that does not nullify the promises made at one's baptism. Why not? Because the power of baptism is not in the mode, nor the time, nor the holiness of the baptizer; rather the power *is found only in the promises of God who raises the dead.* See WCF 28.6.

Thus the WCF says, "not only those that do actually profess faith in and obedience unto Christ, but also the infants of one or both believing parents are to be baptized." Does God love infants? Clearly. Does God include them in the covenant people of the Old Testament? Of course. Are they fully human bearing the image of God? Yes! Thus infant baptism is meaningful, powerful and appropriate.

Now that I have stated the Reformed position on infant baptism, allow me to state some pastoral concerns regarding it. Let us be clear here what infant baptism does NOT do: It does not regenerate the sinner as the Roman Catholic Church and the Lutheran theology suggest. It does not save the infant. Only the blood of Jesus Christ can save fallen human souls. Since infant baptism is not specifically commanded in Scripture, therefore it cannot be THE ONLY imperative form. We respect those brothers and sisters in Christ who, out of conscience, adhere to believers' baptism only.

in water, we are reminded that water is the great biblical sign of washing, cleansing and purifying. As I perform a baptism, or view one being performed, I like to think of the water representing God's unfailing love pouring over us. This type of love is found nowhere else. Consider Isaiah 49 for instance. While many in Israel felt that God had abandoned their cause at the time of the exile, God reminded the faithful of His unfailing love through the words of the prophet Isaiah.

> But Zion said, 'The Lord has forsaken me; my Lord has forgotten me.' Can a woman forget her nursing child, that she should have no compassion on the son of her womb? Even these may forget, yet I will not forget you. Behold I have engraved you on the palms of my hands (Isaiah 49:14-16).

How amazing is the capacity of God's love! In this passage from Isaiah, God tells us that He loves us so deeply that He has our very names engraved on the palms of His hands! Into such love are we "immersed" and plunged in Jesus Christ.

Search Inward

Not only do the Scriptures speak of water baptism, but also of baptism with fire and with the Holy Spirit (Matthew 3:11). This experience is not necessarily the same as water baptism. When John the Baptist served God as a wild, camel-skin-wearing prophet in the wilderness proclaiming a baptism for the repentance of sins, he made a clear distinction that Jesus would usher in another form of "baptism" (remember: the Greek word usually means to immerse). John made this promise; "I have baptized you with water, but he will baptize you with the Holy Spirit" (Mark 1:8).

Some teach that being "baptized with the Holy Spirit" is some sort of "secondary blessing" and must come subsequent to conversion. Many Pentecostals for instance teach that there are two "steps" to conversion. The first is being saved by faith. But, they say, a second step is necessary: believers must also be filled with the Holy Spirit *subsequent to conversion.* Many hold that the true evidence for this second level is speaking in tongues. Both of these "steps" are seen as necessary for salvation. Reformed churches do not teach such a "two level" system.

Nevertheless, it is clear that being baptized with the Holy Spirit is a distinct experience from water baptism alone. Many times that a person is filled with the Spirit in the New Testament, they immediately speak the Gospel with boldness.[77] This infilling of love with God's Spirit drives our hearts heavenward in such a manner that we begin to be enamored more and more with the glory of God, our sin begins to seem more and more volatile and putrid in our own eyes, and our desire for intimacy with God increases on exponential levels. Hence we proclaim the Gospel with a special zeal by His filling.

John Piper, Senior Pastor of Bethlehem Baptist Church in Minnesota, makes a helpful analogy when he states that baptism in the Holy Spirit is similar to a child taking a walk with his father. For the entire walk, the child is safe in his father's presence. His relationship with him is secure. And yet there are times when the father will swoop up the child, hold him tight in his arms, rejoice over him, and smother him with his love![78] This is baptism in the Holy Spirit! If you have not felt that type of intimacy with the Savior in a while, seek it ardently in prayer.

Step Out—Entering the Water

While water baptism is to be administered to a person only one time, its effects are far-reaching. First of all, it is a reminder that the believer has been saved by God's grace. Neither suffering, nor temptation, nor failure, nor the devil himself is able to wrench a believer out of God's hands (Romans 8:37-38). Baptism reminds us of Him to whom we belong.

Secondly, baptism is a symbol that the believer has died to his or her former way of life. When facing times of extreme temptation, it might be helpful for the believer to rehearse this simple truth in her mind, *"I am baptized!"* This is another way of saying *"I belong to Jesus! I cannot be destroyed by my sinful desires; sin has no hold over my life any longer!"* When we rehearse our identity in Christ in such ways, it actually begins to strengthen our desire for holiness in the heart, and melts away our desire for sin—whatever it may be at that moment.

Thirdly, while baptism means that we are immersed into the Body of Christ, it also signifies being incorporated into the Church, His bride. Christ has chosen the Church to be His Body here on earth. If we are baptized into Him, we owe the Church our allegiance, our support (financial and otherwise) our commitment, and our submission to its discipline.

---

77 Consider Stephen's martyrdom in Acts 7:55 for instance.

78 John Piper. "A Passion for Christ Exalting Power." Sermon. www.desiringgod.com/resourcelibrary/topicindex/42. August 23, 2007.

Finally, we ought to begin to reformulate our view of baptism if we view it merely ceremonially. Far more than a mere formal procedure to be attended in some sort of weak perfunctory manner, being baptized (immersed) into the body of Christ must become a complete way of life. We can never forget that its primary meaning is death to our old lives, and resurrection into the new.

The Confession Chapter Twenty-nine:

Of the Lord's Supper

1. Our Lord Jesus, in the night wherein he was betrayed, instituted the sacrament of his body and blood, called the Lord's Supper, to be observed in his Church unto the end of the world; for the perpetual remembrance of the sacrifice of himself in his death, the sealing all benefits thereof unto true believers, their spiritual nourishment and growth in him, their further engagement in and to all duties which they owe unto him; and to be a bond and pledge of their communion with him, and with each other, as members of his mystical body.

2. In this sacrament Christ is not offered up to his Father, nor any real sacrifice made at all for remission of sins of the quick or dead, but a commemoration of that one offering up of himself, by himself, upon the cross, once for all, and a spiritual oblation of all possible praise unto God for the same; so that the Popish sacrifice of the mass, as they call it, is most abominably injurious to Christ's one only sacrifice, the only propitiation for all the sins of the elect.

3. The Lord Jesus has, in this ordinance, appointed his ministers to declare his word of institution to the people, to pray, and bless the elements of bread and wine, and thereby to set them apart from a common to an holy use; and to take and break the bread, to take the cup, and (they communicating also themselves) to give both to the communicants; but to none who are not then present in the congregation.

4. Private masses, or receiving this sacrament by a priest, or any other, alone; as likewise the denial of the cup to the people; worshipping the elements, the lifting them up, or carrying them about for adoration, and the reserving them for any pretended religious use, are all contrary to the nature of this sacrament, and to the institution of Christ.

5. The outward elements in this sacrament, duly set apart to the uses ordained by Christ, have such relation to him crucified, as that truly, yet sacramentally only, they are sometimes called by the name of the things they represent, to wit, the body and blood of Christ; albeit, in substance and nature, they still remain truly, and only, bread and wine, as they were before.

6. That doctrine which maintains a change of the substance of bread and wine, into the substance of Christ's body and blood (commonly called transubstantiation) by consecration of a priest, or by any other way, is repugnant, not only to Scripture alone, but even to common-sense and reason; overthrows the nature of the sacrament; and has been, and is, the cause of manifold superstitions, yea, of gross idolatries.

7. Worthy receivers, outwardly partaking of the visible elements in this sacrament, do then also inwardly by faith, really and indeed, yet not carnally and corporally, but spiritually, receive and feed upon Christ crucified, and all benefits of his death: the body and blood of Christ being then not corporally or carnally in, with, or under the bread and wine; yet as really, but spiritually, present to the faith of believers in that ordinance, as the elements themselves are to their outward senses.

8. Although ignorant and wicked men receive the outward elements in this sacrament, yet they receive not the thing signified thereby; but by their unworthy coming thereunto are guilty of the body and blood of the Lord, to their own damnation. Wherefore all ignorant and ungodly persons, as they are unfit to enjoy communion with him, so are they unworthy of the Lord's table, and can not, without great sin against Christ, while they remain such, partake of these holy mysteries, or be admitted thereunto.

Prepare in Prayer
God, as we study this sacrament in the Bible and in the Confession today, help our spirits to understand and receive Communion for what its signs truly portray: the body and blood of Christ given for us. Amen.

Into the Scriptures
Read John 6:22-71 and 1 Corinthians 11:17-34.

Reach Back
Rereading the Westminster Confession to prepare for writing this section, I was struck by the holy awe retained in the hearts of the Puritans. As we

study this document together, and the Scriptures that the Puritans loved, let us not forget the gravity and the magnitude of the glory of Jesus Christ as He reveals Himself to us through the sacrament of communion. Notice how often in this twenty-ninth chapter of the Confession, that when the writers spoke of holy things such as the Lord's Table, how they seemed to be keenly aware that the realities of heaven and hell hung in the balance.

To the Westminster Divines, the sacrament of Holy Communion stood for that great chasm finally breached through the blood and body of Christ. This meal is no trifle. On the contrary it is of eternal consequence that we, by faith alone, participate in this great reality of the atonement. That utter conviction molded the writers' views on communion and for this reason the Confession sounds so bold and strong in this chapter.

The writers totally rejected the Catholic view of transubstantiation: the view that the wine and bread literally turned into the body and blood of Jesus Christ (WCF 29.2, 4, 6). Not only is this view absent from Scripture, but it led to the abuses of those who held the elements up and began to worship the elements at the Table rather than the God who gave them. Instead, the Westminster Divines held that the body and blood truly convey the reality of Jesus' death, but spiritually. In this understanding they avoided the implication that Jesus' sacrificial death on the cross was in any way being repeated, as the atonement was a once-and-for-all sacrifice for the sins of the elect. His presence then, is real but not physical. Christ is truly manifest at the Lord's Table, but not in the physical, literal way the Roman Church conceived of it. After all, it is to the divine nature of Jesus Christ (not His human nature) that the characteristic of omnipresence belongs.

Yet even John Calvin, the theologian par excellence of the Reformation, when trying to describe this mystery of Christ's presence in the holy meal could only say,

> If anyone asks me about the process (of how Christ is present), I do not mind admitting that it is too high a mystery for my mind to grasp or my words to express. I feel rather than understand it. I can rest safely in the truth of God and embrace it without question. He declares that his flesh is the food, his blood is the drink for my soul. I give my soul to him to be fed with such food.[79]

---

79. John Calvin, The Institutes of the Christian Religion. 4.17.32.
Edited by Tony Lane and Hilary Osborne. (Grand Rapids MI: Baker, 1978) P.270.

There is real power in the sacrament of the Lord's Table. The Confession points out that in eating this meal together, believers are given a tangible reminder of the death and resurrection of Jesus through the symbols of bread and cup, are united together as a community through this shared meal, are strengthened for the journey of faith by feasting upon Christ (John 6:52-56), and are set apart from the world as a faithful witness. Thus the Lord's Table:

> Represents the body and blood of Jesus Christ, shed on the cross of Calvary,

> Presents believers with the real (yet spiritual) presence of Jesus Christ and

> Reminds believers, not only of their commitment to each other, but of Christ's commitment to them.

Gaze Upwards

In today's society, the realities represented by the Lord's Table (body and blood) are seen as vile, gross, and unnecessary. Many decry Christians' adherence to a bloody Christ and a bloody cross. Our culture is fixated on health, healing, and wellness, not nails and crossbeams. Think of the way our culture is fixed on products like band-aids, sanitizing gels, and insurance policies to ensure that we don't have to think of blood, wounds, or death more often than we must. And yet, in communion we are posed with the question: what kind of God would choose this way—this cross—to save the world? What kind of God is He that requires us to contemplate the road to Calvary in such graphic terms as pictured by this strange meal? What kind of God would put His own Son through such a torture as an ancient crucifixion? The only answer can be a God who loves humanity enough to endure this suffering on our behalf. The next time your church celebrates the Lord's Supper together, ask yourself, "What kind of God would do this for me?" The only answer can be one who takes sin dead seriously, and yet has grace immeasurable to cover it.

Search Inwards

Not only does Communion represent the body and blood of Jesus, but it was given to the disciples in the context of the Passover's paschal meal. In the

Passover, the Jews customarily celebrated that great event in their history when God delivered His people from the horrors of Egyptian slavery. Not only did the Jews experience deliverance from an oppressive enemy, but God also "passed over" the homes of the faithful that were marked with the blood of the Lamb, saving them from death and the hands of a destroying angel. They were commanded to,

> Go and select lambs for yourselves according to the clans, and kill the Passover lamb. Take a bunch of hyssop and dip it in the blood that is in the basin, and touch the lintel and the two *doorposts* with the blood that is in the basin...For the LORD will pass through to strike the Egyptians, and when he sees the blood on the lintel and on the two *doorposts*, the LORD will pass over the door and not allow the destroyer to enter your houses and strike you (Exodus 12:22-23).

As with baptism, deep and penetrating questions ought to be rippling through our hearts as we sit at the table. One of those questions that the Lord's Table (and the Passover before it) prompts is this; "From what have I been delivered?" What are the sins that no longer have a hold over you? What are some areas that God has taken the sinful passions from you? For instance, as you begin to grow in your relationship to Christ, you may notice that your sexual cravings no longer have dominion over your mind as they once did. For others, they will feel their ambitious desire to attain more and more wealth slowly begin to lessen. Still others may notice their resentments towards others dissipating. As the Passover celebrated God's people being delivered from the evil taskmaster Pharaoh, so also we celebrate our deliverance from our former masters of sin and death at the Lord's Table.

Step Out—Feasting on Christ

When the people of God join together to receive the Lord's Supper, they are themselves being nourished by the Lord Jesus Christ. In a true, yet mysterious way, we actually draw strength, faith, and hope through and from Jesus Christ in a spiritual, but no less real, way. Jonathan Edwards says,

> (The Lord's Supper) was appointed to draw forth the longings of our souls towards Jesus Christ. Here are the glorious objects of spiritual desire by visible signs represented to our view. We have Christ evidently set forth as crucified. Here we have that spiritual meat and drink represented and offered to excite our hunger and thirst; here

we have all that spiritual feast represented which God has provided for poor souls; and here we may hope in some measure to have our longing souls satisfied in this world by the gracious communications of the Spirit of God.[80]

The Bible says "Blessed are those who hunger and thirst for righteousness, for they shall be satisfied" (Matthew 5:6). We shall be satisfied, of course in Christ alone. Remarkably Jesus even said, "Whoever feeds on my flesh and drinks my blood abides in me and I in him" (John 6:56). Apparently spiritual feasting is a lot like physical feasting. Think for a moment about eating a big meal such as Thanksgiving dinner. If you hurry, rush the moment, and gorge yourself, you are prone to indigestion. You will be full, but you will not have likely enjoyed the process much. And yet when we wait, slow down, and allow each bite to be tasted and savored, not only is the dinner more enjoyable, but our bodies receive it, digest it, and use it more effectively.

Jesus Christ said, "I am the bread of life" (John 6:46). In an amazing but true way, our spiritual strength is derived by consuming Jesus; by feasting upon His words. We do this through devouring His love into our anatomical systems. We do this as we absorb His teaching, His beauty, and even His presence into our own lifeblood. We do this in the act of believing worship.

80 Quoted in Gary Crampton, A Conversation with Jonathan Edwards. (Grand Rapids MI: Reformation Heritage Books, 2006) p. 163-164.

The Confession Chapter Thirty:

Of Church Censures

1. The Lord Jesus, as king and head of his Church, has therein appointed a government in the hand of Church officers, distinct from the civil magistrate.

2. To these officers the keys of the Kingdom of Heaven are committed, by virtue whereof they have power respectively to retain and remit sins, to shut that kingdom against the impenitent, both by the word and censures; and to open it unto penitent sinners, by the ministry of the gospel, and by absolution from censures, as occasion shall require.

3. Church censures are necessary for the reclaiming and gaining of offending brethren; for deterring of others from like offenses; for purging out of that leaven which might infect the whole lump; for vindicating the honor of Christ, and the holy profession of the gospel; and for preventing the wrath of God, which might justly fall upon the Church, if they should suffer his covenant, and the seals thereof, to be profaned by notorious and obstinate offenders.

4. For the better attaining of these ends, the officers of the Church are to proceed by admonition, suspension from the sacrament of the Lord's Supper for a season, and by excommunication from the Church, according to the nature of the crime, and demerit of the person.

Prepare in Prayer
God, as we study this delicate topic today, please help us to realize how often You must bring us back to the fold again by means of discipline. By any means, keep us in a state of obedience! Amen.

Into the Scriptures
Read Matthew 18:15-20 and 1 Corinthians 5.

Reach Back
Most of us will remember reading the work "The Scarlet Letter" in high school or college. It is about a young woman who has committed a sexual sin (we later find out it is with the pastor!) and is branded as an adulteress by the community. In brazen style, the community forces her to wear a red letter "A" to remind all, including the offending parties, of her adulterous ways. Many young students remember that the reading of this famous work also came with equally memorable lectures against "intolerance," "judgmentalism," and "puritanical ways." This work brings up an interesting dilemma: how can the church admonish its congregants without becoming intolerable or harsh? This question is the inquiry of this chapter of the Westminster and is also the subject addressed in today's Scriptures.

At first blush, 1 Corinthians chapter five is a frightening chapter. "Blush" is probably the right choice of words since, in context, this passage is speaking about dealing with a brother in the church who has been caught in a sexual sin of the worst kind—he has been caught sleeping with his step-mother! And yet the prescription of Paul in dealing with this situation seems difficult as well. He states, "purge the evil person from among you" and barely bats an eye in doing so. Apparently, Paul is not willing to spare the rod of discipline. Nevertheless, when it comes to church discipline regarding gross, overt, and blatant sins, this passage must be taken along with Matthew 18. This gospel teaching of Jesus prescribes a three-step format by which believers can confront their brothers with grace. Together, these two passages form a grace-filled, but uncompromisingly firm-handed stance on sin within the fellowship of believers. The Confession's reading for today is helpful as it reminds us that "church censures are necessary for the reclaiming and gaining of offending brethren; for deterring others from like offenses," and also for "purging out the leaven which might infect the whole lump" (WCF 30.3).

So how do we deal with sin that has become a public affair and yet maintain our grace at the same time? In this section, the Westminster Confession makes several key points to which we must attune ourselves. 1) First, Jesus Christ has given the church authority to deal with sinning brethren (WCF 30.2. See also Matthew 16:19-20). Ignoring actions that may destroy the fellowship is *not in the end* the most peaceable option. 2) Secondly, as we have just stated, church discipline is intended to *reclaim* erring brethren, not drive them away (WCF 30.3 cf. Matthew 18:15). 3) Finally, Church discipline must be in accordance with the true weight of the crime (WCF 30.4), but when necessary, may require the denial of some privileges of Christian fellowship—including the sacraments in extreme cases. While these measures may seem overly harsh in our day, the writers of the Westminster considered it far less dangerous to deny an unrepentant sinner to the Table than to risk tarnishing the reputation of Christ, His Church, or His sacraments.

Gaze Upwards

As we have studied this Confession together, we have noticed how each section of the Westminster Confession of Faith holds up another aspect of God's character to the light, just as one might hold up a diamond to clear light in order to consider its perfections. Here we consider God's Fatherly concern in discipline.

While it is popular for many theologians, pastors, and teachers today to speak exclusively of God's love, to the neglect of His justice, the Bible presents a much more dimensional understanding of God. Over and over again, the Scriptures remind us "the Lord disciplines the one he loves and chastises every son whom he receives" (Hebrews 12:6). Repeatedly the Bible teaches that God admonishes those whom He calls as His own, especially in the book of Proverbs (cf. 3:11; 5:23; 12:1; 13:24; 22:15; 23:13-14; 29:17). Many of the preceding passages from Proverbs are encouragements for human parents to discipline their children. If mothers and fathers are bid not to withhold their discipline from their earthly children, how much more will our Heavenly Father take measured care to correct us when we go astray?

Many parents have had the agony of having to spank their children when they run into the street where dangerous cars whiz by. Though it hurts us considerably to spank them for this "crime," we know that we must make an impression upon them lest they run into the dangerous road again. In the same way, God often disciplines us through the words of a friend, the correction of a superior in the workplace, or even the gentle yet relentless whisper of the Holy Spirit.

Consider the training of one disciple, Peter. Where would Peter have been had not the Lord rebuked him strongly several times? "Get behind me

Satan! You are a hindrance to me," Jesus said after Peter scoffed at His prediction of death and resurrection (Matthew 16:23). More than that, after Jesus was arrested and Peter denied knowing His master, mere eye contact was enough to remind Peter of his grave error (Luke 22:61). Finally, Jesus' three-fold challenge to Peter after the resurrection to "feed my sheep" (John 21:15-19) stood as a lasting corrective before Peter was prepared to preach with power weeks later at Pentecost. One could only speculate what kind of leader Peter would have been without Jesus' loving yet stern correction. Without this constant discipline, Peter surely would never have become the useful tool that he became as the new Church was launched that Pentecost morning.

Search Inward

We understand that tools and weapons need to be sharpened to be effective. We laud athletes, fighters, and dancers when they discipline themselves before their competition or performance. And yet, many of us are sluggish of heart when it comes to receiving correction and rebuke. Consider Proverbs 12:1, "Whoever loves discipline loves knowledge, but he who hates reproof is stupid." I don't know about you, but it would be very difficult for me to say truthfully that I love discipline! This is especially true when it comes to the discipline of another believer's rebuke. And yet this is exactly what the Scriptures teach us we are to grow to welcome.

I remember as I was learning to preach how my senior pastor Dr. Wayne Bogue would correct me. "Watch your transitions!" he would often scold me privately after a sermon. "Keep your message focused, you are trying to do too much!" he might also say. I began to dread those post-sermon chats. What had I done wrong *this* time? And yet it was putting his words of wisdom into practice that helped to mold and form my skill from the pulpit. While I often disliked receiving those correcting words (in my ignorance I had always thought I did rather well) I have to admit that it was his insight that helped me to hone my skills much more than my own myopic perspective would have allowed.

What kinds of emotions do you experience when you receive words of correction, rebuke, or challenge? Do you find yourself getting angry with the message-bearer rather than with the message? Do you find yourself striking back verbally, or perhaps worse—by lashing back in repeated *unspoken* conversations in your own mind? Let us endeavor to become the kind of people that Proverbs 12:1 aims for. When we receive just criticism for our actions, let us receive it with praise and thanksgiving for "better is open rebuke than hidden love" (Proverbs 27:5).

Step Out—Receiving Rebuke

One of the measures of Christian maturity is our ability to receive criticism for what it is worth. Often criticism and discipline are exactly what we need to sharpen our ministry tools, shake corrosion off of our hearts, and turn us again to prayer and to Christ. And yet the mature Christian must learn that there are correct ways and incorrect ways to receive criticism. An obvious example of an incorrect way to receive criticism is to despise your critic. Equally bad is to let the harsh words of others destroy us.

So how do we receive confrontation well? First of all, the believer ought to ask a series of questions.

1. Does my critic know the field that he is advising me in? In the example I gave from my own life, I knew Pastor Bogue to be an expert preacher. His experience and his credentials were top notch. I knew that he was many times the preacher I was, and so his criticism was valid.

2. Secondly, does the person have my best interests in mind? Does the person love me in the Lord? If we know that this person has our best interests at heart, we can value his or her criticism much more than the person that we do not know well, or the person that we suspect *does not* have our best interests in mind.

3. Thirdly, is the criticism just? This analysis takes objectivity on our part, as none of us like to receive criticism. Here we may have to do a bit of digging into our own words and actions, viewing them from a third-person perspective, and maybe even asking another party their opinion if necessary. If we find that the person is knowledgeable in their field, has our interests at heart, and also the criticism seems to be warranted, we must not allow our own stubborn pride to prevent us from absorbing the challenge. If any of these three questions come up negative, this does not necessarily negate the truth-value of the criticism, but it is a sign that we ought to put on the brakes slightly before receiving their word as gospel truth.[81]

---

81 These three questions were given to me by Mark Van Drunen, a wise friend of mine and a deacon in my home church.

When we receive criticism or confrontation in moral areas of our lives, this is called rebuke. Usually this is a much more difficult form of confrontation to receive than mere criticism. When we are "called out" for a word or deed of questionable morality or integrity, this strikes even deeper to our core than other forms of confrontation. The reason is intrinsically linked to our sinful nature. In our limited-scope, we often tend to view the world through our own moral lenses, which have not yet been fully sanctified in the love of Christ.

When evaluating our own words and actions, we almost always give ourselves the benefit of the doubt. For instance, when arguing with my wife I expect her to judge my words literally. "I said, I *will* take out the trash!" If my tone of voice is challenged, I demand her to judge me on my words alone. And yet I will often turn around and attack her merely for the *tone* of her voice, even if her words themselves were faultless. "Well you didn't have to ask me like *that!*" In the same way, we expect others to judge us by our *intentions* and not our actions alone. "But I *meant* to be to your soccer game on time." And yet we flip the coin and judge others by their actions alone and negate their possible intentions. "Besides, *you* were late for dinner last night too!"

Thus, when we receive criticism, rebuke, or outright confrontation, especially from our brothers and sisters in Christ, we must learn to ask ourselves a few pointed questions, do some serious self-reflection to understand the offense, and when necessary be bold enough to repent and turn from our sin. When we are strong enough to do this, we will become the kind of person described in Proverbs 12:1, "who loves discipline" and knowledge as well.

The Confession Chapter Thirty-one:

Of Synods and Councils

1. For the better government and further edification of the Church, there ought to be such assemblies as are commonly called synods or councils.

2. As magistrates may lawfully call a synod of ministers and other fit persons to consult and advise with about matters of religion; so, if magistrates be open enemies of the Church, the ministers of Christ, of themselves, by virtue of their office, or they, with other fit persons, upon delegation from their churches, may meet together in such assemblies.

3. It belongs to synods and councils, pastorally, to determine controversies of faith, and cases of conscience; to set down rules and directions for the better ordering of the public worship of God, and government of his Church; to receive complaints in cases of misadministration, and authoritatively to determine the same: which decrees and determinations, if consonant to the Word of God, are to be received with reverence and submission, not only for their agreement with the Word, but also for the power whereby they are made, as being an ordinance of God, appointed thereunto in his Word.

4. All synods or councils since the apostles' times, whether general or particular, may err, and many have erred; therefore they are not to be made the rule of faith or practice, but to be used as a help in both.

5. Synods and councils are to handle or conclude nothing but that which is ecclesiastical: and are not to intermeddle with civil affairs which concern the commonwealth, unless by way of humble petition in cases extraordinary; or by way of advice for satisfaction of conscience, if they be thereunto required by the civil magistrate.

Prepare in Prayer

God, today as we study, show us some ways that Your Spirit has moved though the councils of men in the past, in order that we might be obedient to Your Word today in the present. Amen.

Into the Scriptures

Read Acts 15 and Titus 1-2.

Reach Back

In church life there are nor shortage of controversies that can and do occur. Unfortunately, Church history is full of them. Many of these controversies rip apart congregations and leave sincere believers in a wake of confusion. What should happen if a pastor or church leader is found guilty of a sin or a crime? Does anyone have the power to confront such fallen leaders, or even to *remove* them? Sometimes there are strong differences *between* churches. Should churches work together cooperatively, or strike out on their own? How should churches resolve their difficulties if irreconcilable differences arise between congregations? How should a theological controversy be resolved when matters of doctrine become disputed? Is there any way to gather the leaders to a summit to arrive at a conclusion?

All of the above examples are reasons why the Westminster Confession of Faith includes Chapter 31 "Of Synods and Councils." Simply stated, the Confession holds that individual leaders and pastors should and must submit to a greater authority beyond their own. For this reason, the Confession suggests that churches may bind themselves together in cooperative networks often called today "presbyteries," "districts," or "synods." Here, the community of churches represents a broader spectrum of the Body of Christ than any individual leader or congregation. Ideally, this helps to prevent rogue leaders from straying from the faith, curtails ostentatious personalities, and hopefully keeps the greater community of faith moored to solid Christian doctrine.

While synods, councils and other regional bodies can and often do err (WCF 31.4), and sometimes even stray collectively from the faith, this living network of believers makes such occasions fewer and often less severe. One example of a council of churches working together well can be given. In the early church, believers debated the nature of Jesus Christ vigorously. Some, following the teaching of Arius, a priest in the church in Alexandria, believed that Jesus Christ was created by God, and not fully divine to the same measure as the Father. Many others including his rival Athanasius, held that Jesus Christ is both fully God and fully human, being of the same substance as the Father. This controversy irked Constantine, the Roman Emperor, who eventually sparked the calling of a church-wide council to debate the issue at Nicaea in 325. After much discussion, the conclusion was reached that the testimony of Scripture clearly adheres to both the divine and human nature of Jesus Christ. Later in 381 at a subsequent council in Constantinople, the Nicene Creed as we know it today was revised and expanded. Thus, the council at Nicaea served to solidify the Church's Christology which has stood firmly upon this foundation ever since.

This example of the early church's cooperative spirit to resolve this plaguing doctrinal matter serves as a stinging counterpoint to today's rugged individualism.

Search Inwards
We live in an age that could be defined as "ragingly individualistic." A number of examples could be given.

> Professional athletes and their fans often obsess over individual statistics rather than their team's wins and losses.

> We have "personal pan pizzas," "personal computers," "personal ads," "personal identification numbers," "personal trainers" and many more "personals."

> Nearly every product from automobiles to hamburgers to sneakers are customized in order to give the consumer exactly what he or she wants. We are bombarded by advertising slogans like "Have it your way" (Burger King).

> Millions post their thoughts, writings, pictures, and videos on personalized blogs and social networking websites.

> Email, text-messaging, and instant messaging have drastically reduced our need to visit others' homes, make phone calls, and write hand-written letters.

Many evangelical churches have even adopted the language of a "personal relationship with Jesus Christ," "personal devotions," and "personal prayer languages."

A.W. Tozer says, "To be specific, the self-sins are self-righteousness, self-pity, self-confidence, self-sufficiency, self-admiration, self-love, and a host of others like them."[82] Martin Luther said that the human soul is "curved in on itself." And yet as we read the Scriptures we are hit again and again over the head with the fact that God deals with humanity not *merely* as individuals, but also as a covenant community. Paul for instance was a master at networking. He communicated regularly (visiting when possible) with believers in Colossae, Galatia, Ephesus, Corinth and even had friends in Rome to whom he wrote before he made it there. Clearly his vision for the Body of Christ was much broader than his "home church."

It is no wonder then, that when the New Testament church ran into a controversy in Acts 15 regarding the admission of non-Jews into the Christian faith, the believers were able to rally together at the Jerusalem council and hammer out the issues. Through faith, prayer, discussion, and humility, the believers concluded that God's plan for salvation was available for all who trust in Jesus Christ—gentiles did not need to first become observant Jews in order to be saved. And yet it took a church council in order for the doctrine to become fully clarified!

Look into your own heart for a few minutes. How much of your 24-hour day is fixated on yourself. Add together the time you think about your outfit before breakfast, the time grooming before the mirror, the time you think about how others perceive your words, the effort you spend managing your reputation, the time you spend praying for yourself, agonizing over your regrets, posting photos of yourself on your webpage—add it all together and we must admit that we are an individually fixated people.

For this reason, we need the Holy Spirit working through other people: yes through our own pastors and elders and teachers, but also through the guidance and correction of other bodies of believers beyond the doors of our home church. (Not only that, but beyond our national borders as well! It is my conviction that every American church ought to have a partner church somewhere else around the globe to help correct our

---

82 A. W. Tozer. The Pursuit of God. (Camp Hill PA: Christian Publications, 1993) p. 42.

vision when it becomes too near-sighted.) This is a particularly strong need for those who belong to non-denominational churches that do not come equipped with a network in place.

If, when looking into your own heart, you are disturbed at your self-centeredness, perhaps the suggestions outlined below will be of aid to your growth in Christ.

Step Out—Spiritual Direction

The most obvious way that we can put the thirty-second chapter of the Confession into practice is to participate in your own denomination. Learn about it online by reading its website and its historical confessions. Familiarize yourself with its functions as a corporate body. Begin to study the missionaries and ministries your denomination leads or supports. If your denomination has an annual convocation or assembly, study the various motions and overtures that are being considered at the national level. Obviously, if you are an elder within your church your responsibility to dutifully participate and attend such meetings is that much greater.

But how can you fight off what Tozer calls the "self sins" if you are not in a connectional denomination, or cannot represent your congregation at the higher church courts? Are there still ways to remain accountable to others and help preserve pure doctrine? Here I would recommend the process of spiritual direction.

Spiritual direction is a guided mentorship with another believer who is further along the walk of faith than you are. The relationship can be casual or formal. It can take place under the auspices of a church or school (i.e. a confirmation or discipleship program, a seminary education, or ministry training preparation) or else it can spontaneously develop, naturally. Spiritual directors may serve in a personal advisory capacity for a long term such as a decade or even a lifetime, or a short term such as a weekend retreat.

Clearly the greatest example we have of this form of guided person-to-person discipleship is with Jesus Christ Himself. Jesus chose twelve men to follow Him from place to place and to learn from His example, but more than that, He chose three men of those twelve to walk even closer. John, James, and Peter were enabled to study at Jesus' feet and were privy to several events that the others did not see, including the

Transfiguration (Mark 9:2), the healing of a dead girl (Mark 5:37), and the agony in the garden of Gethsemane (Mark 14:33).

The purpose of such spiritual directors is to give us suggestions as to ways that we can seek God's greater glory in our lives. If they know us well, they will also be asked to help identify our strengths and also (and probably more importantly) our weaknesses. Often the spiritual director will recommend that the student observe some of the other spiritual disciplines such as fasting, prayer, or guided study through the Scriptures. At times their meetings will serve to reflect on the student's life, particularly when he or she undergoes a "dark night of the soul" or a challenging dilemma. Often the mentor will simply serve as a sounding board for the student's joys and frustrations.

If you feel that the Holy Spirit is leading you to find, or even to *become* a spiritual director, act on that prompting immediately! It has been said that each believer in their lifetime should be a Barnabus (who introduced Paul to the Jerusalem Church in Acts 9:26-27) and a Timothy (a young pastor whom Paul later mentored); a mentor and a mentee. To whom are you a Barnabus? To whom are you a Timothy?

The Confession Chapter Thirty-two:

Of the State of Man After Death, and of the Resurrection of the Dead

1. The bodies of men, after death, return to dust, and see corruption; but their souls (which neither die nor sleep), having an immortal subsistence, immediately return to God who gave them. The souls of the righteous, being then made perfect in holiness, are received into the highest heavens, where they behold the face of God in light and glory, waiting for the full redemption of their bodies; and the souls of the wicked are cast into hell, where they remain in torments and utter darkness, reserved to the judgment of the great day. Besides these two places for souls separated from their bodies, the Scripture acknowledges none.

2. At the last day, such as are found alive shall not die, but be changed: and all the dead shall be raised up with the self-same bodies, and none other, although with different qualities, which shall be united again to their souls forever.

3. The bodies of the unjust shall, by the power of Christ, be raised to dishonor; the bodies of the just, by his Spirit, unto honor, and be made conformable to his own glorious body.

Prepare in Prayer

God, no matter how ready we may feel to stand in Your presence, the prospect of our death still frightens us tremendously. Show us in this study how completely You have defeated this enemy! Amen.

Into the Scriptures

Read 1 Corinthians 15 and 1 Thessalonians 4.

Reach Back

This section of the Confession has a two-banded theme running throughout in that it is concerned both with the temporal (the here and now) as well as the eternal (the timeless). Note the instances of time-bound language: there are no less than four references to our physical, flesh-and-blood bodies. These bodies die, and "return to dust." But observe also the timeless: there are nearly a dozen references to: souls, immortal subsistence, being made perfect, full redemption, different qualities, and being raised. Clearly the Confession, expositing the New Testament's great theme of resurrection, is begging us to remember that we are much more than a collection of vertebrae, tonsils, cartilage, and gray matter. This changes our entire scope on living.

The warning is of course that everything we do now, every course of action we choose, every wound we inflict on others, every word that we speak echoes for eternity. By speaking of the "just" and the "unjust" (WCF 32.3), the Confession is by no means teaching a resurrection based upon our efforts in this life. Rather these phrases should be taken as the "justified" and the "unjustified" for it is only through a personal, substitutionary atonement that one is finally and fully vindicated at the resurrection.

The resurrection is no auxiliary theme in Christian theology. It is the sum of Christian theology. It is for this reason Paul makes clear in 1 Corinthians 15 that, if not for the resurrection of the dead through Jesus Christ, Christians are "without hope," and above all men to be pitied for their foolish, wasted lives. But, if indeed Christ Jesus defeated death by His own resurrection—making not only possible, but certain a resurrection for those who cleave to Him—then the resurrection is the final vindication for a life of faith, endurance, suffering, hardship, and joy.

Gaze Upwards

There is much in our hope of resurrection that awes and inspires us to give praise to God through Jesus Christ. First of all, through the resurrection of the dead, God demonstrates His victory over the whole of creation and not just humanity—both the things that are physical, gritty, earthy, "material" (our bodies), and also the things that are "immaterial," subject to the spiritual realm. Regarding the material world, the apostle Paul teaches in Romans 8:21 that "we know that the creation itself will be set free from its bondage to decay and obtain the freedom of the glory of the children of God." Notice that in this strange passage the redemption of the world itself (vs. 21) is somehow tied to the resurrection of our own bodies (vs. 23). So then, if the physical universe which now convulses in pain by means of hurricanes, tidal waves, tornados, and black holes; if this universe *itself* will share in the redemption of the universe through God's Son, how much greater will be the rejoicing of those whom He purchased with His blood! Exactly *how* the cosmos will participate in the redemption of the world, as promised in Isaiah 65:17 and repeated in Revelation 21:1, is yet to be seen.

More than that, the repercussions of the resurrection also result in reverberations throughout the *spiritual realms* since angels long to look into these things (1 Peter 1:2). I take this to mean that God's incarnation and resurrection poured into humanity through the love of His Son is so baffling to the angels that they cannot help to peer into the mystery of this passion. Finally, the demons as well shudder with fear (James 2:19) at the beauty of God. Thus what the Old Testament refers to as the "hosts of heaven" (Psalm 148:2) or the "mighty ones" (Psalm 103:20)—these too will also exalt in God's Son Jesus Christ at the time of the resurrection of the dead.

Finally, as hinted above, the *individual* has great reason to be personally exuberant in the hope of resurrection. The resurrection represents the greatest of the "already/not yet" mystery of the Kingdom of God. As for the individual soul, he or she will participate in the new reality of our resurrected bodies promised in 1 Corinthians 15:35-49. Now, what we have begun to experience in a limited way (the "already")—things like the possibility of healing, the imputed righteousness of Christ on our behalf, and fellowship with the Holy Spirit—will be finalized and perfected as we experience the fullness of these graces. Then, (the "not yet") we shall experience complete healing, as our limited bodies are made ready for an eternal dwelling, where sickness and disease are banished from existence. Then, we shall have not only the imputed righteousness of Christ that justifies us, but also the full removal of the *possibility* of sin making us ready to live directly in God's presence. Then, we shall not only live with the indwelling of the Holy Spirit, but we shall also be ushered into the fullness of God's manifest presence as Revelation makes clear,

> Behold the dwelling place of God is with man. He will dwell with them, and they will be His people, and God himself will be with them as their God... No longer will there be anything accursed, but the throne of God and the Lamb will be in it, and His

servants will worship Him. They shall see His face... (Revelation 21:3; 22:3-4).

Search Inwards

In some way, we must begin to realize that our mortal bodies are not all that God has created for us. So often we think of our human body as our "true self." We look into the mirror and we see "us." And yet there is much more to "us" than we can even see! For many, the appearance or condition of their body reflects heavily on how they perceive themselves. If they find themselves overweight, many begin to hate themselves for it. If they do not like their wrinkles, many will take expensive steps to see them ironed out. If they are bound to a wheelchair or walker, some begin to see their lives as no longer fruitful. But the resurrection denies of all of this foolishness. The resurrection of the dead forces us to acknowledge that life has meaning; much more meaning in fact, than the limitations of our mortal flesh. It is just that, flesh. Clumps of bone and muscle. And yet the true "us" is resident inside of this matter and screams out for meaning, value, and worth far beyond our ability to throw a football, or walk a mile, or run a marathon. The resurrection forces us to focus on the fact that God created our souls for relationship and for His glory. As a matter of fact, should we begin to believe that anything the body can do (such as win a beauty contest, engage in sexual activity, or win a wrestling match) is the end-all be-all purpose of our existence, we must acknowledge that there is a holy "other" for which we are created. If we think the body is the primary purpose of our lives, we lose the treasure of the soul; if we realize that our souls are central to our purpose as created beings, we gain the body.

Christians are not dualists believing that the physical is evil and the spiritual is good. No, God created the world and proclaimed it good. Jesus was incarnated into a real body. The heresy of docetism once proclaimed that Jesus could not be truly incarnate because His physical body would have ruined His soul. This is false. Christians believe that both the body and the soul have redeeming functions, and work best when both are tuned to the glory of God. Consider Psalm 38 for instance, while intimately concerned with the state of his soul, David's prayer is awash with the physical realm, mentioning repeatedly both the body (flesh, bones, wounds) and physical posture (bowed down, prostrate, crushed).

St. Augustine wrote:

> The souls of the departed saints are not troubled by the death in which they are separated from their bodies. This is because their 'flesh rests in hope' (Psalm 16:9). Whatever humiliations it may seem to have suffered, it is now unable to feel them. For they do not (as Plato supposed) desire that their bodies should be forgotten; rather, they remember the promise given them by the one who always keeps his word, and who has given them the assurance of the preservation of the hairs of their head (Luke 21:18)...For this body will not only be better than it was here, in its best estate of health; it will far surpass the bodies of the first human beings before sin.[83]

As you endeavor to live the resurrection life now, continue to ask yourself deep, penetrating questions such as: Does my perception of my body impact my understanding of my value as a person of God? Do I engage in negative or hurtful actions towards my own body (i.e. anorexia, bulimia, or "cutting") because of the spiritual pain of my soul? Is my soul subservient to my body (i.e. gluttony, sexual indiscretion, etc.) or am I periodically able to subject my body to the discipline of my soul's choosing (i.e. fasting, meditation, physical exercise). Do I hope in the one who exercises dominion beyond the grave?

Step Out—Hope

As I write this I have just received the news that one of the precious families in our church is about to experience a great loss. The father of two of my former students in the youth ministry, and the husband of one of our greatest volunteers, Darrel (not his real name) has just discovered that he has liver cancer. Not only that, but the disease is now to the fourth stage, a point from which liver cancer patients rarely return. The doctor has told him that he has about two to three months to live. I have tried to imagine staring death in the face as Darrel is doing. My heart breaks as his wife explains to me how they plan on sharing the news to their daughter, whom he may not see graduate from High School at the end of this year.

If it were not for the resurrection from the dead, this situation would be hopeless from a pastoral perspective. I could do nothing but prepare the

---

83 St. Augustine, "Augustine On the Christian Hope" in The Christian Theology Reader. Ed. by Alister McGrath. (Malden MA: Blackwell Publishing, 2001) p. 620.

survivors for the end result of death. Even as I write, I dread the moments that will lead up to Darrel's final days. What will I say? How can I comfort? As a counselor, I would be next to worthless (if there were no resurrection) as I try to bring them hope. But this is not the case. Death has been defeated!

As believers we have the certainty that we *will* live beyond the grave. We have the certainty of the resurrection promise because of what Christ has done for us through His work on the cross and His resurrection victory over the grave. When we live out our last day and hour, take our least breath, feel the last rhythmic beat of the heart, utter our last good-byes—they will not be the true finale. Christ has made sure that for believers there is no "end." Darrel will see his wife and children again.

The Confession Chapter Thirty-three:

Of the Last Judgment

1. God has appointed a day, wherein he will judge the world in righteousness by Jesus Christ, to whom all power and judgment is given of the Father. In which day, not only the apostate angels shall be judged; but likewise all persons, that have lived upon earth, shall appear before the tribunal of Christ, to give an account of their thoughts, words, and deeds; and to receive according to what they have done in the body, whether good or evil.

2. The end of God's appointing this day, is for the manifestation of the glory of his mercy in the eternal salvation of the elect; and of his justice in the damnation of the reprobate, who are wicked and disobedient. For then shall the righteous go into everlasting life, and receive that fullness of joy and refreshing which shall come from the presence of the Lord: but the wicked, who know not God, and obey not the gospel of Jesus Christ, shall be cast into eternal torments, and punished with everlasting destruction from the presence of the Lord, and from the glory of his power.

3. As Christ would have us to be certainly persuaded that there shall be a day of judgment, both to deter all men from sin, and for the greater consolation of the godly in their adversity: so will he have that day unknown to men, that they may shake off all carnal security, and be always watchful, because they know not at what hour the Lord will come; and may be ever prepared to say, Come, Lord Jesus, come quickly. Amen.

Prepare in Prayer
God, without Your Son Jesus Christ, who could stand at the Judgment? No one! We know this full well, and yet we have the tendency to see ourselves as better than others. Once again, allow us to remember our true position in Christ—justified by faith alone. Amen.

Into the Scriptures

Read 1 Corinthians 3:10-15 and Revelation 19:1-8.

Reach Back

It seems a bit strange for the Westminster Confession to end with a chapter on judgment. Yet, it is not that grace is lacking in this text. There is plenty of peace here. For instance the Confession speaks of "the manifestation of the glory of His mercy in the eternal salvation of the elect," and "the fullness of joy and refreshing which shall come from the presence of the Lord" (33.2). And yet we remember that this is a Puritan document. And so it is quite fitting that this great confession, as it was originally written, ends with a stern warning to obedience and faith. For this reason we are not surprised to hear of hell mentioned in the closing words as well.

Is the concept of hell consistent with a loving God? It is. Jonathan Edwards explains why:

> The crime of one being despising and casting contempt on another, is proportionally more or less heinous, as he was under greater or lesser obligations to obey him. And therefore if there be any being that we are under infinite obligations to love, and honor, and obey, the contrary towards him must be infinitely faulty. Our obligation to love, honor, and obey any being is in proportion to his loveliness, honorableness, and authority...But God is a being infinitely lovely, because he hath infinite excellency and beauty...So sin against God, being a violation of infinite obligations must be infinitely heinous...and therefore renders no more than proportional to the heinousness of what they are guilty of.[84]

The Christian faith is no "lollipop religion." It is not the chaff of popular self-esteem banter. It is not the easy-to-digest frivolity of "do it yourself" religion. And the Westminster Confession of Faith makes no pretensions of recommending such glitter. The Christian faith does, however, remit serious warnings of judgment as often as it promises incomprehensible rewards; often in the same breath. And so the Confession ends here, a bit like the Apostle John ends his first epistle, with a staunch reminder of the sheer weightiness of the matters presented within the rest of the document.

---

84 Jonathan Edwards, quoted in John Piper, Desiring God: Meditations of a Christian Hedonist. (Sisters OR: Multnomah Publishers, 2003) p. 60.

Gaze Upwards

When we decide to worship and serve the Lord Jesus Christ with our lives, we have also decided to worship and serve the one who will judge us on that last day (John 5:22, 27). This is wonderful news. The one who will judge us is also our Savior! If our own judge took off His garments of honor and nobility to condescend to be our Savior, how much more then will His judgment be according to His own mercy.

As we consider the sternness and mercy of God today, let us pray with the Reformer John Calvin regarding this great and terrible doctrine of the judgment,

> Almighty God, our heavenly Father, grant us the grace that, being warned by so many examples of Your wrath and vengeance (in the Bible), the memory of which You have willed should endure until the end of the world, we might learn thereby how redoubtable and terrible a Judge You are against the obstinate and those who have hardened their hearts. Grant us also the grace that, today we might not be deaf to this doctrine which we have heard from the mouth of your prophet. Rather, grant that we might apply all our studies in order to appease You and find favor in Your sight, and, abandoning all hope in mankind, present ourselves directly to You. Moreover, being supported by Your loving kindness alone, which You have promised us in Jesus Christ, may we never doubt again that You are our true Father. May we be so touched by a spirit of repentance, that, even if we have been bad examples for one another, and scandalized each other, we might rather become banner-bearers, or guides, to the right way of salvation. And may we strive to help our neighbors by living a good and well-ordered life, so that all together we might attain that heavenly and happy life which Your only Son, our Lord Jesus Christ, has dearly acquired for us by His blood. Amen.[85]

Search Inwards

Go ahead and read 1 Corinthians 3:10-15. Allow yourself to begin to look over your entire life; all the goals and accomplishments that you attained, all the rewards and medals and blue ribbons that you have won, the structures (to remain with Paul's metaphor), both material and immaterial,

---

85 John Calvin, quoted in Steven J. Lawson, The Expository Genius of John Calvin. (Orlando FL: Reformation Trust Publishing, 2007) p. 127-128.

that you have built. Consider all of the relationships that you have fostered, or damaged. Think of the diplomas and the degrees that you have earned. Look back over all of your writings; letters of encouragement or criticism, get well cards, school papers, stories, novels, or books. Think deeply about the way you have treated your parents and raised your children. Envision the faces that you know, both acquaintances and intimate friends; those that you have loved, those that you have spurned. And then, having meditated over the sum of your existence, ask yourself this question: *Of all that I have thought, said, and done, what of these things will be found to be of lasting value as Paul describes them in this Scripture?* What things will be revealed to have been made of gold and silver (vs. 12)? What things will have been constructed with wood, hay, and stubble?

I have sitting on my desk a tiny trophy that I "earned" for playing T-ball as a young boy. T-ball is the kind of baseball that is played before children are able to hit and pitch the ball on their own. The baseball just sits there on the tee waiting for the batter to strike it. At the end of my first season playing for the "T-ball Tornados" the coach handed us each a small, itty-bitty trophy no higher than six inches. It sits modestly on a 1-inch high pedestal of plastic. What seemed to me a more than generous reward for my efforts as a child, now seems to me a humorous reminder of the irony of my achievements. Our earthly trophies are so small and ignoble compared to the righteousness of Jesus, aren't they?

Step Out—Holy Fear

Often I have found that the more I can meditate on the day of my own judgment, the more I am able to ferret out the wood and hay before I am foolish enough to try to build something out of them. Philippians 2:12 warns us to "work out your own salvation with fear and trembling, for it is God who works in you, both to will and to work for His good pleasure." We fear, not because we are concerned that God will destroy us, for there is no longer any condemnation for those who are in Christ Jesus (Romans 8:1); rather we fear because our hearts have been regenerated in order to love Him more and more. Our fear is not that we would ourselves be condemned, but we fear that we would live in such a way that the honor of God is tarnished. Similarly, we tremble not because we are afraid of punishment, but with the ground-shaking responsibility of carrying His name-plate on our hearts.

A man or woman who fears the Lord with a godly fear continues to step out into the world with boldness for the name of Jesus Christ, confident of His completed work on the cross, passionate for the magnitude of His glory, enraptured with a sense of the majesty and holiness of His nature.

George Whitefield, the 18th century Anglican evangelist uttered the following prayer. As you read it, slowly meditate over each and every line, comparing it to your own life:

> "Yeah that we shall see the great Head of the Church once more . . . raise up unto Himself certain young men whom He may use in this glorious employ. And what manner of men will they be? Men mighty in the Scriptures, their lives dominated by a sense of the greatness, the majesty and holiness of God, and their minds and hearts aglow with the great truths of the doctrines of grace. They will be men who have learned what it is to die to self, to human aims and personal ambitions; men who are willing to be 'fools for Christ's sake', who will bear reproach and falsehood, who will labor and suffer, and whose supreme desire will be, not to gain earth's accolades, but to win the Master's approbation when they appear before His awesome judgment seat. They will be men who will preach with broken hearts and tear-filled eyes, and upon whose ministries God will grant an extraordinary effusion of the Holy Spirit, and who will witness 'signs and wonders following' in the transformation of multitudes of human lives."

May God continue to raise up men and women of this generation who have experienced exactly this kind of "Copernican Revolution" of the soul. Amen.

Appendix A:

Two Additional Chapters to the Westminster Confession of Faith

In 1903 many Presbyterians conferred to add two additional chapters to the Westminster Confession of Faith. I have chosen to add them here as Appendix A rather than in the main body of the text because, where possible, I have attempted to preserve this historic document in its original form. The history of this revision is complicated by the splits and mergers that the Presbyterian tradition has endured.[86] Let it suffice to say that the current Evangelical Presbyterian Church (EPC), the Presbyterian Church (USA), and Associate Reformed Presbyterian Church (ARP) include these additional chapters, while the Presbyterian Church in America (PCA) and the Orthodox Presbyterian Church (OPC) do not.

---

86 In 1903 the Westminster Confession of Faith was amended. Two more chapters were written and added; the Presbyterian Church in the United States (PCUS; the southern branch) regarded them as chapters 9 "Of the Holy Spirit" and 10 "Of the Gospel," thus bumping each subsequent chapter up in order. The United Presbyterian Church in the United States of America (the northern branch) regarded the addition as chapters 34 "Of the Holy Spirit" and 35 "Of the Gospel of the Love of God and Missions." These two denominations later merged in 1983 to become the current Presbyterian Church (USA) whose Book of Order includes both versions of these additions in its Book of Confessions.

When the Presbyterian Church of America, a more conservative branch of Reformed believers, split off from the PCUS in the early 1970's they decided, for the sake of historical integrity, to adopt virtually the same version of the Confession as was adopted by the first American Presbyterian Assembly of 1789. For this reason the PCA does *not* include these two additional chapters.

Two other branches of conservative Presbyterianism, the Evangelical Presbyterian Church (or the EPC, formed in 1981) and the Associate Reformed Presbyterian Church (the ARP, formed in 1782) decided to adopt the version of the Westminster Confession which *does* include these additional chapters. Viewing them as consistent supplements to the Confession as written by the Westminster Divines, the EPC and ARP stay in line with PCUS tradition of adding these chapters to the end of the Confession as Chapters 34 and 35.

The Confession Chapter Thirty-four:

Of the Holy Spirit

1. The Holy Spirit, the third Person in the Trinity, proceeding from the Father and the Son, of the same substance and equal in power and glory, is, together with the Father and the Son, to be believed in, loved, obeyed, and worshiped throughout all ages.

2. He is the Lord and Giver of life, everywhere present, and is the source of all good thoughts, pure desires, and holy counsels in men. By him the prophets were moved to speak the Word of God, and all the writers of the Holy Scriptures inspired to record infallibly the mind and will of God. The dispensation of the gospel is especially committed to him. He prepares the way for it, accompanies it with his persuasive power, and urges its message upon the reason and conscience of men, so that they who reject its merciful offer are not only without excuse, but are also guilty of resisting the Holy Spirit.

3. The Holy Spirit, whom the Father is ever willing to give to all who ask him, is the only efficient agent in the application of redemption. He regenerates men by his grace, convicts them of sin, moves them to repentance, and persuades and enables them to embrace Jesus Christ by faith. He unites all believers to Christ, dwells in them as their Comforter and Sanctifier, gives to them the Spirit of adoption and prayer, and performs all these gracious offices by which they are sanctified and sealed unto the day of redemption.

4. By the indwelling of the Holy Spirit all believers being vitally united to Christ, who is the head, are thus united one to another in the Church, which is his body. He calls and anoints ministers for their holy office, qualifies all other officers in the Church for their special work, and imparts various gifts and graces to its members. He gives efficacy to the Word and to the ordinances of the gospel. By him the Church will be preserved, in-creased, purified, and at last made perfectly holy in the presence of God.

The Confession Chapter Thirty-five:

Of the Gospel of the Love of God and Missions

1. God in infinite and perfect love, having provided in the covenant of grace, through the mediation and sacrifice of the Lord Jesus Christ, a way of life and salvation, sufficient for and adapted to the whole lost race of man, doth freely offer this salvation to all men in the gospel.

2. In the gospel God declares his love for the world and his desire that all men should be saved; reveals fully and clearly the only way of salvation; promises eternal life to all who truly repent and believe in Christ; invites and commands all to embrace the offered mercy; and by his Spirit accompanying the Word pleads with men to accept his gracious invitation.

3. It is the duty and privilege of everyone who hears the gospel immediately to accept its merciful provisions; and they who continue in impenitence and unbelief incur aggravated guilt and perish by their own fault.

4. Since there is no other way of salvation than that revealed in the gospel, and since in the divinely established and ordinary method of grace faith cometh by hearing the Word of God, Christ hath commissioned his Church to go into all the world and to make disciples of all nations. All believers are, therefore, under obligation to sustain the ordinance of the Christian religion where they are already established, and to contribute by their prayers, gifts, and personal efforts to the extension of the Kingdom of Christ throughout the whole earth.

Appendix B:

Introduction to the Shorter and Larger Catechisms

Appended to the main body of the Westminster Confession of Faith are two additional tools for the doctrinal instruction of Reformed Christian believers. They are two catechisms known, for obvious reasons, as the "Shorter Catechism" and the "Larger Catechism." Essentially, both were devised for the purposeful, intentional, instruction of God's people in matters of personal faith and theology.

The word "catechism" comes from the Greek word *katakismos* meaning "instruction." The use of catechisms to instruct believers goes back to the early church as confessing candidates were prepared for baptism. Baptismal services were, in many places, held only once per year, likely at Easter. Many candidates for baptism were required to memorize large portions of Scripture to prepare for this monumental day. During the time of the Reformation, more formal and detailed catechisms sprung up, notably Luther's own Larger and Smaller Catechisms, and the Heidelberg Catechism. John Calvin as well had prepared a catechism for his exhortation and usage in Geneva.

Alongside the Body of the Westminster Confession, the Divines of the Assembly saw fit to prepare two new catechisms for use in Reformed churches. The Shorter Catechism is primarily an instructional devise for children and youth.[87] The outline of the Smaller Catechism is roughly:

---

87 As mentioned in the introduction to this work, the Shorter Catechism was included in the New England Primer, the schoolbook through which many American colonial schoolchildren learned to read.

Questions 1-10: God, the Scriptures, and Creation

Questions 11-29: Christ and His Work

Questions 30-38: The Holy Spirit and Redemption

Questions 39-85: The Law and the Ten Commandments

Questions 86-97: Personal Faith and the Sacraments

Questions 98-107: The Lord's Prayer.[88]

The Larger Catechism is longer, more complicated, and detailed. Its primary usage was as a guide for preaching and teaching systematic theology, by which pastors would be equipped to educate their people. The Larger Catechism is roughly outlined in three sections:

(Questions 1-5): Man's Purpose and the Scriptures

(Questions 6-90): "What Man Ought to Believe Concerning God." Here the Catechism delves deeply into matters such as the Trinity, providence, the Fall, the covenants, the incarnation and work of Jesus Christ, His death and resurrection, the Church, the ordo salutis[89], and our final judgment.

(Questions 91-196): "Having Seen What the Scriptures Principally Teach Us to Believe Concerning God, It Follows to Consider What They Require as the Duty of Man." In this last section, the Catechism works through the moral law, the Ten Commandments, the application of the Word of God, the sacraments, and the Lord's Prayer.

Both catechisms are similar in that their theology is parallel to that of the main body of the Confession itself. As a whole, both are consumed with a passion for the glory and sovereignty of God. Both, like many catechisms before them, use a "question and answer" style that could readily be adapted to family, small group, large group, or individual study purposes. Neither catechism elaborates upon the Apostles Creed, which was a derivation from the standard inclusion of this universal statement of faith in other

88 These are my own divisions.

89 See my introduction to this work.

catechisms. Both catechisms, however, include reflection on the Ten Commandments as well as the Lord's Prayer.

Both catechisms are also noted for their beautiful (and similar) first questions; "What is the chief end of man?" Answer: "Man's chief end is to glorify God, and to enjoy Him forever" (WSC #1).

Unfortunately, the usage of the catechisms has fallen out of favor. Professor Charles Hodge, one of the great venerable Princeton theologians of the 1800's lamented in his own time, "It is within memory of many now living that in almost every Presbyterian and Congregationalist family in the land, as a matter of course, the children were regularly taught the 'Westminster Catechism.' It is not so now."[90] Nevertheless, while it is true that the catechisms are no longer used as frequently as they once were, there are still many ways that they can be of service to Reformed Christian people.

1) The catechisms are helpful in defining and summing complex theological ideas. These documents are very helpful in placing succinct, accurate, and pointed definitions of Scriptural ideas into the hands of believers. Often, when defining and defending the Christian faith, we are in need of brief definitions of theological concepts. The catechisms provide us with these concise truths. For instance, consider the definition of sin in question #14 of the Shorter,

"Q #24. What is sin? A: Sin is any want of conformity unto, or transgression of, the law of God."

Or consider the Larger Catechism's definition of justification, a complex theological notion that often requires much development. Here, a portable, compact definition is offered:

> Q #70. What is justification? A: Justification is an act of God's free grace unto sinners, in which he pardons all their sins, accepts and accounts their persons righteous in his sight; not for anything wrought in them, or done by them, but only for the perfect obedience and full satisfaction of Christ, by God imputed to them, and received by faith alone.

2) Secondly, the catechisms are vital for helping everyday laypersons to

---

90 Charles Hodge. Systematic Theology. Volume III. (Peabody MA: Hendrickson, 2003) p. 572.

delineate the difference between Reformed branches of Christianity and non-Reformed branches of Christianity. While the differences here can be considered "in-house debates," the distinction between branches of the Christian family tree are not without importance. By way of example, suppose a Bible study is studying the book of Acts and comes upon the question of whether infants and children should be baptized. A believer from a Baptist church asks her Presbyterian friend why her church baptizes infants. Not sure how to respond, she looks for a pointed answer, perhaps finding it in the Larger Confession's question #166. "We baptize infants," she explains,

> Baptism is not to be administered to any that are out of the visible church, and so strangers from the covenant of promise, till they profess their faith in Christ, and obedience to him, but infants descending from parents, either both, or but one of them, professing faith in Christ, and obedience to him, are in that respect within the covenant, and to be baptized.

3) Thirdly, the catechisms are valuable for personal devotional use, for prompting and enhancing our prayer lives, and for the commitment of Scriptural truths to heart and memory. Because much of the content in the catechisms has a "devotional feel" to them, they read with a pastoral pathos. Many of the answers contained in the catechisms are full of personal assurance, grace-filled language, and confirming confidence.

Consider for example the words of Question #185 of the Larger Catechism,

> We are to pray with an awful apprehension of the majesty of God, and deep sense of our own unworthiness, necessities, and sins; with penitent, thankful, and enlarged hearts; with understanding, faith, sincerity, fervency, love, and perseverance, waiting upon him, with humble submission to his will.

4) Finally, while they may have fallen out of favor in our generation, the timeless truths of the catechisms ought not to be discarded, as they are useful for discipling the younger generations, instructing new believers in the faith, and confirming the hearts and minds of the elders within the Body of Christ. Although rote memorization is a difficult thing for most of us, the freedom that comes through the godly discipline of memorization is unparalleled. Would that God would raise up a new generation of pastors that are not afraid to introduce theological depth to their young people,

elders that are concerned to bring a well-articulated theology to their new church members, and church members that would not back down from the hard, difficult work of apprehending the doctrines of grace.

Appendix C:

The Westminster Shorter Catechism

Q. 1. *What is the chief end of man?*
A. Man's chief end is to glorify God, and to enjoy him forever.

Q. 2. *What rule has God given to direct us how we may glorify and enjoy him?*
A. The word of God, which is contained in the scriptures of the Old and New Testaments, is the only rule to direct us how we may glorify and enjoy him.

Q. 3. *What do the scriptures principally teach?*
A. The scriptures principally teach what man is to believe concerning God, and what duty God requires of man.

Q. 4. *What is God?*
A. God is a spirit, infinite, eternal, and unchangeable, in his being, wisdom, power, holiness, justice, goodness and truth.

Q. 5. *Are there more Gods than one?*
A. There is but one only, the living and true God.

Q. 6. *How many persons are there in the godhead?*
A. There are three persons in the Godhead; the Father, the Son, and the Holy Ghost; and these three are one God, the same in substance, equal in power and glory.

Q. 7. *What are the decrees of God?*
A. The decrees of God are his eternal purpose, according to the counsel of his will, whereby, for his own glory, he has foreordained whatsoever comes to pass.

Q. 8. *How does God execute his decrees?*
A. God executes his decrees in the works of creation and providence.

Q. 9. *What is the work of creation?*
A. The work of creation is God's making all things of nothing, by the word of his power, in the space of six days, and all very good.

Q. 10. *How did God create man?*
A. God created man male and female, after his own image, in knowledge, righteousness and holiness, with dominion over the creatures.

Q. 11. *What are God's works of providence?*
A. God's works of providence are his most holy, wise and powerful preserving and governing all his creatures, and all their actions.

Q. 12. *What special act of providence did God exercise toward man in the estate wherein he was created?*
A. When God had created man, he entered into a covenant of life with him, upon condition of perfect obedience; forbidding him to eat of the tree of the knowledge of good and evil, upon the pain of death.

Q. 13. *Did our first parents continue in the estate wherein they were created?*
A. Our first parents, being left to the freedom of their own will, fell from the estate wherein they were created, by sinning against God.

Q. 14. *What is sin?*
A. Sin is any want of conformity unto, or transgression of, the law of God.

Q. 15. *What was the sin whereby our first parents fell from the estate wherein they were created?*
A. The sin whereby our first parents fell from the estate wherein they were created was their eating the forbidden fruit.

Q. 16. *Did all mankind fall in Adam's first transgression?*
A. The covenant being made with Adam, not only for himself, but for his posterity; all mankind, descending from him by ordinary generation, sinned in him, and fell with him, in his first transgression.

Q. 17. *Into what estate did the fall bring mankind?*
A. The fall brought mankind into an estate of sin and misery.

Q. 18. *Wherein consists the sinfulness of that estate whereinto man fell?*
A. The sinfulness of that estate whereinto man fell consists in the guilt of Adam's first sin, the want of original righteousness, and the corruption of his whole nature, which is commonly called original sin; together with all actual transgressions which proceed from it.

Q. 19. *What is the misery of that estate whereinto man fell?*
A. All mankind by their fall lost communion with God, are under his wrath and curse, and so made liable to all miseries in this life, to death itself, and to the pains of hell forever.

Q. 20. *Did God leave all mankind to perish in the estate of sin and misery?*
A. God having, out of his mere good pleasure, from all eternity, elected some to everlasting life, did enter into a covenant of grace, to deliver them out of the estate of sin and misery, and to bring them into an estate of salvation by a redeemer.

Q. 21. *Who is the redeemer of God's elect?*
A. The only redeemer of God's elect is the Lord Jesus Christ, who, being the eternal Son of God, became man, and so was, and continues to be, God and man in two distinct natures, and one person, forever.

Q. 22. *How did Christ, being the Son of God, become man?*
A. Christ, the Son of God, became man, by taking to himself a true body and a reasonable soul, being conceived by the power of the Holy Ghost in the womb of the Virgin Mary, and born of her, yet without sin.

Q. 23. *What offices does Christ execute as our redeemer?*
A. Christ, as our redeemer, executes the offices of a prophet, of a priest, and of a king, both in his estate of humiliation and exaltation.

Q. 24. *How does Christ execute the office of a prophet?*
A. Christ executes the office of a prophet, in revealing to us, by his word and Spirit, the will of God for our salvation.

Q. 25. *How does Christ execute the office of a priest?*
A. Christ executes the office of a priest, in his once offering up of himself a sacrifice to satisfy divine justice, and reconcile us to God; and in making continual intercession for us.

Q. 26. *How does Christ execute the office of a king?*
A. Christ executes the office of a king, in subduing us to himself, in ruling and defending us, and in restraining and conquering all his and our enemies.

Q. 27. *Wherein did Christ's humiliation consist?*
A. Christ's humiliation consisted in his being born, and that in a low condition, made under the law, undergoing the miseries of this life, the wrath of God, and the cursed death of the cross; in being buried, and continuing under the power of death for a time.

Q. 28. *What consists of Christ's exaltation?*
A. Christ's exaltation consists in his rising again from the dead on the third day, in ascending up into heaven, in sitting at the right hand of God the Father, and in coming to judge the world at the last day.

Q. 29. *How are we made partakers of the redemption purchased by Christ?*
A. We are made partakers of the redemption purchased by Christ, by the effectual application of it to us by his Holy Spirit.

Q. 30. *How does the Spirit apply to us the redemption purchased by Christ?*
A. The Spirit applies to us the redemption purchased by Christ, by working faith in us, and thereby uniting us to Christ in our effectual calling.

Q. 31. *What is effectual calling?*
A. Effectual calling is the work of God's Spirit, whereby, convincing us of our sin and misery, enlightening our minds in the knowledge of Christ, and renewing our wills, he does persuade and enable us to embrace Jesus Christ, freely offered to us in the gospel.

Q. 32. *What benefits do they that are effectually called partake of in this life?*
A. They that are effectually called do in this life partake of justification, adoption and sanctification, and the several benefits that in this life do either accompany or flow from them.

Q. 33. *What is justification?*
A. Justification is an act of God's free grace, wherein he pardons all our sins, and accepts us as righteous in his sight, only for the righteousness of Christ imputed to us, and received by faith alone.

Q. 34. *What is adoption?*
A. Adoption is an act of God's free grace, whereby we are received into the

number, and have a right to all the privileges of, the sons of God.

Q. 35. *What is sanctification?*
A. Sanctification is the work of God's free grace, whereby we are renewed in the whole man after the image of God, and are enabled more and more to die unto sin, and live unto righteousness.

Q. 36. *What are the benefits that in this life do accompany or flow from justification, adoption and sanctification?*
A. The benefits that in this life do accompany or flow from justification, adoption and sanctification, are, assurance of God's love, peace of conscience, joy in the Holy Ghost, increase of grace, and perseverance therein to the end.

Q. 37. *What benefits do believers receive from Christ at death?*
A. The souls of believers are at their death made perfect in holiness, and do immediately pass into glory; and their bodies, being still united to Christ, do rest in their graves till the resurrection.

Q. 38. *What benefits do believers receive from Christ at the resurrection?*
A. At the resurrection, believers being raised up in glory, shall be openly acknowledged and acquitted in the day of judgment, and made perfectly blessed in the full enjoying of God to all eternity.

Q. 39. *What is the duty that God requires of man?*
A. The duty that God requires of man is obedience to his revealed will.

Q. 40. *What did God at first reveal to man for the rule of his obedience?*
A. The rule that God at first revealed to man for his obedience was the moral law.

Q. 41. *Where is the moral law summarily comprehended?*
A. The moral law is summarily comprehended in the Ten Commandments.

Q. 42. *What is the sum of the Ten Commandments?*
A. The sum of the Ten Commandments is to love the Lord our God with all our heart, with all our soul, with all our strength, and with all of our mind; and our neighbor as ourselves.

Q. 43. *What is the preface to the Ten Commandments?*
A. The preface to the ten commandments is in these words, I am the Lord

your God, which have brought thee out of the land of Egypt, out of the house of bondage.

Q. 44. *What does the preface to the Ten Commandments teach us?*
A. The preface to the Ten Commandments teaches us that because God is the Lord, and our God, and redeemer, therefore we are bound to keep all his commandments.

Q. 45. *Which is the first commandment?*
A. The first commandment is, You shall have no other gods before me.

Q. 46. *What is required in the first commandment?*
A. The first commandment requires us to know and acknowledge God to be the only true God, and our God; and to worship and glorify him accordingly.

Q. 47. *What is forbidden in the first commandment?*
A. The first commandment forbids the denying, or not worshiping and glorifying the true God as God, and our God; and the giving of that worship and glory to any other, which is due to him alone.

Q. 48. *What are we specially taught by these words before me in the first commandment?*
A. These words before me in the first commandment teach us that God, who sees all things, takes notice of, and is much displeased with, the sin of having any other god.

Q. 49. *Which is the second commandment?*
A. The second commandment is, You shall not make unto thee any graven image, or any likeness of anything that is in heaven above, or that is in the earth beneath, or that is in the water under the earth: you shall not bow down yourself to them, nor serve them: for I the Lord your God am a jealous God, visiting the iniquity of the fathers upon the children unto the third and fourth generation of them that hate me; and showing mercy unto thousands of them that love me, and keep my commandments.

Q. 50. *What is required in the second commandment?*
A. The second commandment requires the receiving, observing, and keeping pure and entire, all such religious worship and ordinances as God has appointed in his word.

Q. 51. *What is forbidden in the second commandment?*
A. The second commandment forbids the worshiping of God by images, or any other way not appointed in his word.

Q. 52. *What are the reasons annexed to the second commandment?*
A. The reasons annexed to the second commandment are, God's sovereignty over us, his propriety in us, and the zeal he has to his own worship.

Q. 53. *Which is the third commandment?*
A. The third commandment is, You shall not take the name of the Lord your God in vain: for the Lord will not hold him guiltless that takes his name in vain.

Q. 54. *What is required in the third commandment?*
A. The third commandment requires the holy and reverent use of God's names, titles, attributes, ordinances, word and works.

Q. 55. *What is forbidden in the third commandment?*
A. The third commandment forbids all profaning or abusing of anything whereby God makes himself known.

Q. 56. *What is the reason annexed to the third commandment?*
A. The reason annexed to the third commandment is that however the breakers of this commandment may escape punishment from men, yet the Lord our God will not suffer them to escape his righteous judgment.

Q. 57. *Which is the fourth commandment?*
A. The fourth commandment is, Remember the Sabbath day, to keep it holy. Six days shall you labor, and do all your work: but the seventh day is the Sabbath of the Lord your God: in it you shall not do any work, you, nor your son, nor your daughter, your manservant, nor your maidservant, nor your cattle, nor your stranger that is within your gates: for in six days the Lord made heaven and earth, the sea, and all that in them is, and rested the seventh day: wherefore the Lord blessed the Sabbath day, and hallowed it.

Q. 58. *What is required in the fourth commandment?*
A. The fourth commandment requires the keeping holy to God such set times as he has appointed in his word; expressly one whole day in seven, to be a holy Sabbath to himself.

Q. 59. *Which day of the seven has God appointed to be the weekly Sabbath?*
A. From the beginning of the world to the resurrection of Christ, God appointed the seventh day of the week to be the weekly Sabbath; and the first day of the week ever since, to continue to the end of the world, which is the Christian Sabbath.

Q. 60. *How is the Sabbath to be sanctified?*
A. The Sabbath is to be sanctified by a holy resting all that day, even from such worldly employments and recreations as are lawful on other days; and spending the whole time in the public and private exercises of God's worship, except so much as is to be taken up in the works of necessity and mercy.

Q. 61. *What is forbidden in the fourth commandment?*
A. The fourth commandment forbids the omission or careless performance of the duties required, and the profaning the day by idleness, or doing that which is in itself sinful, or by unnecessary thoughts, words or works, about our worldly employments or recreations.

Q. 62. *What are the reasons annexed to the fourth commandment?*
A. The reasons annexed to the fourth commandment are, God's allowing us six days of the week for our own employments, his challenging a special propriety in the seventh, his own example, and his blessing the Sabbath day.

Q. 63. *Which is the fifth commandment?*
A. The fifth commandment is, Honor your father and your mother; that your days may be long upon the land which the Lord your God gives thee.

Q. 64. *What is required in the fifth commandment?*
A. The fifth commandment requires the preserving the honor, and performing the duties, belonging to every one in their several places and relations, as superiors, inferiors or equals.

Q. 65. *What is forbidden in the fifth commandment?*
A. The fifth commandment forbids the neglecting of, or doing anything against, the honor and duty which belongs to every one in their several places and relations.

Q. 66. *What is the reason annexed to the fifth commandment?*
A. The reason annexed to the fifth commandment is a promise of long life and prosperity (as far as it shall serve for God's glory and their own good) to all such as keep this commandment.

Q. 67. *Which is the sixth commandment?*
A. The sixth commandment is, You shall not kill.

Q. 68. *What is required in the sixth commandment?*
A. The sixth commandment requires all lawful endeavors to preserve our own life, and the life of others.

Q. 69. *What is forbidden in the sixth commandment?*
A. The sixth commandment forbids the taking away of our own life, or the life of our neighbor unjustly, or whatsoever tends thereunto.

Q. 70. *Which is the seventh commandment?*
A. The seventh commandment is, You shall not commit adultery.

Q. 71. *What is required in the seventh commandment?*
A. The seventh commandment requires the preservation of our own and our neighbor's chastity, in heart, speech and behavior.

Q. 72. *What is forbidden in the seventh commandment?*
A. The seventh commandment forbids all unchaste thoughts, words and actions.

Q. 73. *Which is the eighth commandment?*
A. The eighth commandment is, You shall not steal.

Q. 74. *What is required in the eighth commandment?*
A. The eighth commandment requires the lawful procuring and furthering the wealth and outward estate of ourselves and others.

Q. 75. *What is forbidden in the eighth commandment?*
A. The eighth commandment forbids whatsoever does or may unjustly hinder our own or our neighbor's wealth or outward estate.

Q. 76. *Which is the ninth commandment?*
A. The ninth commandment is, You shall not bear false witness against your neighbor.

Q. 77. *What is required in the ninth commandment?*
A. The ninth commandment requires the maintaining and promoting of truth between man and man, and of our own and our neighbor's good name, especially in witness-bearing.

Q. 78. *What is forbidden in the ninth commandment?*
A. The ninth commandment forbids whatsoever is prejudicial to truth, or injurious to our own or our neighbor's good name.

Q. 79. *Which is the tenth commandment?*
A. The tenth commandment is, You shall not covet your neighbor's house, you shall not covet your neighbor's wife, nor his manservant, nor his maidservant, nor his ox, nor his ass, nor anything that is your neighbor's.

Q. 80. *What is required in the tenth commandment?*
A. The tenth commandment requires full contentment with our own condition, with a right and charitable frame of spirit toward our neighbor, and all that is his.

Q. 81. *What is forbidden in the tenth commandment?*
A. The tenth commandment forbids all discontentment with our own estate, envying or grieving at the good of our neighbor, and all inordinate motions and affections to anything that is his.

Q. 82. *Is any man able perfectly to keep the commandments of God?*
A. No mere man since the fall is able in this life perfectly to keep the commandments of God, but does daily break them in thought, word and deed.

Q. 83. *Are all transgressions of the law equally heinous?*
A. Some sins in themselves, and by reason of several aggravations, are more heinous in the sight of God than others.

Q. 84. *What does every sin deserve?*
A. Every sin deserves God's wrath and curse, both in this life, and that which is to come.

Q. 85. *What does God require of us that we may escape his wrath and curse due to us for sin?*
A. To escape the wrath and curse of God due to us for sin, God requires of us faith in Jesus Christ, repentance unto life, with the diligent use of all the outward means whereby Christ communicates to us the benefits of redemption.

Q. 86. *What is faith in Jesus Christ?*
A. Faith in Jesus Christ is a saving grace, whereby we receive and rest upon

him alone for salvation, as he is offered to us in the gospel.

Q. 87. *What is repentance unto life?*
A. Repentance unto life is a saving grace, whereby a sinner, out of a true sense of his sin, and apprehension of the mercy of God in Christ, does, with grief and hatred of his sin, turn from it unto God, with full purpose of, and endeavor after, new obedience.

Q. 88. *What are the outward means whereby Christ communicates to us the benefits of redemption?*
A. The outward and ordinary means whereby Christ communicates to us the benefits of redemption, are his ordinances, especially the word, sacraments, and prayer; all which are made effectual to the elect for salvation.

Q. 89. *How is the word made effectual to salvation?*
A. The Spirit of God makes the reading, but especially the preaching, of the word, an effectual means of convincing and converting sinners, and of building them up in holiness and comfort, through faith, unto salvation.

Q. 90. *How is the word to be read and heard, that it may become effectual to salvation?*
A. That the word may become effectual to salvation, we must attend thereunto with diligence, preparation and prayer; receive it with faith and love, lay it up in our hearts, and practice it in our lives.

Q. 91. *How do the sacraments become effectual means of salvation?*
A. The sacraments become effectual means of salvation, not from any virtue in them, or in him that does administer them; but only by the blessing of Christ, and the working of his Spirit in them that by faith receive them.

Q. 92. *What is a sacrament?*
A. A sacrament is an holy ordinance instituted by Christ; wherein, by sensible signs, Christ, and the benefits of the new covenant, are represented, sealed, and applied to believers.

Q. 93. *Which are the sacraments of the New Testament?*
A. The sacraments of the New Testament are baptism and the Lord's supper.

Q. 94. *What is baptism?*
A. Baptism is a sacrament, wherein the washing with water in the name

of the Father, and of the Son, and of the Holy Ghost, does signify and seal our ingrafting into Christ, and partaking of the benefits of the covenant of grace, and our engagement to be the Lord's.

Q. 95. *To whom is baptism to be administered?*
A. Baptism is not to be administered to any that are out of the visible church, till they profess their faith in Christ, and obedience to him; but the infants of such as are members of the visible church are to be baptized.

Q. 96. *What is the Lord's Supper?*
A. The Lord's supper is a sacrament, wherein, by giving and receiving bread and wine according to Christ's appointment, his death is showed forth; and the woryour receivers are, not after a corporal and carnal manner, but by faith, made partakers of his body and blood, with all his benefits, to their spiritual nourishment and growth in grace.

Q. 97. *What is required to the woryour receiving of the Lord's Supper?*
A. It is required of them that would worthily partake of the Lord's supper, that they examine themselves of their knowledge to discern the Lord's body, of their faith to feed upon him, of their repentance, love, and new obedience; lest, coming unworthily, they eat and drink judgment to themselves.

Q. 98. *What is prayer?*
A. Prayer is an offering up of our desires unto God, for things agreeable to his will, in the name of Christ, with confession of our sins, and thankful acknowledgment of his mercies.

Q. 99. *What rule has God given for our direction in prayer?*
A. The whole word of God is of use to direct us in prayer; but the special rule of direction is that form of prayer that Christ taught his disciples, commonly called the Lord's Prayer.

Q. 100. *What does the preface of the Lord's Prayer teach us?*
A. The preface of the Lord's prayer, which is, Our Father which art in heaven, teaches us to draw near to God with all holy reverence and confidence, as children to a father able and ready to help us; and that we should pray with and for others.

Q. 101. *What do we pray for in the first petition?*
A. In the first petition, which is, Hallowed be your name, we pray that God

would enable us and others to glorify him in all that whereby he makes himself known; and that he would dispose all things to his own glory.

Q. 102. *What do we pray for in the second petition?*
A. In the second petition, which is, Your kingdom come, we pray that Satan's kingdom may be destroyed; and that the kingdom of grace may be advanced, ourselves and others brought into it, and kept in it; and that the kingdom of glory may be hastened.

Q. 103. *What do we pray for in the third petition?*
A. In the third petition, which is, Your will be done in earth, as it is in heaven, we pray that God, by his grace, would make us able and willing to know, obey and submit to his will in all things, as the angels do in heaven.

Q. 104. *What do we pray for in the fourth petition?*
A. In the fourth petition, which is, Give us this day our daily bread, we pray that of God's free gift we may receive a competent portion of the good things of this life, and enjoy his blessing with them.

Q. 105. *What do we pray for in the fifth petition?*
A. In the fifth petition, which is, And forgive us our debts, as we forgive our debtors, we pray that God, for Christ's sake, would freely pardon all our sins; which we are the rather encouraged to ask, because by his grace we are enabled from the heart to forgive others.

Q. 106. *What do we pray for in the sixth petition?*
A. In the sixth petition, which is, And lead us not into temptation, but deliver us from evil, we pray that God would either keep us from being tempted to sin, or support and deliver us when we are tempted.

Q. 107. *What does the conclusion of the Lord's Prayer teach us?*
A. The conclusion of the Lord's prayer, which is, For thine is the kingdom, and the power, and the glory, forever, Amen, teaches us to take our encouragement in prayer from God only, and in our prayers to praise him, ascribing kingdom, power and glory to him. And in testimony of our desire, and assurance to be heard, we say, Amen.

Appendix D:

The Westminster Larger Catechism

Q. 1. *What is the chief and highest end of man?*
A. Man's chief and highest end is to glorify God, and fully to enjoy him forever.

Q. 2. *How does it appear that there is a God?*
A. The very light of nature in man, and the works of God, declare plainly that there is a God; but his word and Spirit only do sufficiently and effectually reveal him unto men for their salvation.

Q. 3. *What is the Word of God?*
A. The holy Scriptures of the Old and New Testament are the Word of God, the only rule of faith and obedience.

Q. 4. *How does it appear that the Scriptures are the Word of God?*
A. The Scriptures manifest themselves to be the Word of God, by their majesty and purity; by the consent of all the parts, and the scope of the whole, which is to give all glory to God; by their light and power to convince and convert sinners, to comfort and build up believers unto salvation: but the Spirit of God bearing witness by and with the Scriptures in the heart of man, is alone able fully to persuade it that they are the very Word of God.

Q. 5. *What do the Scriptures principally teach?*
A. The Scriptures principally teach what man is to believe concerning God, and what duty God requires of man.

Q. 6. *What do the Scriptures make known of God?*
A. The Scriptures make known what God is, the persons in the Godhead, his decrees, and the execution of his decrees.

Q. 7. *What is God?*
A. God is a Spirit, in and of himself infinite in being, glory, blessedness, and perfection; all-sufficient, eternal, unchangeable, incomprehensible, everywhere present, almighty, knowing all things, most wise, most holy, most just, most merciful and gracious, longsuffering, and abundant in goodness and truth.

Q. 8. *Are there more Gods than one?*
A. There is but one only, the living and true God.

Q. 9. *How many persons are there in the Godhead?*
A. There be three persons in the Godhead, the Father, the Son, and the Holy Ghost; and these three are one true, eternal God, the same in substance, equal in power and glory; although distinguished by their personal properties.

Q. 10. *What are the personal properties of the three persons in the Godhead?*
A. It is proper to the Father to beget the Son, and to the Son to be begotten of the Father, and to the Holy Ghost to proceed from the Father and the Son from all eternity.

Q. 11. *How does it appear that the Son and the Holy Ghost are God equal with the Father?*
A. The Scriptures manifest that the Son and the Holy Ghost are God equal with the Father, ascribing unto them such names, attributes, works, and worship, as are proper to God only.

Q. 12. *What are the decrees of God?*
A. God's decrees are the wise, free, and holy acts of the counsel of his will, whereby, from all eternity, he hath, for his own glory, unchangeably foreordained whatsoever comes to pass in time, especially concerning angels and men.

Q. 13. *What hath God especially decreed concerning angels and men?*
A. God, by an eternal and immutable decree, out of his mere love, for the praise of his glorious grace, to be manifested in due time, hath elected some angels to glory; and in Christ hath chosen some men to eternal life, and the means thereof: and also, according to his sovereign power, and the

unsearchable counsel of his own will (whereby he extends or withholds favor as he pleases), hath passed by and foreordained the rest to dishonor and wrath, to be for their sin inflicted, to the praise of the glory of his justice.

Q. 14. *How does God execute his decrees?*
A. God executes his decrees in the works of creation and providence, according to his infallible foreknowledge, and the free and immutable counsel of his own will.

Q. 15. *What is the work of creation?*
A. The work of creation is that wherein God did in the beginning, by the word of his power, make of nothing the world, and all things therein, for himself, within the space of six days, and all very good.

Q. 16. *How did God create angels?*
A. God created all the angels spirits, immortal, holy, excelling in knowledge, mighty in power, to execute his commandments, and to praise his name, yet subject to change.

Q. 17. *How did God create man?*
A. After God had made all other creatures, he created man male and female; formed the body of the man of the dust of the ground, and the woman of the rib of the man, endued them with living, reasonable, and immortal souls; made them after his own image, in knowledge, righteousness, and holiness; having the law of God written in their hearts, and power to fulfill it, and dominion over the creatures; yet subject to fall.

Q. 18. *What are God's works of providence?*
A. God's works of providence are his most holy, wise, and powerful preserving and governing all his creatures; ordering them, and all their actions, to his own glory.

Q. 19. *What is God's providence towards the angels?*
A. God by his providence permitted some of the angels, willfully and irrecoverably, to fall into sin and damnation, limiting and ordering that, and all their sins, to his own glory; and established the rest in holiness and happiness; employing them all, at his pleasure, in the administrations of his power, mercy, and justice.

Q. 20. *What was the providence of God toward man in the estate in which he was created?*

A. The providence of God toward man in the estate in which he was created, was the placing him in paradise, appointing him to dress it, giving him liberty to eat of the fruit of the earth; putting the creatures under his dominion, and ordaining marriage for his help; affording him communion with himself; instituting the Sabbath; entering into a covenant of life with him, upon condition of personal, perfect, and perpetual obedience, of which the tree of life was a pledge; and forbidding to eat of the tree of the knowledge of good and evil, upon the pain of death.

Q. 21. *Did man continue in that estate wherein God at first created him?*

A. Our first parents being left to the freedom of their own will, through the temptation of Satan, transgressed the commandment of God in eating the forbidden fruit; and thereby fell from the estate of innocence wherein they were created.

Q. 22. *Did all mankind fall in that first transgression?*

A. The covenant being made with Adam as a public person, not for himself only, but for his posterity, all mankind descending from him by ordinary generation, sinned in him, and fell with him in that first transgression.

Q. 23. *Into what estate did the fall bring mankind?*

A. The fall brought mankind into an estate of sin and misery.

Q. 24. *What is sin?*

A. Sin is any want of conformity unto, or transgression of, any law of God, given as a rule to the reasonable creature.

Q. 25. *Wherein consists the sinfulness of that estate whereinto man fell?*

A. The sinfulness of that estate whereinto man fell, consists in the guilt of Adam's first sin, the want of that righteousness wherein he was created, and the corruption of his nature, whereby he is utterly indisposed, disabled, and made opposite unto all that is spiritually good, and wholly inclined to all evil, and that continually; which is commonly called original sin, and from which do proceed all actual transgressions.

Q. 26. *How is original sin conveyed from our first parents unto their posterity?*

A. Original sin is conveyed from our first parents unto their posterity by natural generation, so as all that proceed from them in that way are conceived and born in sin.

Q. 27. *What misery did the fall bring upon mankind?*

A. The fall brought upon mankind the loss of communion with God, his displeasure and curse; so as we are by nature children of wrath, bond slaves to Satan, and justly liable to all punishments in this world, and that which is to come.

Q. 28. *What are the punishments of sin in this world?*

A. The punishments of sin in this world are either inward, as blindness of mind, a reprobate sense, strong delusions, hardness of heart, horror of conscience, and vile affections; or outward, as the curse of God upon the creatures for our sakes, and all other evils that befall us in our bodies, names, estates, relations, and employments; together with death itself.

Q. 29. *What are the punishments of sin in the world to come?*

A. The punishments of sin in the world to come, are everlasting separation from the comfortable presence of God, and most grievous torments in soul and body, without intermission, in hell-fire forever.

Q. 30. *Does God leave all mankind to perish in the estate of sin and misery?*

A. God does not leave all men to perish in the estate of sin and misery, into which they fell by the breach of the first covenant, commonly called the covenant of works; but of his mere love and mercy delivers his elect out of it, and brings them into an estate of salvation by the second covenant, commonly called the covenant of grace.

Q. 31. *With whom was the covenant of grace made?*

A. The covenant of grace was made with Christ as the second Adam, and in him with all the elect as his seed.

Q. 32. *How is the grace of God manifested in the second covenant?*

A. The grace of God is manifested in the second covenant, in that he freely provides and offers to sinners a mediator, and life and salvation by him; and requiring faith as the condition to interest them in him, promises and gives his Holy Spirit to all his elect, to work in them that faith, with all other saving graces; and to enable them unto all holy obedience, as the evidence of the truth of their faith and thankfulness to God, and as the way which he hath appointed them to salvation.

Q. 33. *Was the covenant of grace always administered after one and the same manner?*

A. The covenant of grace was not always administered after the same manner, but the administrations of it under the Old Testament were different from those under the New.

Q. 34. *How was the covenant of grace administered under the Old Testament?*
A. The covenant of grace was administered under the Old Testament, by promises, prophecies, sacrifices, circumcision, the Passover, and other types and ordinances, which did all foresignify Christ then to come, and were for that time sufficient to build up the elect in faith in the promised messiah, by whom they then had full remission of sin, and eternal salvation.

Q. 35. *How is the covenant of grace administered under the New Testament?*
A. Under the New Testament, when Christ the substance was exhibited, the same covenant of grace was and still is to be administered in the preaching of the word, and the administration of the sacraments of baptism and the Lord's supper; in which grace and salvation are held forth in more fullness, evidence, and efficacy, to all nations.

Q. 36. *Who is the mediator of the covenant of grace?*
A. The only mediator of the covenant of grace is the Lord Jesus Christ, who, being the eternal Son of God, of one substance and equal with the Father, in the fullness of time became man, and so was and continues to be God and man, in two entire distinct natures, and one person, forever.

Q. 37. *How did Christ, being the Son of God, become man?*
A. Christ the Son of God became man, by taking to himself a true body, and a reasonable soul, being conceived by the power of the Holy Ghost in the womb of the virgin Mary, of her substance, and born of her, yet without sin.

Q. 38. *Why was it requisite that the mediator should be God?*
A. It was requisite that the mediator should be God, that he might sustain and keep the human nature from sinking under the infinite wrath of God, and the power of death; give worth and efficacy to his sufferings, obedience, and intercession; and to satisfy God's justice, procure his favor, purchase a peculiar people, give his Spirit to them, conquer all their enemies, and bring them to everlasting salvation.

Q. 39. *Why was it requisite that the mediator should be man?*
A. It was requisite that the mediator should be man, that he might advance our nature, perform obedience to the law, suffer and make intercession

for us in our nature, have a fellow-feeling of our infirmities; that we might receive the adoption of sons, and have comfort and access with boldness unto the throne of grace.

Q. 40. *Why was it requisite that the mediator should be God and man in one person?*
A. It was requisite that the mediator, who was to reconcile God and man, should himself be both God and man, and this in one person, that the proper works of each nature might be accepted of God for us, and relied on by us, as the works of the whole person.

Q. 41. *Why was our mediator called Jesus?*
A. Our mediator was called Jesus, because he saves his people from their sins.

Q. 42. *Why was our mediator called Christ?*
A. Our mediator was called Christ, because he was anointed with the Holy Ghost above measure; and so set apart, and fully furnished with all authority and ability, to execute the offices of prophet, priest, and king of his church, in the estate both of his humiliation and exaltation.

Q. 43. *How does Christ execute the office of a prophet?*
A. Christ executes the office of a prophet, in his revealing to the church, in all ages, by his Spirit and word, in divers ways of administration, the whole will of God, in all things concerning their edification and salvation.

Q. 44. *How does Christ execute the office of a priest?*
A. Christ executes the office of a priest, in his once offering himself a sacrifice without spot to God, to be a reconciliation for the sins of the people; and in making continual intercession for them.

Q. 45. *How does Christ execute the office of a king?*
A. Christ executes the office of a king, in calling out of the world a people to himself, and giving them officers, laws, and censures, by which he visibly governs them; in bestowing saving grace upon his elect, rewarding their obedience, and correcting them for their sins, preserving and supporting them under all their temptations and sufferings, restraining and overcoming all their enemies, and powerfully ordering all things for his own glory, and their good; and also in taking vengeance on the rest, who know not God, and obey not the gospel.

Q. 46. *What was the estate of Christ's humiliation?*
A. The estate of Christ's humiliation was that low condition, wherein he

for our sakes, emptying himself of his glory, took upon him the form of a servant, in his conception and birth, life, death, and after his death, until his resurrection.

Q. 47. *How did Christ humble himself in his conception and birth?*
A. Christ humbled himself in his conception and birth, in that, being from all eternity the Son of God, in the bosom of the Father, he was pleased in the fullness of time to become the son of man, made of a woman of low estate, and to be born of her; with divers circumstances of more than ordinary abasement.

Q. 48. *How did Christ humble himself in his life?*
A. Christ humbled himself in his life, by subjecting himself to the law, which he perfectly fulfilled; and by conflicting with the indignities of the world, temptations of Satan, and infirmities in his flesh, whether common to the nature of man, or particularly accompanying that his low condition.

Q. 49. *How did Christ humble himself in his death?*
A. Christ humbled himself in his death, in that having been betrayed by Judas, forsaken by his disciples, scorned and rejected by the world, condemned by Pilate, and tormented by his persecutors; having also conflicted with the terrors of death, and the powers of darkness, felt and borne the weight of God's wrath, he laid down his life an offering for sin, enduring the painful, shameful, and cursed death of the cross.

Q. 50. *Wherein consisted Christ's humiliation after his death?*
A. Christ's humiliation after his death consisted in his being buried, and continuing in the state of the dead, and under the power of death till the third day; which hath been otherwise expressed in these words, He descended into hell.

Q. 51. *What was the estate of Christ's exaltation?*
A. The estate of Christ's exaltation comprehends his resurrection, ascension, sitting at the right hand of the Father, and his coming again to judge the world.

Q. 52. *How was Christ exalted in his resurrection?*
A. Christ was exalted in his resurrection, in that, not having seen corruption in death (of which it was not possible for him to be held), and having the very same body in which he suffered, with the essential properties thereof

(but without mortality, and other common infirmities belonging to this life), really united to his soul, he rose again from the dead the third day by his own power; whereby he declared himself to be the Son of God, to have satisfied divine justice, to have vanquished death, and him that had power of it, and to be Lord of quick and dead: all which he did as a public person, the head of his church, for the justification, quickening in grace, support against enemies, and to assure them of their resurrection from the dead at the last day.

Q. 53. *How was Christ exalted in his ascension?*

A. Christ was exalted in his ascension, in that having after his resurrection often appeared unto and conversed with his apostles, speaking to them of the things pertaining to the kingdom of God, and giving them commission to preach the gospel to all nations, forty days after his resurrection, he, in our nature, and as our head, triumphing over enemies, visibly went up into the highest heavens, there to receive gifts for men, to raise up our affections thither, and to prepare a place for us, where himself is, and shall continue till his second coming at the end of the world.

Q. 54. *How is Christ exalted in his sitting at the right hand of God?*

A. Christ is exalted in his sitting at the right hand of God, in that as God-man he is advanced to the highest favor with God the Father, with all fullness of joy, glory, and power over all things in heaven and earth; and does gather and defend his church, and subdue their enemies; furnishes his ministers and people with gifts and graces, and makes intercession for them.

Q. 55. *How does Christ make intercession?*

A. Christ makes intercession, by his appearing in our nature continually before the Father in heaven, in the merit of his obedience and sacrifice on earth, declaring his will to have it applied to all believers; answering all accusations against them, and procuring for them quiet of conscience, notwithstanding daily failings, access with boldness to the throne of grace, and acceptance of their persons and services.

Q. 56. *How is Christ to be exalted in his coming again to judge the world?*

A. Christ is to be exalted in his coming again to judge the world, in that he, who was unjustly judged and condemned by wicked men, shall come again at the last day in great power, and in the full manifestation of his own glory, and of his Father's, with all his holy angels, with a shout, with the voice of the archangel, and with the trumpet of God, to judge the world in righteousness.

Q. 57. *What benefits hath Christ procured by his mediation?*
A. Christ, by his mediation, hath procured redemption, with all other benefits of the covenant of grace.

Q. 58. *How do we come to be made partakers of the benefits which Christ hath procured?*
A. We are made partakers of the benefits which Christ hath procured, by the application of them unto us, which is the work especially of God the Holy Ghost.

Q. 59. *Who are made partakers of redemption through Christ?*
A. Redemption is certainly applied, and effectually communicated, to all those for whom Christ hath purchased it; who are in time by the Holy Ghost enabled to believe in Christ according to the gospel.

Q. 60. *Can they who have never heard the gospel, and so know not Jesus Christ, nor believe in him, be saved by their living according to the light of nature?*
A. They who, having never heard the gospel, know not Jesus Christ, and believe not in him, cannot be saved, be they never so diligent to frame their lives according to the light of nature, or the laws of that religion which they profess; neither is there salvation in any other, but in Christ alone, who is the Savior only of his body the church.

Q. 61. *Are all they saved who hear the gospel, and live in the church?*
A. All that hear the gospel, and live in the visible church, are not saved; but they only who are true members of the church invisible.

Q. 62. *What is the visible church?*
A. The visible church is a society made up of all such as in all ages and places of the world do profess the true religion, and of their children.

Q. 63. *What are the special privileges of the visible church?*
A. The visible church hath the privilege of being under God's special care and government; of being protected and preserved in all ages, notwithstanding the opposition of all enemies; and of enjoying the communion of saints, the ordinary means of salvation, and offers of grace by Christ to all the members of it in the ministry of the gospel, testifying, that whosoever believes in him shall be saved, and excluding none that will come unto him.

Q. 64. *What is the invisible church?*
A. The invisible church is the whole number of the elect, that have been, are, or shall be gathered into one under Christ the head.

Q. 65. *What special benefits do the members of the invisible church enjoy by Christ?*
A. The members of the invisible church by Christ enjoy union and communion with him in grace and glory.

Q. 66. *What is that union which the elect have with Christ?*
A. The union that the elect have with Christ is the work of God's grace, whereby they are spiritually and mystically, yet really and inseparably, joined to Christ as their head and husband; which is done in their effectual calling.

Q. 67. *What is effectual calling?*
A. Effectual calling is the work of God's almighty power and grace, whereby (out of his free and special love to his elect, and from nothing in them moving him thereunto) he does, in his accepted time, invite and draw them to Jesus Christ, by his word and Spirit; savingly enlightening their minds, renewing and powerfully determining their wills, so as they (although in themselves dead in sin) are hereby made willing and able freely to answer his call, and to accept and embrace the grace offered and conveyed therein.

Q. 68. *Are the elect only effectually called?*
A. All the elect, and they only, are effectually called; although others may be, and often are, outwardly called by the ministry of the word, and have some common operations of the Spirit; who, for their willful neglect and contempt of the grace offered to them, being justly left in their unbelief, do never truly come to Jesus Christ.

Q. 69. *What is the communion in grace that the members of the invisible church have with Christ?*
A. The communion in grace that the members of the invisible church have with Christ, is their partaking of the virtue of his mediation, in their justification, adoption, sanctification, and whatever else, in this life, manifests their union with him.

Q. 70. *What is justification?*
A. Justification is an act of God's free grace unto sinners, in which he pardons all their sins, accepts and accounts their persons righteous in his sight; not for anything wrought in them, or done by them, but only for the

perfect obedience and full satisfaction of Christ, by God imputed to them, and received by faith alone.

Q. 71. *How is justification an act of God's free grace?*

A. Although Christ, by his obedience and death, did make a proper, real, and full satisfaction to God's justice in the behalf of them that are justified; yet inasmuch as God accepts the satisfaction from a surety, which he might have demanded of them, and did provide this surety, his own only Son, imputing his righteousness to them, and requiring nothing of them for their justification but faith, which also is his gift, their justification is to them of free grace.

Q. 72. *What is justifying faith?*

A. Justifying faith is a saving grace, wrought in the heart of a sinner by the Spirit and Word of God, whereby he, being convinced of his sin and misery, and of the disability in himself and all other creatures to recover him out of his lost condition, not only assents to the truth of the promise of the gospel, but receives and rests upon Christ and his righteousness, therein held forth, for pardon of sin, and for the accepting and accounting of his person righteous in the sight of God for salvation.

Q. 73. *How does faith justify a sinner in the sight of God?*

A. Faith justifies a sinner in the sight of God, not because of those other graces which do always accompany it, or of good works that are the fruits of it, nor as if the grace of faith, or any act thereof, were imputed to him for his justification; but only as it is an instrument by which he receives and applies Christ and his righteousness.

Q. 74. *What is adoption?*

A. Adoption is an act of the free grace of God, in and for his only Son Jesus Christ, whereby all those that are justified are received into the number of his children, have his name put upon them, the Spirit of his Son given to them, are under his fatherly care and dispensations, admitted to all the liberties and privileges of the sons of God, made heirs of all the promises, and fellow-heirs with Christ in glory.

Q. 75. *What is sanctification?*

A. Sanctification is a work of God's grace, whereby they whom God hath, before the foundation of the world, chosen to be holy, are in time, through the powerful operation of his Spirit applying the death and resurrection of Christ unto them, renewed in their whole man after the image of God; having the seeds of repentance unto life, and all other saving graces, put into their hearts, and those graces so stirred up, increased, and strengthened, as that they more and more die unto sin, and rise unto newness of life.

Q. 76. *What is repentance unto life?*
A. Repentance unto life is a saving grace, wrought in the heart of a sinner by the Spirit and Word of God, whereby, out of the sight and sense, not only of the danger, but also of the filthiness and odiousness of his sins, and upon the apprehension of God's mercy in Christ to such as are penitent, he so grieves for and hates his sins, as that he turns from them all to God, purposing and endeavoring constantly to walk with him in all the ways of new obedience.

Q. 77. *Wherein do justification and sanctification differ?*
A. Although sanctification be inseparably joined with justification, yet they differ, in that God in justification imputes the righteousness of Christ; in sanctification his Spirit infuses grace, and enables to the exercise thereof; in the former, sin is pardoned; in the other, it is subdued: the one does equally free all believers from the revenging wrath of God, and that perfectly in this life, that they never fall into condemnation; the other is neither equal in all, nor in this life perfect in any, but growing up to perfection.

Q. 78. *Whence arises the imperfection of sanctification in believers?*
A. The imperfection of sanctification in believers arises from the remnants of sin abiding in every part of them, and the perpetual lusts of the flesh against the spirit; whereby they are often foiled with temptations, and fall into many sins, are hindered in all their spiritual services, and their best works are imperfect and defiled in the sight of God.

Q. 79. *May not true believers, by reason of their imperfections, and the many temptations and sins they are overtaken with, fall away from the state of grace?*
A. True believers, by reason of the unchangeable love of God, and his decree and covenant to give them perseverance, their inseparable union with Christ, his continual intercession for them, and the Spirit and seed of God abiding in them, can neither totally nor finally fall away from the state of grace, but are kept by the power of God through faith unto salvation.

Q. 80. *Can true believers be infallibly assured that they are in the estate of grace, and that they shall persevere therein unto salvation?*
A. Such as truly believe in Christ, and endeavor to walk in all good conscience before him, may, without extraordinary revelation, by faith grounded upon

the truth of God's promises, and by the Spirit enabling them to discern in themselves those graces to which the promises of life are made, and bearing witness with their spirits that they are the children of God, be infallibly assured that they are in the estate of grace, and shall persevere therein unto salvation.

Q. 81. *Are all true believers at all times assured of their present being in the estate of grace, and that they shall be saved?*
A. Assurance of grace and salvation not being of the essence of faith, true believers may wait long before they obtain it; and, after the enjoyment thereof, may have it weakened and intermitted, through manifold distempers, sins, temptations, and desertions; yet are they never left without such a presence and support of the Spirit of God as keeps them from sinking into utter despair.

Q. 82. *What is the communion in glory that the members of the invisible church have with Christ?*
A. The communion in glory that the members of the invisible church have with Christ, is in this life, immediately after death, and at last perfected at the resurrection and day of judgment.

Q. 83. *What is the communion in glory with Christ that the members of the invisible church enjoy in this life?*
A. The members of the invisible church have communicated to them in this life the firstfruits of glory with Christ, as they are members of him their head, and so in him are interested in that glory which he is fully possessed of; and, as an earnest thereof, enjoy the sense of God's love, peace of conscience, joy in the Holy Ghost, and hope of glory; as, on the contrary, sense of God's revenging wrath, horror of conscience, and a fearful expectation of judgment, are to the wicked the beginning of their torments which they shall endure after death.

Q. 84. *Shall all men die?*
A. Death being threatened as the wages of sin, it is appointed unto all men once to die; for that all have sinned.

Q. 85. *Death being the wages of sin, why are not the righteous delivered from death, seeing all their sins are forgiven in Christ?*
A. The righteous shall be delivered from death itself at the last day, and even in death are delivered from the sting and curse of it; so that, although they die, yet it is out of God's love, to free them perfectly from sin and

misery, and to make them capable of further communion with Christ in glory, which they then enter upon.

Q. 86. *What is the communion in glory with Christ that the members of the invisible church enjoy immediately after death?*
A. The communion in glory with Christ which the members of the invisible church enjoy immediately after death, is, in that their souls are then made perfect in holiness, and received into the highest heavens, where they behold the face of God in light and glory, waiting for the full redemption of their bodies, which even in death continue united to Christ, and rest in their graves as in their beds, till at the last day they be again united to their souls. Whereas the souls of the wicked are at their death cast into hell, where they remain in torments and utter darkness, and their bodies kept in their graves, as in their prisons, till the resurrection and judgment of the great day.

Q. 87. *What are we to believe concerning the resurrection?*
A. We are to believe that at the last day there shall be a general resurrection of the dead, both of the just and unjust: when they that are then found alive shall in a moment be changed; and the selfsame bodies of the dead which were laid in the grave, being then again united to their souls forever, shall be raised up by the power of Christ. The bodies of the just, by the Spirit of Christ, and by virtue of his resurrection as their head, shall be raised in power, spiritual, incorruptible, and made like to his glorious body; and the bodies of the wicked shall be raised up in dishonor by him, as an offended judge.

Q. 88. *What shall immediately follow after the resurrection?*
A. Immediately after the resurrection shall follow the general and final judgment of angels and men; the day and hour whereof no man knows, that all may watch and pray, and be ever ready for the coming of the Lord.

Q. 89. *What shall be done to the wicked at the Day of Judgment?*
A. At the day of judgment, the wicked shall be set on Christ's left hand, and, upon clear evidence, and full conviction of their own consciences, shall have the fearful but just sentence of condemnation pronounced against them; and thereupon shall be cast out from the favorable presence of God, and the glorious fellowship with Christ, his saints, and all his holy angels, into hell, to be punished with unspeakable torments, both of body and soul, with the devil and his angels forever.

Q. 90. *What shall be done to the righteous at the Day of Judgment?*

A. At the day of judgment, the righteous, being caught up to Christ in the clouds, shall be set on his right hand, and there openly acknowledged and acquitted, shall join with him in the judging of reprobate angels and men, and shall be received into heaven, where they shall be fully and forever freed from all sin and misery; filled with inconceivable joys, made perfectly holy and happy both in body and soul, in the company of innumerable saints and holy angels, but especially in the immediate vision and fruition of God the Father, of our Lord Jesus Christ, and of the Holy Spirit, to all eternity. And this is the perfect and full communion that the members of the invisible church shall enjoy with Christ in glory, at the resurrection and Day of Judgment.

HAVING SEEN WHAT THE SCRIPTURES PRINCIPALLY TEACH US TO BELIEVE CONCERNING GOD, IT FOLLOWS TO CONSIDER WHAT THEY REQUIRE AS THE DUTY OF MAN

Q. 91. *What is the duty that God requires of man?*
A. The duty that God requires of man, is obedience to his revealed will.

Q. 92. *What did God first reveal unto man as the rule of his obedience?*
A. The rule of obedience revealed to Adam in the estate of innocence, and to all mankind in him, besides a special command not to eat of the fruit of the tree of the knowledge of good and evil, was the moral law.

Q. 93. *What is the moral law?*
A. The moral law is the declaration of the will of God to mankind, directing and binding every one to personal, perfect, and perpetual conformity and obedience thereunto, in the frame and disposition of the whole man, soul, and body, and in performance of all those duties of holiness and righteousness which he owes to God and man: promising life upon the fulfilling, and threatening death upon the breach of it.

Q. 94. *Is there any use of the moral law since the fall?*
A. Although no man, since the fall, can attain to righteousness and life by the moral law; yet there is great use thereof, as well common to all men, as peculiar either to the unregenerate, or the regenerate.

Q. 95. *Of what use is the moral law to all men?*
A. The moral law is of use to all men, to inform them of the holy nature and will of God, and of their duty, binding them to walk accordingly; to convince them of their disability to keep it, and of the sinful pollution of their nature, hearts, and lives: to humble them in the sense of their sin and

misery, and thereby help them to a clearer sight of the need they have of Christ, and of the perfection of his obedience.

Q. 96. *What particular use is there of the moral law to unregenerate men?*
A. The moral law is of use to unregenerate men, to awaken their consciences to flee from the wrath to come, and to drive them to Christ; or, upon the continuance in the estate and way of sin, to leave them inexcusable, and under the curse thereof.

Q. 97. *What special use is there of the moral law to the regenerate?*
A. Although they that are regenerate, and believe in Christ, be delivered from the moral law as a covenant of works, so as thereby they are neither justified nor condemned; yet besides the general uses thereof common to them with all men, it is of special use, to show them how much they are bound to Christ for his fulfilling it, and enduring the curse thereof in their stead, and for their good; and thereby to provoke them to more thankfulness, and to express the same in their greater care to conform themselves thereunto as the rule of their obedience.

Q. 98. *Where is the moral law summarily comprehended?*
A. The moral law is summarily comprehended in the Ten Commandments, which were delivered by the voice of God upon mount Sinai, and written by him in two tables of stone; and are recorded in the twentieth chapter of Exodus; the four first commandments containing our duty to God, and the other six our duty to man.

Q. 99. *What rules are to be observed for the right understanding of the Ten Commandments?*
A. For the right understanding of the Ten Commandments, these rules are to be observed:

> 1. That the law is perfect, and binds every one to full conformity in the whole man unto the righteousness thereof, and unto entire obedience forever; so as to require the utmost perfection of every duty, and to forbid the least degree of every sin.

> 2. That it is spiritual, and so reaches the understanding, will, affections, and all other powers of the soul; as well as words, works, and gestures.

> 3. That one and the same thing, in divers respects, is required or forbidden in several commandments.

4. That as, where a duty is commanded, the contrary sin is forbidden; and, where a sin is forbidden, the contrary duty is commanded: so, where a promise is annexed, the contrary threatening is included; and, where a threatening is annexed, the contrary promise is included.

5. That what God forbids, is at no time to be done; what he commands, is always our duty; and yet every particular duty is not to be done at all times.

6. That under one sin or duty, all of the same kind are forbidden or commanded; together with all the causes, means, occasions, and appearances thereof, and provocations thereunto.

7. That what is forbidden or commanded to ourselves, we are bound, according to our places, to endeavor that it may be avoided or performed by others, according to the duty of their places.

8. That in what is commanded to others, we are bound, according to our places and callings, to be helpful to them; and to take heed of partaking with others in what is forbidden them.

Q. 100. *What special things are we to consider in the Ten Commandments?*
A. We are to consider, in the Ten Commandments, the preface, the substance of the commandments themselves, and several reasons annexed to some of them, the more to enforce them.

Q. 101. *What is the preface to the Ten Commandments?*
A. The preface to the Ten Commandments is contained in these words, I am the LORD your God, which have brought thee out of the land of Egypt, out of the house of bondage. Wherein God manifests his sovereignty, as being JEHOVAH, the eternal, immutable, and almighty God; having his being in and of himself, and giving being to all his words and works: and that he is a God in covenant, as with Israel of old, so with all his people; who, as he brought them out of their bondage in Egypt, so he delivers us from our spiritual thralldom; and that therefore we are bound to take him for our God alone, and to keep all his commandments.

Q. 102. *What is the sum of the four commandments that contain our duty to God?*

A. The sum of the four commandments containing our duty to God, is, to love the Lord our God with all our heart, and with all our soul, and with all our strength, and with all our mind.

Q. 103. *Which is the first commandment?*
A. The first commandment is, You shall have no other gods before me.

Q. 104. *What are the duties required in the first commandment?*
A. The duties required in the first commandment are, the knowing and acknowledging of God to be the only true God, and our God; and to worship and glorify him accordingly, by thinking, meditating, remembering, highly esteeming, honoring, adoring, choosing, loving, desiring, fearing of him; believing him; trusting, hoping, delighting, rejoicing in him; being zealous for him; calling upon him, giving all praise and thanks, and yielding all obedience and submission to him with the whole man; being careful in all things to please him, and sorrowful when in anything he is offended; and walking humbly with him.

Q. 105. *What are the sins forbidden in the first commandment?*
A. The sins forbidden in the first commandment, are, atheism, in denying or not having a God; idolatry, in having or worshiping more gods than one, or any with or instead of the true God; the not having and avouching him for God, and our God; the omission or neglect of anything due to him, required in this commandment; ignorance, forgetfulness, misapprehensions, false opinions, unworthy and wicked thoughts of him; bold and curious searching into his secrets; all profaneness, hatred of God; self-love, self-seeking, and all other inordinate and immoderate setting of our mind, will, or affections upon other things, and taking them off from him in whole or in part; vain credulity, unbelief, heresy, misbelief, distrust, despair, incorrigibleness, and insensibleness under judgments, hardness of heart, pride, presumption, carnal security, tempting of God; using unlawful means, and trusting in lawful means; carnal delights and joys; corrupt, blind, and indiscreet zeal; lukewarmness, and deadness in the things of God; estranging ourselves, and apostatizing from God; praying, or giving any religious worship, to saints, angels, or any other creatures; all compacts and consulting with the devil, and hearkening to his suggestions; making men the lords of our faith and conscience; slighting and despising God and his commands; resisting and grieving of his Spirit, discontent and impatience at his dispensations, charging him foolishly for the evils he inflicts on us; and ascribing the praise of any good we either are, have, or can do, to fortune, idols, ourselves, or any other creature.

Q. 106. What are we specially taught by these words, before me, in the first commandment?
A. These words, before me, or before my face, in the first commandment, teach us, that God, who sees all things, takes special notice of, and is much displeased with, the sin of having any other God: that so it may be an argument to dissuade from it, and to aggravate it as a most impudent provocation: as also to persuade us to do as in his sight, whatever we do in his service.

Q. 107. Which is the second commandment?
A. The second commandment is, You shall not make unto thee any graven image, or any likeness of anything that is in heaven above, or that is in the earth beneath, or that is in the water under the earth. You shall not bow down yourself to them, nor serve them: for I the LORD your God am a jealous God, visiting the iniquity of the fathers upon the children unto the third and fourth generation of them that hate me; and showing mercy unto thousands of them that love me, and keep my commandments.

Q. 108. What are the duties required in the second commandment?
A. The duties required in the second commandment are, the receiving, observing, and keeping pure and entire, all such religious worship and ordinances as God hath instituted in his word; particularly prayer and thanksgiving in the name of Christ; the reading, preaching, and hearing of the word; the administration and receiving of the sacraments; church government and discipline; the ministry and maintenance thereof; religious fasting; swearing by the name of God, and vowing unto him: as also the disapproving, detesting, opposing, all false worship; and, according to each one's place and calling, removing it, and all monuments of idolatry.

Q. 109. What sins are forbidden in the second commandment?
A. The sins forbidden in the second commandment are, all devising, counseling, commanding, using, and any wise approving, any religious worship not instituted by God himself; the making any representation of God, of all or of any of the three persons, either inwardly in our mind, or outwardly in any kind of image or likeness of any creature whatsoever; all worshiping of it, or God in it or by it; the making of any representation of feigned deities, and all worship of them, or service belonging to them; all superstitious devices, corrupting the worship of God, adding to it, or taking from it, whether invented and taken up of ourselves, or received by tradition from others, though under the title of antiquity, custom, devotion, good intent, or any other pretense whatsoever; simony; sacrilege; all neglect, contempt, hindering, and opposing the worship and ordinances which God hath appointed.

Q. 110. *What are the reasons annexed to the second commandment, the more to enforce it?*
A. The reasons annexed to the second commandment, the more to enforce it, contained in these words, For I the LORD your God am a jealous God, visiting the iniquity of the fathers upon the children unto the third and fourth generation of them that hate me; and showing mercy unto thousands of them that love me, and keep my commandments; are, besides God's sovereignty over us, and propriety in us, his fervent zeal for his own worship, and his revengeful indignation against all false worship, as being a spiritual whoredom; accounting the breakers of this commandment such as hate him, and threatening to punish them unto divers generations; and esteeming the observers of it such as love him and keep his commandments, and promising mercy to them unto many generations.

Q. 111. *Which is the third commandment?*
A. The third commandment is, You shall not take the name of the LORD your God in vain: for the LORD will not hold him guiltless that takes his name in vain.

Q. 112. *What is required in the third commandment?*
A. The third commandment requires, that the name of God, his titles, attributes, ordinances, the word, sacraments, prayer, oaths, vows, lots, his works, and whatsoever else there is whereby he makes himself known, be holily and reverently used in thought, meditation, word, and writing; by an holy profession, and answerable conversation, to the glory of God, and the good of ourselves, and others.

Q. 113. *What are the sins forbidden in the third commandment?*
A. The sins forbidden in the third commandment are, the not using of God's name as is required; and the abuse of it in an ignorant, vain, irreverent, profane, superstitious, or wicked mentioning or otherwise using his titles, attributes, ordinances, or works, by blasphemy, perjury; all sinful cursing, oaths, vows, and lots; violating of our oaths and vows, if lawful; and fulfilling them, if of things unlawful; murmuring and quarreling at, curious prying into, and misapplying of God's decrees and providences; misinterpreting, misapplying, or any way perverting the word, or any part of it, to profane jests, curious or unprofitable questions, vain janglings, or the maintaining of false doctrines; abusing it, the creatures, or anything contained under the name of God, to charms, or sinful lusts and practices; the maligning, scorning, reviling, or any wise opposing of God's truth, grace, and ways; making profession of religion in hypocrisy, or for sinister ends; being ashamed of it, or a shame to it, by

unconformable, unwise, unfruitful, and offensive walking, or backsliding from it.

Q. 114. *What reasons are annexed to the third commandment?*

A. The reasons annexed to the third commandment, in these words, The LORD your God, and, For the LORD will not hold him guiltless that takes his name in vain, are, because he is the Lord and our God, therefore his name is not to be profaned, or any way abused by us; especially because he will be so far from acquitting and sparing the transgressors of this commandment, as that he will not suffer them to escape his righteous judgment, albeit many such escape the censures and punishments of men.

Q. 115. *Which is the fourth commandment?*

A. The fourth commandment is, Remember the Sabbath day, to keep it holy. Six days shall you labor, and do all your work; but the seventh day is the Sabbath of the LORD your God: in it you shall not do any work, you, nor your son, nor your daughter, your manservant, nor your maidservant, nor your cattle, nor your stranger that is within your gates. For in six days the LORD made heaven and earth, the sea, and all that in them is, and rested the seventh day: wherefore the LORD blessed the Sabbath day, and hallowed it.

Q. 116. *What is required in the fourth commandment?*

A. The fourth commandment requires of all men the sanctifying or keeping holy to God such set times as he hath appointed in his word, expressly one whole day in seven; which was the seventh from the beginning of the world to the resurrection of Christ, and the first day of the week ever since, and so to continue to the end of the world; which is the Christian Sabbath, and in the New Testament called The Lord's Day.

Q. 117. *How is the Sabbath or the Lord's Day to be sanctified?*

A. The Sabbath or Lord's day is to be sanctified by an holy resting all the day, not only from such works as are at all times sinful, but even from such worldly employments and recreations as are on other days lawful; and making it our delight to spend the whole time (except so much of it as is to be taken up in works of necessity and mercy) in the public and private exercises of God's worship: and, to that end, we are to prepare our hearts, and with such foresight, diligence, and moderation, to dispose and seasonably dispatch our worldly business, that we may be the more free and fit for the duties of that day.

Q. 118. *Why is the charge of keeping the Sabbath more specially directed to governors of families, and other superiors?*
A. The charge of keeping the Sabbath is more specially directed to governors of families, and other superiors, because they are bound not only to keep it themselves, but to see that it be observed by all those that are under their charge; and because they are prone often times to hinder them by employments of their own.

Q. 119. What are the sins forbidden in the fourth commandment?
A. The sins forbidden in the fourth commandment are, all omissions of the duties required, all careless, negligent, and unprofitable performing of them, and being weary of them; all profaning the day by idleness, and doing that which is in itself sinful; and by all needless works, words, and thoughts, about our worldly employments and recreations.

Q. 120. *What are the reasons annexed to the fourth commandment, the more to enforce it?*
A. The reasons annexed to the fourth commandment, the more to enforce it, are taken from the equity of it, God allowing us six days of seven for our own affairs, and reserving but one for himself, in these words, Six days shall you labor, and do all your work: from God's challenging a special propriety in that day, The seventh day is the Sabbath of the LORD your God: from the example of God, who in six days ... made heaven and earth, the sea, and all that in them is, and rested the seventh day: and from that blessing which God put upon that day, not only in sanctifying it to be a day for his service, but in ordaining it to be a means of blessing to us in our sanctifying it; Wherefore the LORD blessed the Sabbath day, and hallowed it.

Q. 121. *Why is the word Remember set in the beginning of the fourth commandment?*
A. The word Remember is set in the beginning of the fourth commandment, partly, because of the great benefit of remembering it, we being thereby helped in our preparation to keep it, and, in keeping it, better to keep all the rest of the commandments, and to continue a thankful remembrance of the two great benefits of creation and redemption, which contain a short abridgment of religion; and partly, because we are very ready to forget it, for that there is less light of nature for it, and yet it restraineth our natural liberty in things at other times lawful; that it cometh but once in seven days, and many worldly businesses come between, and too often take off our minds from thinking of it, either to prepare for it, or to sanctify it; and that Satan with his instruments much labor to blot out the glory, and even the memory of it, to bring in all irreligion and impiety.

Q. 122. *What is the sum of the six commandments which contain our duty to man?*
A. The sum of the six commandments which contain our duty to man, is, to love our neighbor as ourselves, and to do to others what we would have them do to us.

Q. 123. *Which is the fifth commandment?*
A. The fifth commandment is, Honor your father and your mother: that your days may be long upon the land which the Lord your God gives thee.

Q. 124. *Who are meant by father and mother in the fifth commandment?*
A. By father and mother, in the fifth commandment, are meant, not only natural parents, but all superiors in age and gifts; and especially such as, by God's ordinance, are over us in place of authority, whether in family, church, or commonwealth.

Q. 125. *Why are superiors styled Father and Mother?*
A. Superiors are styled Father and Mother, both to teach them in all duties toward their inferiors, like natural parents, to express love and tenderness to them, according to their several relations; and to work inferiors to a greater willingness and cheerfulness in performing their duties to their superiors, as to their parents.

Q. 126. *What is the general scope of the fifth commandment?*
A. The general scope of the fifth commandment is, the performance of those duties which we mutually owe in our several relations, as inferiors, superiors or equals.

Q. 127. *What is the honor that inferiors owe to their superiors?*
A. The honor which inferiors owe to their superiors is, all due reverence in heart, word, and behavior; prayer and thanksgiving for them; imitation of their virtues and graces; willing obedience to their lawful commands and counsels; due submission to their corrections; fidelity to, defense, and maintenance of their persons and authority, according to their several ranks, and the nature of their places; bearing with their infirmities, and covering them in love, that so they may be an honor to them and to their government.

Q. 128. *What are the sins of inferiors against their superiors?*
A. The sins of inferiors against their superiors are, all neglect of the duties required toward them; envying at, contempt of, and rebellion against their persons and places, in their lawful counsels, commands, and corrections;

cursing, mocking, and all such refractory and scandalous carriage, as proves a shame and dishonor to them and their government.

Q. 129. *What is required of superiors towards their inferiors?*
A. It is required of superiors, according to that power they receive from God, and that relation wherein they stand, to love, pray for, and bless their inferiors; to instruct, counsel, and admonish them; countenancing, commending, and rewarding such as do well; and discountenancing, reproving, and chastising such as do ill; protecting, and providing for them all things necessary for soul and body: and by grave, wise, holy, and exemplary carriage, to procure glory to God, honor to themselves, and so to preserve that authority which God hath put upon them.

Q. 130. *What are the sins of superiors?*
A. The sins of superiors are, besides the neglect of the duties required of them, an inordinate seeking of themselves, their own glory, ease, profit, or pleasure; commanding things unlawful, or not in the power of inferiors to perform; counseling, encouraging, or favoring them in that which is evil; dissuading, discouraging, or discountenancing them in that which is good; correcting them unduly; careless exposing, or leaving them to wrong, temptation, and danger; provoking them to wrath; or any way dishonoring themselves, or lessening their authority, by an unjust, indiscreet, rigorous, or remiss behavior.

Q. 131. *What are the duties of equals?*
A. The duties of equals are, to regard the dignity and worth of each other, in giving honor to go one before another; and to rejoice in each other's gifts and advancement, as their own.

Q. 132. *What are the sins of equals?*
A. The sins of equals are, besides the neglect of the duties required, the undervaluing of the worth, envying the gifts, grieving at the advancement or prosperity one of another; and usurping preeminence one over another.

Q. 133. *What is the reason annexed to the fifth commandment, the more to enforce it?*
A. The reason annexed to the fifth commandment, in these words, That your days may be long upon the land which the LORD your God gives thee, is an express promise of long life and prosperity, as far as it shall serve for God's glory and their own good, to all such as keep this commandment.

Q. 134. *Which is the sixth commandment?*
A. The sixth commandment is, You shall not kill.

Q. 135. *What are the duties required in the sixth commandment?*
A. The duties required in the sixth commandment are, all careful studies, and lawful endeavors, to preserve the life of ourselves and others by resisting all thoughts and purposes, subduing all passions, and avoiding all occasions, temptations, and practices, which tend to the unjust taking away the life of any; by just defense thereof against violence, patient bearing of the hand of God, quietness of mind, cheerfulness of spirit; a sober use of meat, drink, physic, sleep, labor, and recreations; by charitable thoughts, love, compassion, meekness, gentleness, kindness; peaceable, mild and courteous speeches and behavior; forbearance, readiness to be reconciled, patient bearing and forgiving of injuries, and requiting good for evil; comforting and succoring the distressed, and protecting and defending the innocent.

Q. 136. *What are the sins forbidden in the sixth commandment?*
A. The sins forbidden in the sixth commandment are, all taking away the life of ourselves, or of others, except in case of public justice, lawful war, or necessary defense; the neglecting or withdrawing the lawful and necessary means of preservation of life; sinful anger, hatred, envy, desire of revenge; all excessive passions, distracting cares; immoderate use of meat, drink, labor, and recreations; provoking words, oppression, quarreling, striking, wounding, and whatsoever else tends to the destruction of the life of any.

Q. 137. *Which is the seventh commandment?*
A. The seventh commandment is, You shall not commit adultery.

Q. 138. *What are the duties required in the seventh commandment?*
A. The duties required in the seventh commandment are, chastity in body, mind, affections, words, and behavior; and the preservation of it in ourselves and others; watchfulness over the eyes and all the senses; temperance, keeping of chaste company, modesty in apparel; marriage by those that have not the gift of continency, conjugal love, and cohabitation; diligent labor in our callings; shunning all occasions of uncleanness, and resisting temptations thereunto.

Q. 139. *What are the sins forbidden in the seventh commandment?*
A. The sins forbidden in the seventh commandment, besides the neglect of the duties required, are, adultery, fornication, rape, incest, sodomy,

and all unnatural lusts; all unclean imaginations, thoughts, purposes, and affections; all corrupt or filthy communications, or listening thereunto; wanton looks, impudent or light behavior, immodest apparel; prohibiting of lawful, and dispensing with unlawful marriages; allowing, tolerating, keeping of stews, and resorting to them; entangling vows of single life, undue delay of marriage; having more wives or husbands than one at the same time; unjust divorce, or desertion; idleness, gluttony, drunkenness, unchaste company; lascivious songs, books, pictures, dancing, stage plays; and all other provocations to, or acts of uncleanness, either in ourselves or others.

Q. 140. *Which is the eighth commandment?*
A. The eighth commandment is, You shall not steal.

Q. 141. *What are the duties required in the eighth commandment?*
A. The duties required in the eighth commandment are, truth, faithfulness, and justice in contracts and commerce between man and man; rendering to every one his due; restitution of goods unlawfully detained from the right owners thereof; giving and lending freely, according to our abilities, and the necessities of others; moderation of our judgments, wills, and affections concerning worldly goods; a provident care and study to get, keep, use, and dispose these things which are necessary and convenient for the sustentation of our nature, and suitable to our condition; a lawful calling, and diligence in it; frugality; avoiding unnecessary lawsuits, and suretyship, or other like engagements; and an endeavor, by all just and lawful means, to procure, preserve, and further the wealth and outward estate of others, as well as our own.

Q. 142. *What are the sins forbidden in the eighth commandment?*
A. The sins forbidden in the eighth commandment, besides the neglect of the duties required, are, theft, robbery, man-stealing, and receiving anything that is stolen; fraudulent dealing, false weights and measures, removing landmarks, injustice and unfaithfulness in contracts between man and man, or in matters of trust; oppression, extortion, usury, bribery, vexatious lawsuits, unjust enclosures and depredation; engrossing commodities to enhance the price; unlawful callings, and all other unjust or sinful ways of taking or withholding from our neighbor what belongs to him, or of enriching ourselves; covetousness; inordinate prizing and affecting worldly goods; distrustful and distracting cares and studies in getting, keeping, and using them; envying at the prosperity of others; as likewise idleness, prodigality, wasteful gaming; and all other ways whereby we do unduly

prejudice our own outward estate, and defrauding ourselves of the due use and comfort of that estate which God hath given us.

Q. 143. *Which is the ninth commandment?*
A. The ninth commandment is, You shall not bear false witness against your neighbor.

Q. 144. *What are the duties required in the ninth commandment?*
A. The duties required in the ninth commandment are, the preserving and promoting of truth between man and man, and the good name of our neighbor, as well as our own; appearing and standing for the truth; and from the heart, sincerely, freely, clearly, and fully, speaking the truth, and only the truth, in matters of judgment and justice, and in all other things whatsoever; a charitable esteem of our neighbors; loving, desiring, and rejoicing in their good name; sorrowing for and covering of their infirmities; freely acknowledging of their gifts and graces, defending their innocence; a ready receiving of a good report, and unwillingness to admit of an evil report, concerning them; discouraging talebearers, flatterers, and slanderers; love and care of our own good name, and defending it when need requires; keeping of lawful promises; studying and practicing of whatsoever things are true, honest, lovely, and of good report.

Q. 145. *What are the sins forbidden in the ninth commandment?*
A. The sins forbidden in the ninth commandment are, all prejudicing the truth, and the good name of our neighbors, as well as our own, especially in public judicature; giving false evidence, suborning false witnesses, wittingly appearing and pleading for an evil cause, outfacing and overbearing the truth; passing unjust sentence, calling evil good, and good evil; rewarding the wicked according to the work of the righteous, and the righteous according to the work of the wicked; forgery, concealing the truth, undue silence in a just cause, and holding our peace when iniquity calls for either a reproof from ourselves, or complaint to others; speaking the truth unseasonably, or maliciously to a wrong end, or perverting it to a wrong meaning, or in doubtful or equivocal expressions, to the prejudice of the truth or justice; speaking untruth, lying, slandering, backbiting, detracting, gossip, whispering, scoffing, reviling, rash, harsh, and partial censuring; misconstructing intentions, words, and actions; flattering, vainglorious boasting, thinking or speaking too highly or too meanly of ourselves or others; denying the gifts and graces of God; aggravating smaller faults; hiding, excusing, or extenuating of sins, when called to a free confession; unnecessary discovering of infirmities; raising false rumors, receiving and

countenancing evil reports, and stopping our ears against just defense; evil suspicion; envying or grieving at the deserved credit of any; endeavoring or desiring to impair it, rejoicing in their disgrace and infamy; scornful contempt, fond admiration; breach of lawful promises; neglecting such things as are of good report, and practicing, or not avoiding ourselves, or not hindering what we can in others, such things as procure an ill name.

Q. 146. *Which is the tenth commandment?*
A. The tenth commandment is, You shall not covet your neighbor's house, you shall not covet your neighbor's wife, nor his manservant, nor his maidservant, nor his ox, nor his ass, nor anything that is your neighbor's.

Q. 147. *What are the duties required in the tenth commandment?*
A. The duties required in the tenth commandment are, such a full contentment with our own condition, and such a charitable frame of the whole soul toward our neighbor, as that all our inward motions and affections touching him, tend unto, and further all that good which is his.

Q. 148. *What are the sins forbidden in the tenth commandment?*
A. The sins forbidden in the tenth commandment are, discontentment with our own estate; envying and grieving at the good of our neighbor, together with all inordinate motions and affections to anything that is his.

Q. 149. *Is any man able perfectly to keep the commandments of God?*
A. No man is able, either of himself, or by any grace received in this life, perfectly to keep the commandments of God; but does daily break them in thought, word, and deed.

Q. 150. *Are all transgressions of the law of God equally heinous in themselves, and in the sight of God?*
A. All transgressions of the law are not equally heinous; but some sins in themselves, and by reason of several aggravations, are more heinous in the sight of God than others.

Q. 151. *What are those aggravations that make some sins more heinous than others?*
A. Sins receive their aggravations,

> 1. From the persons offending; if they be of riper age, greater experience or grace, eminent for profession, gifts, place, office,

guides to others, and whose example is likely to be followed by others.

2. From the parties offended: if immediately against God, his attributes, and worship; against Christ, and his grace; the Holy Spirit, his witness, and workings; against superiors, men of eminency, and such as we stand especially related and engaged unto; against any of the saints, particularly weak brethren, the souls of them, or any other, and the common good of all or many.

3. From the nature and quality of the offence: if it be against the express letter of the law, break many commandments, contain in it many sins: if not only conceived in the heart, but breaks forth in words and actions, scandalize others, and admit of no reparation: if against means, mercies, judgments, light of nature, conviction of conscience, public or private admonition, censures of the church, civil punishments; and our prayers, purposes, promises, vows, covenants, and engagements to God or men: if done deliberately, willfully, presumptuously, impudently, boastingly, maliciously, frequently, obstinately, with delight, continuance, or relapsing after repentance.

4. From circumstances of time, and place: if on the Lord's day, or other times of divine worship; or immediately before or after these, or other helps to prevent or remedy such miscarriages: if in public, or in the presence of others, who are thereby likely to be provoked or defiled.

Q. 152. *What does every sin deserve at the hands of God?*
A. Every sin, even the least, being against the sovereignty, goodness, and holiness of God, and against his righteous law, deserves his wrath and curse, both in this life, and that which is to come; and cannot be expiated but by the blood of Christ.

Q. 153. *What does God require of us, that we may escape his wrath and curse due to us by reason of the transgression of the law?*
A. That we may escape the wrath and curse of God due to us by reason of the transgression of the law, he requires of us repentance toward God, and faith toward our Lord Jesus Christ, and the diligent use of the outward means whereby Christ communicates to us the benefits of his mediation.

Q. 154. *What are the outward means whereby Christ communicates to us the benefits of his mediation?*
A. The outward and ordinary means whereby Christ communicates to his church the benefits of his mediation, are all his ordinances; especially the word, sacraments, and prayer; all which are made effectual to the elect for their salvation.

Q. 155. *How is the word made effectual to salvation?*
A. The Spirit of God makes the reading, but especially the preaching of the word, an effectual means of enlightening, convincing, and humbling sinners; of driving them out of themselves, and drawing them unto Christ; of conforming them to his image, and subduing them to his will; of strengthening them against temptations and corruptions; or building them up in grace, and establishing their hearts in holiness and comfort through faith unto salvation.

Q. 156. *Is the Word of God to be read by all?*
A. Although all are not to be permitted to read the word publicly to the congregation, yet all sorts of people are bound to read it apart by themselves, and with their families: to which end, the holy Scriptures are to be translated out of the original into vulgar languages.

Q. 157. *How is the Word of God to be read?*
A. The holy Scriptures are to be read with an high and reverent esteem of them; with a firm persuasion that they are the very Word of God, and that he only can enable us to understand them; with desire to know, believe, and obey the will of God revealed in them; with diligence, and attention to the matter and scope of them; with meditation, application, self-denial, and prayer.

Q. 158. *By whom is the Word of God to be preached?*
A. The Word of God is to be preached only by such as are sufficiently gifted, and also duly approved and called to that office.

Q. 159. *How is the Word of God to be preached by those that are called thereunto?*
A. They that are called to labor in the ministry of the word, are to preach sound doctrine, diligently, in season and out of season; plainly, not in the enticing words of man's wisdom, but in demonstration of the Spirit, and of power; faithfully, making known the whole counsel of God; wisely, applying themselves to the necessities and capacities of the hearers; zealously, with fervent love to God and the souls of his people; sincerely, aiming at his glory, and their conversion, edification, and salvation.

Q. 160. *What is required of those that hear the word preached?*

A. It is required of those that hear the word preached, that they attend upon it with diligence, preparation, and prayer; examine what they hear by the Scriptures; receive the truth with faith, love, meekness, and readiness of mind, as the Word of God; meditate, and confer of it; hide it in their hearts, and bring forth the fruit of it in their lives.

Q. 161. *How do the sacraments become effectual means of salvation?*

A. The sacraments become effectual means of salvation, not by any power in themselves, or any virtue derived from the piety or intention of him by whom they are administered, but only by the working of the Holy Ghost, and the blessing of Christ, by whom they are instituted.

Q. 162. *What is a sacrament?*

A. A sacrament is an holy ordinance instituted by Christ in his church, to signify, seal, and exhibit unto those that are within the covenant of grace, the benefits of his mediation; to strengthen and increase their faith, and all other graces; to oblige them to obedience; to testify and cherish their love and communion one with another; and to distinguish them from those that are without.

Q. 163. *What are the parts of a sacrament?*

A. The parts of a sacrament are two; the one an outward and sensible sign, used according to Christ's own appointment; the other an inward and spiritual grace thereby signified.

Q. 164. *How many sacraments hath Christ instituted in his church under the New Testament?*

A. Under the New Testament Christ hath instituted in his church only two sacraments, baptism and the Lord's Supper.

Q. 165. *What is baptism?*

A. Baptism is a sacrament of the New Testament, wherein Christ hath ordained the washing with water in the name of the Father, and of the Son, and of the Holy Ghost, to be a sign and seal of ingrafting into himself, of remission of sins by his blood, and regeneration by his Spirit; of adoption, and resurrection unto everlasting life; and whereby the parties baptized are solemnly admitted into the visible church, and enter into an open and professed engagement to be wholly and only the Lord's.

Q. 166. *Unto whom is baptism to be administered?*
A. Baptism is not to be administered to any that are out of the visible church, and so strangers from the covenant of promise, till they profess their faith in Christ, and obedience to him, but infants descending from parents, either both, or but one of them, professing faith in Christ, and obedience to him, are in that respect within the covenant, and to be baptized.

Q. 167. *How is baptism to be improved by us?*
A. The needful but much neglected duty of improving our baptism, is to be performed by us all our life long, especially in the time of temptation, and when we are present at the administration of it to others; by serious and thankful consideration of the nature of it, and of the ends for which Christ instituted it, the privileges and benefits conferred and sealed thereby, and our solemn vow made therein; by being humbled for our sinful defilement, our falling short of, and walking contrary to, the grace of baptism, and our engagements; by growing up to assurance of pardon of sin, and of all other blessings sealed to us in that sacrament; by drawing strength from the death and resurrection of Christ, into whom we are baptized, for the mortifying of sin, and quickening of grace; and by endeavoring to live by faith, to have our conversation in holiness and righteousness, as those that have therein given up their names to Christ; and to walk in brotherly love, as being baptized by the same Spirit into one body.

Q. 168. *What is the Lord's Supper?*
A. The Lord's supper is a sacrament of the New Testament, wherein, by giving and receiving bread and wine according to the appointment of Jesus Christ, his death is showed forth; and they that worthily communicate feed upon his body and blood, to their spiritual nourishment and growth in grace; have their union and communion with him confirmed; testify and renew their thankfulness, and engagement to God, and their mutual love and fellowship each with other, as members of the same mystical body.

Q. 169. *How hath Christ appointed bread and wine to be given and received in the sacrament of the Lord's Supper?*
A. Christ hath appointed the ministers of his word, in the administration of this sacrament of the Lord's supper, to set apart the bread and wine from common use, by the word of institution, thanksgiving, and prayer; to take and break the bread, and to give both the bread and the wine to the communicants: who are, by the same appointment, to take and eat the bread, and to drink the wine, in thankful remembrance that the body of Christ was broken and given, and his blood shed, for them.

Q. 170. *How do they that worthily communicate in the Lord's Supper feed upon the body and blood of Christ therein?*

A. As the body and blood of Christ are not corporally or carnally present in, with, or under the bread and wine in the Lord's supper, and yet are spiritually present to the faith of the receiver, no less truly and really than the elements themselves are to their outward senses; so they that worthily communicate in the sacrament of the Lord's supper, do therein feed upon the body and blood of Christ, not after a corporal and carnal, but in a spiritual manner; yet truly and really, while by faith they receive and apply unto themselves Christ crucified, and all the benefits of his death.

Q. 171. *How are they that receive the sacrament of the Lord's supper to prepare themselves before they come unto it?*

A. They that receive the sacrament of the Lord's supper are, before they come, to prepare themselves thereunto, by examining themselves of their being in Christ, of their sins and wants; of the truth and measure of their knowledge, faith, repentance; love to God and the brethren, charity to all men, forgiving those that have done them wrong; of their desires after Christ, and of their new obedience; and by renewing the exercise of these graces, by serious meditation, and fervent prayer.

Q. 172. *May one who doubts of his being in Christ, or of his due preparation, come to the Lord's Supper?*

A. One who doubts of his being in Christ, or of his due preparation to the sacrament of the Lord's supper, may have true interest in Christ, though he be not yet assured thereof; and in God's account hath it, if he be duly affected with the apprehension of the want of it, and unfeignedly desires to be found in Christ, and to depart from iniquity: in which case (because promises are made, and this sacrament is appointed, for the relief even of weak and doubting Christians) he is to bewail his unbelief, and labor to have his doubts resolved; and, so doing, he may and ought to come to the Lord's supper, that he may be further strengthened.

Q. 173. *May any who profess the faith, and desire to come to the Lord's Supper, be kept from it?*

A. Such as are found to be ignorant or scandalous, notwithstanding their profession of the faith, and desire to come to the Lord's supper, may and ought to be kept from that sacrament, by the power which Christ hath left in his church, until they receive instruction, and manifest their reformation.

Q. 174. *What is required of them that receive the sacrament of the Lord's Supper in the time of the administration of it?*

A. It is required of them that receive the sacrament of the Lord's supper, that, during the time of the administration of it, with all holy reverence and attention they wait upon God in that ordinance, diligently observe the sacramental elements and actions, heedfully discern the Lord's body, and affectionately meditate on his death and sufferings, and thereby stir up themselves to a vigorous exercise of their graces; in judging themselves, and sorrowing for sin; in earnest hungering and thirsting after Christ, feeding on him by faith, receiving of his fullness, trusting in his merits, rejoicing in his love, giving thanks for his grace; in renewing of their covenant with God, and love to all the saints.

Q. 175. *What is the duty of Christians, after they have received the sacrament of the Lord's Supper?*

A. The duty of Christians, after they have received the sacrament of the Lord's supper, is seriously to consider how they have behaved themselves therein, and with what success; if they find quickening and comfort, to bless God for it, beg the continuance of it, watch against relapses, fulfill their vows, and encourage themselves to a frequent attendance on that ordinance: but if they find no present benefit, more exactly to review their preparation to, and carriage at, the sacrament; in both which, if they can approve themselves to God and their own consciences, they are to wait for the fruit of it in due time: but, if they see they have failed in either, they are to be humbled, and to attend upon it afterwards with more care and diligence.

Q. 176. *Wherein do the sacraments of baptism and the Lord's Supper agree?*

A. The sacraments of baptism and the Lord's supper agree, in that the author of both is God; the spiritual part of both is Christ and his benefits; both are seals of the same covenant, are to be dispensed by ministers of the gospel, and by none other; and to be continued in the church of Christ until his second coming.

Q. 177. *Wherein do the sacraments of baptism and the Lord's Supper differ?*

A. The sacraments of baptism and the Lord's supper differ, in that baptism is to be administered but once, with water, to be a sign and seal of our regeneration and ingrafting into Christ, and that even to infants; whereas the Lord's supper is to be administered often, in the elements of bread and wine, to represent and exhibit Christ as spiritual nourishment to the soul, and to confirm our continuance and growth in him, and that only to such as are of years and ability to examine themselves.

Q. 178. *What is prayer?*
A. Prayer is an offering up of our desires unto God, in the name of Christ, by the help of his Spirit; with confession of our sins, and thankful acknowledgement of his mercies.

Q. 179. *Are we to pray unto God only?*
A. God only being able to search the hearts, hear the requests, pardon the sins, and fulfill the desires of all; and only to be believed in, and worshiped with religious worship; prayer, which is a special part thereof, is to be made by all to him alone, and to none other.

Q. 180. *What is it to pray in the name of Christ?*
A. To pray in the name of Christ is, in obedience to his command, and in confidence on his promises, to ask mercy for his sake; not by bare mentioning of his name, but by drawing our encouragement to pray, and our boldness, strength, and hope of acceptance in prayer, from Christ and his mediation.

Q. 181. *Why are we to pray in the name of Christ?*
A. The sinfulness of man, and his distance from God by reason thereof, being so great, as that we can have no access into his presence without a mediator; and there being none in heaven or earth appointed to, or fit for, that glorious work but Christ alone, we are to pray in no other name but his only.

Q. 182. *How does the Spirit help us to pray?*
A. We not knowing what to pray for as we ought, the Spirit helps our infirmities, by enabling us to understand both for whom, and what, and how prayer is to be made; and by working and quickening in our hearts (although not in all persons, nor at all times, in the same measure) those apprehensions, affections, and graces which are requisite for the right performance of that duty.

Q. 183. *For whom are we to pray?*
A. We are to pray for the whole church of Christ upon earth; for magistrates, and ministers; for ourselves, our brethren, yea, our enemies; and for all sorts of men living, or that shall live hereafter; but not for the dead, nor for those that are known to have sinned the sin unto death.

Q. 184. *For what things are we to pray?*
A. We are to pray for all things tending to the glory of God, the welfare of the church, our own or others' good; but not for anything that is unlawful.

Q. 185. *How are we to pray?*
A. We are to pray with an awful apprehension of the majesty of God, and deep sense of our own unworthiness, necessities, and sins; with penitent, thankful, and enlarged hearts; with understanding, faith, sincerity, fervency, love, and perseverance, waiting upon him, with humble submission to his will.

Q. 186. *What rule hath God given for our direction in the duty of prayer?*
A. The whole Word of God is of use to direct us in the duty of prayer; but the special rule of direction is that form of prayer that our Savior Christ taught his disciples, commonly called The Lord's Prayer.

Q. 187. *How is the Lord's Prayer to be used?*
A. The Lord's prayer is not only for direction, as a pattern, according to which we are to make other prayers; but may also be used as a prayer, so that it be done with understanding, faith, reverence, and other graces necessary to the right performance of the duty of prayer.

Q. 188. *Of how many parts does the Lord's Prayer consist?*
A. The Lord's Prayer consists of three parts; a preface, petitions, and a conclusion.

Q. 189. *What does the preface of the Lord's Prayer teach us?*
A. The preface of the Lord's prayer (contained in these words, Our Father which art in heaven) teaches us, when we pray, to draw near to God with confidence of his fatherly goodness, and our interest therein; with reverence, and all other childlike dispositions, heavenly affections, and due apprehensions of his sovereign power, majesty, and gracious condescension: as also, to pray with and for others.

Q. 190. *What do we pray for in the first petition?*
A. In the first petition (which is, Hallowed be your name), acknowledging the utter inability and indisposition that is in ourselves and all men to honor God aright, we pray, that God would by his grace enable and incline us and others to know, to acknowledge, and highly to esteem him, his titles, attributes, ordinances, word, works, and whatsoever he is pleased to make himself known by; and to glorify him in thought, word, and deed: that he would prevent and remove atheism, ignorance, idolatry, profaneness, and

whatsoever is dishonorable to him; and, by his overruling providence, direct and dispose of all things to his own glory.

Q. 191. *What do we pray for in the second petition?*
A. In the second petition (which is, Your kingdom come), acknowledging ourselves and all mankind to be by nature under the dominion of sin and Satan, we pray, that the kingdom of sin and Satan may be destroyed, the gospel propagated throughout the world, the Jews called, the fullness of the Gentiles brought in; the church furnished with all gospel officers and ordinances, purged from corruption, countenanced and maintained by the civil magistrate; that the ordinances of Christ may be purely dispensed, and made effectual to the converting of those that are yet in their sins, and the confirming, comforting, and building up of those that are already converted: that Christ would rule in our hearts here, and hasten the time of his second coming, and our reigning with him forever: and that he would be pleased so to exercise the kingdom of his power in all the world, as may best conduce to these ends.

Q. 192. *What do we pray for in the third petition?*
A. In the third petition (which is, Your will be done in earth, as it is in heaven), acknowledging that by nature we and all men are not only utterly unable and unwilling to know and to do the will of God, but prone to rebel against his word, to repine and murmur against his providence, and wholly inclined to do the will of the flesh, and of the devil: we pray, that God would by his Spirit take away from ourselves and others all blindness, weakness, indisposedness, and perverseness of heart; and by his grace make us able and willing to know, do, and submit to his will in all things, with the like humility, cheerfulness, faithfulness, diligence, zeal, sincerity, and constancy, as the angels do in heaven.

Q. 193. *What do we pray for in the fourth petition?*
A. In the fourth petition (which is, Give us this day our daily bread), acknowledging that in Adam, and by our own sin, we have forfeited our right to all the outward blessings of this life, and deserve to be wholly deprived of them by God, and to have them cursed to us in the use of them; and that neither they of themselves are able to sustain us, nor we to merit, or by our own industry to procure them; but prone to desire, get, and use them unlawfully: we pray for ourselves and others, that both they and we, waiting upon the providence of God from day to day in the use of lawful means, may, of his free gift, and as to his fatherly wisdom shall seem best, enjoy a competent portion of them; and have the same continued and blessed unto

us in our holy and comfortable use of them, and contentment in them; and be kept from all things that are contrary to our temporal support and comfort.

Q. 194. *What do we pray for in the fifth petition?*

A. In the fifth petition (which is, Forgive us our debts, as we forgive our debtors), acknowledging that we and all others are guilty both of original and actual sin, and thereby become debtors to the justice of God; and that neither we, nor any other creature, can make the least satisfaction for that debt: we pray for ourselves and others, that God of his free grace would, through the obedience and satisfaction of Christ, apprehended and applied by faith, acquit us both from the guilt and punishment of sin, accept us in his Beloved; continue his favor and grace to us, pardon our daily failings, and fill us with peace and joy, in giving us daily more and more assurance of forgiveness; which we are the rather emboldened to ask, and encouraged to expect, when we have this testimony in ourselves, that we from the heart forgive others their offenses.

Q. 195. *What do we pray for in the sixth petition?*

A. In the sixth petition (which is, And lead us not into temptation, but deliver us from evil), acknowledging that the most wise, righteous, and gracious God, for divers holy and just ends, may so order things, that we may be assaulted, foiled, and for a time led captive by temptations; that Satan, the world, and the flesh, are ready powerfully to draw us aside, and ensnare us; and that we, even after the pardon of our sins, by reason of our corruption, weakness, and want of watchfulness, are not only subject to be tempted, and forward to expose ourselves unto temptations, but also of ourselves unable and unwilling to resist them, to recover out of them, and to improve them; and worthy to be left under the power of them; we pray, that God would so overrule the world and all in it, subdue the flesh, and restrain Satan, order all things, bestow and bless all means of grace, and quicken us to watchfulness in the use of them, that we and all his people may by his providence be kept from being tempted to sin; or, if tempted, that by his Spirit we may be powerfully supported and enabled to stand in the hour of temptation; or when fallen, raised again and recovered out of it, and have a sanctified use and improvement thereof: that our sanctification and salvation may be perfected, Satan trodden under our feet, and we fully freed from sin, temptation, and all evil, forever.

Q. 196. *What does the conclusion of the Lord's Prayer teach us?*

A. The conclusion of the Lord's Prayer (which is, For thine is the kingdom, and the power, and the glory, forever. Amen.) teaches us to enforce our petitions with arguments, which are to be taken, not from any worthiness in ourselves, or in any other creature, but from God; and with our prayers to join praises, ascribing to God alone eternal sovereignty, omnipotence, and glorious excellency; in regard whereof, as he is able and willing to help us, so we by faith are emboldened to plead with him that he would, and quietly to rely upon him, that he will fulfill our requests. And, to testify of our desire and assurance, we say, Amen.

Matthew Everhard is the Senior Pastor of Faith Evangelical Presbyterian Church (EPC) in Brooksville, Florida.

Native Ohioans from the Akron area, he and his lovely wife Kelly have three children, Soriah (age 10, an aspiring artist and writer), Elijah (age 8, an aspiring ninja), and Simone (age 3, an aspiring lawyer). Besides preaching, teaching, and writing, Matthew enjoys riding bikes with the family and playing in the backyard or on the living room floor with the children.

Matthew is a graduate of Ashland Theological Seminary (Ashland Ohio) and Malone University (Canton Ohio). Matthew is also pursuing post-graduate study at Reformed Theological Seminary (Orlando Florida).

Matthew also is deeply interested in missions, having served on the mission fields of Equatorial Guinea (Central West Africa), El Salvador, Mexico, Ukraine, the Cayman Islands, and the Bahamas (yes, really).

His other books include: *Abortion: The Evangelical Perspective* (BIBAL PRESS, 2007); *Rock Solid: Helping Teens Discover the Truth of Christianity* (Reformation Press, 2005), *The Children's Catechism: A Parent's Resource for Scripture Memorization* (Faith Church Publishing, 2010), and *Christ Our Supreme Joy: Encountering the Glory of Jesus Christ*. Kindle Edition. (Faith Church Publishing, 2010).

His greatest passion and supreme treasure, however, is the Lord Jesus Christ who captured his heart in 1990 and has not let go since.